ELIZABETH, LADY HOLLAND TO HER SON

1821—1845

Edited by
THE EARL OF ILCHESTER

pub. 1946

With a Frontispiece

LONDON
JOHN MURRAY, ALBEMARLE STREET, W.

First Edition . *March 1946*
Reprinted . . *April 1946*

Made and Printed in Great Britain by Butler & Tanner Ltd., Frome and London

ELIZABETH, LADY HOLLAND TO HER SON

BOOK
PRODUCTION
WAR ECONOMY
STANDARD

THIS BOOK IS PRODUCED
IN COMPLETE CONFORMITY WITH
THE AUTHORIZED ECONOMY STANDARDS

HENRY FOX, FIRST LORD HOLLAND
His Family and Relations

THE HOME OF THE HOLLANDS
1605–1820

CHRONICLES OF HOLLAND HOUSE
1820–1900

LORD AND LADY HOLLAND, DR ALLEN AND W. DOGGETT IN THE
LIBRARY AT HOLLAND HOUSE

From a mezzotint by S. W. Reynolds, after C. R. Leslie

CONTENTS

INTRODUCTION

THE problem of selection from a series of over 1,350 letters, few of which lack interest of some kind or another, is always difficult, even under normal conditions. But during a war, when paper supplies are strictly limited, the operation has become a major one. So much has necessarily to be omitted, when one volume might be expanded into two, that it is not easy to maintain a just proportion between the multifarious subjects upon which Lady Holland has touched in these letters addressed to her son, Henry Edward Fox, later fourth Lord Holland. To fill these pages with society gossip alone, would be to give a false impression of their varied scope; for interwoven with matters of serious family import, we find much that must not be omitted touching the politics of the day, with a strict bias naturally to Whig tenets. The sayings and doings of her husband, as may be expected, form a prominent feature in her narrative of current events. Added to these, are to be found constant allusions to new plays and outspoken criticism of the performers, for Lady Holland was always an inveterate theatre-goer. Comments on books, too, take up further space, indicating the new works with which she was wont to keep her son supplied, when his wanderings on the Continent took him far from home. But since these stern times have not permitted the coveted indulgence in paper, an endeavour must be made to give the space to each topic which it deserves, without ruining the continuity of the letters or spoiling the effect of the diversity of the subject-matter. Explanatory notes, too, have had to be cut to a minimum, and are often produced in an abbreviated form; while even this introduction cannot be given the expansion which could be deemed desirable.

For these reasons I do not propose to inflict on the reader any repetition of my references to Lady Holland in other volumes, and shall confine myself to some short reflections upon the new aspect which seems to emerge from this series of the writer's letters. I have drawn attention to the curiously complex nature of her character, both in her *Journal* published in 1908 and more recently in my books on Holland House. But for those who have not read those volumes, a short résumé of the chief incidents in her career will not come amiss.

Elizabeth Vassall, born in 1771, was the daughter of Richard Vassall (himself the son of Florentius Vassall (1710-79), a planter in

Jamaica), and Mary Anne Clark, of New York, who, a year after her first husband's death in 1795, married Sir Gilbert Affleck, of Dalham Hall, and survived until 1835. The account of her early upbringing given in her *Journal* is supplemented in several passages in these letters, in which she refers feelingly to the joyless existence and almost complete lack of education which was her lot, before at an early age of 15 she was married to Sir Godfrey Webster, of Battle Abbey, a country squire many years her senior. So incongruous an alliance could only have one end, disaster, allowing for her natural talents and precocity; and in due course the catastrophe came about. The counter-attractions of young Henry Richard Fox, third Lord Holland (1773–1840), whom she met in the course of a trip to Italy with Sir Godfrey, altered her whole life. Friendship blossomed into love, and notwithstanding two surviving sons, and a daughter who reappears in these pages as Mrs. Pellew, she decided to throw in her lot with him. Sir Godfrey raised many objections to a divorce; but this was finally arranged, although one condition was the surrender of the fortune left her by her father, in those days some £8,000 a year. The Parliamentary Bill, however, then necessary, was passed too late to legitimize their eldest son, Charles Richard Fox, who therefore could not succeed to the title.

The recipient of the present letters, Henry Edward Fox, was born in 1804; and two daughters followed. The elder married Lord Lilford in 1830, while the younger died at an early age in 1817. Henry Edward was afflicted with some form of hip trouble from birth, and was never a robust child, but succeeded as fourth and last Lord Holland in 1840.

The Hollands had taken up their abode at Holland House shortly after their marriage, and established themselves there, moving to the fashionable quarter of the town for the winter months; in order to be near Lord Holland's Parliamentary work, to the theatres, and to the small social circle in which Lady Holland moved. As a divorcée, she was only received in a limited number of the great houses, comprising those of her husband's relatives and of the great Whig magnates. Consequently, the masculine sex predominated at the gatherings over which she presided. They often spent a month or two every year at Brighton; and besides, after 1818, owned Ampthill Park, near Woburn, bequeathed to Lord Holland by his uncle the second and last Earl of Upper Ossory. The latter's two daughters, Ladies Gertrude and Anne Fitzpatrick, are often referred to in these pages; as is Lord Holland's sister, Miss Caroline Fox, a favourite with all her contemporaries and relatives, and especially adored by the younger generation. She kept house for many years with her relative, Miss Elizabeth Vernon, Lord Upper Ossory's half-sister by his mother's second marriage, at Little Holland House, two old farm-houses, practically in the grounds of the great mansion, especially converted for her use by her devoted brother. The references to Dr. John Allen, family physician, librarian at Holland House and Warden of Dulwich College, a figure indispensable at every Holland House entertainment, large or small, are not so numerous in these letters as one would have expected. But the fact is that Allen and Henry Fox never really hit it off; and the latter, after his father's death, rightly or wrongly imputed to the Doctor's advice many of the slights which he considered were being put upon him.

One is certainly struck in these letters by the moderation of Lady Holland's comments on her contemporaries. She has always borne the reputation of a hard, imperious woman, who always saw the worst side of the characters of those whom she criticized, and was not afraid of expressing her thoughts freely. Imperious in her old age she certainly was; and when she strikes, she strikes without mercy. But in general in the correspondence under review she shows little tendency to accentuate the shortcomings of those on whom she sits in judgment. In dealing with political opponents, her Whiggism comes very near to the surface; but with all that she had friends in the other camp, such as Aberdeen, Eldon and Lyndhurst, and clung to them regardless of party ties, as long as they played the game according to her lights. It should be noted too how closely her relation of political affairs tallies with that of Charles Greville, although the latter was more closely affiliated to the opposite party in politics. Her interest in foreign affairs was always maintained at a high level, owing to her intimacy and that of Lord Holland with the diplomats accredited to the British Court.

As regards family matters, the first thing which impresses one in the course of these letters is the genuine adoration with which Lady Holland regarded her husband. She might order him about, she might bully him (and incidentally he usually gave way to her whims): but her delight in his society, and her gratitude for a life of happiness, are unmistakable, while the void which his death created was to her irreparable. To sum up her relations with her children in a few sentences is a more difficult matter. She posed as a sympathetic, indul-gent mother, and was probably convinced in her own mind that she filled the part. As long as everyone fell in with her wishes, all went reasonably well; though in Mary Fox's case, strict discipline and repression, to which Lady Granville referred in her letters to her sister, Lady Carlisle (*Letters of Harriet, Lady Granville*), might well have had serious after-effects upon the girl's character. Fortunately a blissfully happy marriage negatived all fear of danger in that quarter ; and with Charles Fox too, an early alliance with a woman of great charm though always prone to delicate health, removed him from too close a dependance upon the family circle. In Henry Fox's case, the affectionate tone of these letters makes it hard to realize that things were not quite as they appear on the surface. But so it was ; yet the extent is not easily definable, as many of his early replies have been destroyed. Certain it is, however, notwithstanding his highly successful marriage to Lady Mary Augusta Coventry in 1833, that, especially after the death of the father whom he and his brother and sister worshipped, the position reached a stage very near to breaking point, when he realized that his mother had been left in full control of the estate, and that she was using that control in directions of which he did not approve. Yet the faults were by no means all on one side. Henry was undeniably difficult. He was precocious, as one realizes from his *Journal*, published in 1923 : he was self-willed, and he resented any attempts to drive him. He was romantically inclined from an early age, and proved so susceptible to the charms of certain young ladies in society, that his parents thought it advisable to pack him off abroad. But the effect was far more far-reaching than they had ever imagined. On the Continent, he found emancipation from home restraints ; and seeds were sown which established a preference for a life abroad which to his dying day was never extinguished.

But throughout these letters runs a continual under-current of complaint that her children were not doing enough for her. Henry especially, she wrote, was deserting her by remaining so long abroad. He should return, and gladden the last years of her life. How happy she would be if he was more with her. Yet when he was at home nothing seemed to run smoothly ; and a suspicion becomes inevitable that he found it best for his own peace of mind and everyone else's to stay away.

With increasing years Lady Holland's idiosyncrasies did not grow less. After 1840 Holland House held too many ghosts of the happy past for her to think of returning there permanently. As long as Miss Fox was alive Little Holland House in close proximity was open to her ; but her place of residence was her " nutshell " in South Street, left to her by her mother. Her friends with great houses, the Lansdownes, the Palmerstons and others, did all they could to distract her, when she could be tempted to overcome her accentuated and physical fears of the railway. But her old friends were dying fast.

Lauderdale and Bedford had gone, then Allen, and finally Sydney and Bobus Smith. Yet she continued to entertain in London to the last; but it was a new set who graced her table, many of whom only knew by hearsay the palmy days in Kensington, with all which that society represented.

Lady Holland's handwriting is not easy to decipher; and words have had to be left out here and there, and are labelled as *illegible*. She announced that she was quite unequal to writing a letter in French, yet she constantly used French words and French idioms. Her style has little literary merit to commend it, though naturally that is hardly to be expected in these intimate family letters; but it has an individuality of its own which is certainly not without a peculiar charm. The letters are as often as not undated; but the dockets made by her son come to the rescue, and as a last resource the "Dinner Books" prove useful to settle the proper sequence. Her method of using stops, too, does not make things any easier. These have been corrected, and also her spelling, except in cases where she constantly uses old forms, in such words as *agreable*, *encrease*, *shew*, *honor* and similar terminations. Omissions from the letters are not indicated, except when the subject under discussion is continued; but a dotted line, when used at the commencement of a letter, signifies that earlier matter has been left out. Square brackets in the text denote explanatory names.

My best thanks are due to Sir John Murray for useful information, suggestions and comments, as well as for looking over the proofs. My wife too has greatly helped me in the elucidation of difficult problems in handwriting. I am obliged also to Messrs. Macmillan and Messrs. Longman Green for permission to quote a few short passages from the new edition of *Charles Greville's Memoirs* (Strachey and Fulford), and from the *Letters of Harriet, Lady Granville*, respectively.

1945   ILCHESTER.

CHAPTER I

1821—1822

WE have taken the year 1821 as a starting point for Lady Holland's letters, as there is nothing of special importance before that date. Henry Edward Fox, born in 1802, was then only 19. His own letters to her, as preserved, commence in 1817 ; while his *Journal*, the writing of a young man of far more mature years, which has already been published, dates from one year later.

The first letter selected for publication refers to General Sir Robert Wilson as the champion and adviser of Queen Caroline, whose trial in the House of Lords had been abandoned in November. Upon this, she demanded the provision of a royal residence. This was refused ; but Parliament on reassembling voted her £50,000 per annum. Some of her friends demurred at her taking this allowance, and attempted to raise an adequate sum for her by private subscription. She was at this time living at Brandenburgh House, near Hammersmith. The purchase of Marlborough House was apparently in contemplation. (*See* Aspinall's *Letters of George IV*, ii, 417.) Creevey (ii, 15) spoke of Cambridge House as bought by her, which Lady Holland corroborates.

Fox, at this time at Christ Church, Oxford, was a college friend and contemporary of Henry Greville (1801–72), younger brother of Charles (" Punch ") Greville, and himself the author of a notable journal.

Monday, 26 February, 1821.

. . . The only sentence of common sense I have heard uttered by Sir Robert Wilson this year was last night, when I asked how his stomach could bear the Queen taking her money, which she is doing for her house, etc. He assured me he had highly disapproved her rejection of the money ; & knew that it was contrary to her own wishes that the message was sent. He came yesterday to allot her apartments, & is to come and reside in the course of the week. Punch Greville dined here yesterday & praised you very much ; but said his brother had complained that you corrupted him by idleness, & prevented his studying, & that he had said so to his family to account for the little proficiency he made, *all* of which he lays upon lounging in your rooms. I was a little piqued, & answered Mr Punch warmly, adding, I was afraid the tables might be turned upon young Tattle.

I questioned him clearly ; & he gave me his honor what he said was true of the complaint.

Your Papa has read the *Chevalier Johnson*,[1] & could not lay it down till he had read it through ; though it has all the interest of one of Walter Scott's Novels, & corroborates the picture of manners so well drawn in those on Scotch ground.   Walter Scott is going into Wales. He has a stubborn boy [2] who will not learn Latin.   To induce him to that pursuit, he is to be placed in a village where Welsh alone is spoken ; & Scott flatters himself he will thus be driven to the language of Cicero in preference to that of Shenkin & Cadwallader.

Wednesday, 28 February, 1821.

. . . Prince Leopold sent for Ld Grey, & shewed all that had passed between him & the Queen relative to M. House.   I am reluctantly obliged to report that Ld G. considers Leopold's conduct is irreproachable ; & that evidently the Queen meant the correspondence for the eye of the public.   The last letter is by the same hand as that to the King.   What, my Love, do you mean by saying the Queen should not take the money ?   How can a person live, without means of paying their subsistence & servants ?   Is it just ; or indeed is it possible ?   Add to that the impossibility of her trusting to subscriptions, which do not flow in at all.   The old maxim " Be just before you are generous " ought to be in one's mind constantly.   By the bye we are so much in that predicament, that I do not buy a single article or give a crown in charity, as our affairs are in a very bad plight ; tho' we try by this to keep down debt.   But the *total* failure for two years of Jamaica, not a shilling from Oxfordshire, & little from Bedfordshire, make even the most rigid economy necessary & hardly equal to the outgoings.

Lady Holland attended the 2nd reading debate of the Catholic Disability Removal Bill in the Commons on March 16.

[1] James Johnstone, Chevalier (1719–1800 ?).   A.D.C. to the Young Pretender in 1745.   Served with the French in Canada.   Extracts from his *Memoirs* were published in 1820.

[2] Charles Scott, Sir Walter's 2nd son (1805–41). He died in Teheran when serving as a diplomatic attaché.   The reference to Scott's Novels is of some interest, for the writer never officially announced his hand in them till 1826.   Yet the authorship was clearly an open secret some years before, and Lady Holland wrote in the autumn, " Mr Murray told your Papa, W. Scott, with whom he spent some days this summer, acknowledged almost that he wrote the whole series of the Novels."

Monday, 19 *March*, 1821.

. . . Mephitic air & heat are bad ; but for the treat I enjoyed more would I undergo. The four speeches were all admirable in their different manners ; & Mr Peel's I was curious to hear, that I might from my own estimate take measure of him. As Marsh [1] says, about him, " we will *talk*." Wilberforce, full of feeling, harmonious sentences, melodious voice, one passage about *prison dress* very happy. Mackintosh, full of just reasoning, illustrated by historical learning, & all apposite. Canning ! beautiful, such diction, such wit, readiness & perfect round periods. He surpassed my expectations. Plunket was supposed to have spoken less well than on the former night ; but it was the most perfectly well-reasoned, clear, distinct argument I ever heard delivered, & gave a conviction of his wonderful abilities & powers. His short speech on the Petition was as neat & witty as Canning himself could have made. What a glorious place is that House of Commons. What an arena for the display of intellectual powers. No wonder all Europe, knowing its construction, are desirous of enjoying a representative Govt. What a glorious field for the understanding, to see the ablest & best informed members of Society using their utmost means to do their *best*. What an admirable school for the rising generation to behold such exertions ; for it is learning in the best shape, & must give a desire in the hearers to acquire knowledge to be on a par with what is said. The next good debate will be on Lambton's motion for Reform on the 10th. I mean to ask to go to that.

On Saturday I was completely overcome, so could not go to the Opera with Lady Cowper, [2] which I should have liked ; tho' I do not hear it is very good ; only Campanese, & one dancer who only dances with one leg the critics say. Mde Vestris is lost in the vastness of the theatre. You should rejoice for my sake that I return home, [3] as these bright, nice days make me long very much to walk about the house & enjoy the daylight. I think London detestable after 10th March. I had a most *brilliant assembly last night*, being my last Sunday. All my friends came, much beauty, etc.

[1] Rev. Matthew Marsh, an old friend of the Hollands, and recently their son's tutor.

[2] Amelia Lamb, Countess Cowper, sister of William, Lord Melbourne, and wife of 5th Earl ; subsequently married to Viscount Palmerston.

[3] To Holland House, from a house in Old Burlington Street. They leased yearly a house in Town, to enable Lord Holland to attend Parliament and Lady Holland to go to the opera and theatre.

H. H. *Wednesday*, 21 *March*, 1821.

. . . We had a very agreable dinner on Monday at Mr Rogers's. His spirits were high & I never saw him happier. The day went off admirably. The only remarkable person was Sir Wm Grant.[1] Others of his cast failed, by being detained in the H. of Commons, but the rest were all our usual friends. Yesterday we had a sumptuous *banquet* in that splendid salon at Devonshire House. Tho' the party was numerous, yet it was lively & very, very pleasant. The King being at the Opera prevented the projected evening party, as the singers could not come & the company wanted to go. Therefore that was given up, & stands for some other evening. I got away in time to see the last scene of the new actress, who is handsome & promises well for the future.[2] She was applauded to the skies. The farce of *Husbands & Wives* made Papa laugh mightily. I had the Ords & Mrs Tierney. Mr Ward,[3] I hear, made a beautiful speech, & was full as personal against the Czar as Papa, more so. The Queen has written to express her wish of going to the D[rawing] Room to Lord Liverpool ; which he has answered as might be expected, no precedent for a Queen going. She may hold one, but cannot attend that held by another. She has possession of Cambridge House.

A reference to affairs connected with the Continent occurs in the next letter, which may require some explanation. This was the restoration of King Ferdinand to the throne of Naples, carried out by the Powers at the Congress of Laybach by means of an Austrian army, notwithstanding the breach of an oath to his subjects to maintain the Constitution.

H. H. *Monday*, 26 *March*, 1821.

. . . On Sunday we had a large party, Bessboroughs, Ponsonbys, Normanbys, & men. John [Russell] came in evening & slept, & is now till Thursday a sojourner. He then goes to Huntingdon, from whence a gentleman has written to offer *you* a bed. Wrio[4] will go to Ch. Ch., as Dr Maltby recommends it far above Cambridge, the good set, & freedom from vices of drinking, gambling & low manners. D. & Dss [of Bedford] dine here today. Poor Plunket set off in a

---

[1] (1752–1832). Master of the Rolls, 1801–17.

[2] Miss Dance (Mrs. Halles), a pupil of Mrs. Siddons.

[3] John William Ward (1780–1833), 4th Viscount Dudley and Ward in 1823 ; created an Earl in 1827, and Foreign Secretary.

[4] Lord Wriothesley Russell (1804–86), the eldest son of the Duke of Bedford's 2nd marriage. He married his first-cousin, Elizabeth, daughter of Lord William Russell in 1843 : and earlier took orders.

state of distraction for Ireland.[1] He was extremely attached to his wife, & lived in the most domestic manner. Mr Ward told me that he lived so entirely in the bosom of his family, that during the period Mr Peel was Secretary in Ireland, tho' he tried to get acquainted with him, he yet never could meet him at dinner but twice. Lord Fife was turned out for voting against the Malt Tax ; fair enough, as his salary came from such taxes. The wags say Lord Castlereagh likes all taxes, but *Syntax*. Where is Wentworth that Lady Worcester is going to stay at so long ? Hardly Lord Fitzwilliam's. Papa is very busy with some Owyee Chiefs, shewing the plates in *Cook's Voyage*. I hear they look intelligent, are very swarthy : but hating smells & itch, I keep out of the way. The Austrian affair at Rieti seems to be no great matter, but Piedmont is anxious. Mons. de Caraman announced an *Ukase* from the Czar that 100,000,000 men were immediately to proceed into Italy. However, it is a bon bout de chemin from Muscovy or Tartary to the frontiers of fair Italy ; & the *sinews* of war are not very ready in these barbarous countries, unless our friend the great Alexander helps with a loan.

The Hollands, accompanied by their son, went abroad early in May. They returned in September, to allow the latter to return to Oxford to keep one more term.

Saturday, October 27, 1821.

. . . Johnny [Russell] will not quit his books & study at Woburn. He enjoys the solitude, & reads incessantly. One is sorry to lose him ; but it is so much the greatest, indeed the only solid happiness to be occupied, that I am fond enough of him to rejoice. Indeed, thank God, I feel myself the benefit of this possession ; as I now have been able to occupy my mind & revert to my old habits of reading. The day is brightly spent ; & the only fault is its' being too short. When once in a course of reading, so many things branch out to be looked to, that there is never a vacant half hour. This conduces to health and cheerfulness, & makes a very narrow society, indeed none, necessary.

In 1820, Canning, being out of sympathy with the Ministerial persecution of Queen Caroline, resigned the Board of Control, and left the Government. After her death, in August, 1821, however, he showed willingness to rejoin, but found himself banned by the

[1] William Conyngham Plunket (1764–1854) : Baron in 1827. Lord Chancellor of Ireland. He is also mentioned in a preceding letter.

King. He accepted India, however ; but before he sailed, the tragedy of Lord Londonderry's death was enacted, and he found himself insisted upon for the Foreign Office. The Lord Chancellor was Lord Eldon.

Lady Holland's reference to Sir Hudson Lowe was in connection with the snuffbox left to her in Napoleon's will. It is now at the British Museum. It was presented to her by Counts Montholon and Bertrand in London, early in September. See *Chronicles of Holland House*, p. 15.

November 14, 1821. Hd H.

The political world are in a bustle. Mr Canning, who was staying quietly at Welbeck, has suddenly appeared on the stage, & is much with Ld Liverpool. The chief obstacles to his success are the Chancellor, King, & Lord Harrowby ; but as the King has spent *immensely*, Ld Liverpool has *him in hand*. The Coronation, estimated at the moderate sum, has exceeded by half a million. His robes alone cost £22,000, ermine, embroidery, velvet, etc. What can Sir Hudson mean by saying I owe the box to him ? Does he insinuate that Montholon meant to steal it ; indeed his own letter to me is a proof to the contrary. Col. Dawson prevented him publishing a justification, & Ld Bathurst advised him not.

Papa goes on Monday to Ampthill. I shall go & sleep in town these two nights, as this house without him or *you* will be insupportable. Lady G. Bathurst & kin are trying hard for Ld Liverpool, &, as he must be ravished to be won, will probably succeed.

19 *November*, 1821. *Monday.*

. . . We yesterday had the G. Lambs, Clifford, S. Bathurst, Ld Lauderdale, Col. Maitland & Brougham. Mr Canning left town on Saturday for Welbeck ; but his friends say the negociation is not over. Lord Conyngham is to be Lord Steward, which Ld Cholmondeley resigns ; & his son, Lord Rocksavage, is to be called up to the House of Lords so that his second & favourite son, Ld Henry, may come into Parlt ; & Ld Chol. has the promise of the first blue ribband, but this is not solid enough to please him. People still believe Ld Wellesley will be Chamberlain ; [1] if so, I think a Ministry to which he is hostile not likely to last, as he will be enabled by the nature of his office to have hourly access to insinuate what he pleases into the royal ear . . . We go to establish in B. Street on Thursday next.

_____
[1] Lord Wellesley was sent to Ireland as Lord-Lieutenant.

Wednesday. Hd H. 21 *Nov.*, 1821.

Dear Papa will return,[1] I trust, before footpad hour. The day has cleared, & a salutary frost will keep off fog & bring him safely at six . . . The old grey horse carried him admirably ; & tho' he did not feel himself as active as the Roe, vide Luttrell, he felt like Santiago, mounted for Victory on his white horse. The Spaniards, you know, always believed in their battles with the Moors that their patron *Santiago* (St James) appeared & fought for them mounted on his milk white steed. *St James, Santiago, Diego, Jayme,* are all the same name, & one or two more which I do not exactly remember. The field was also a scene of glory ; for strange to say, Papa with his own hand killed a pheasant flying ! in Reddings Wood, the only such trophy he ever obtained in all his life. Last night Mr Brougham came, slept & breakfasted. He was very good-natured to relieve our solitude.

I have been reading over again D'Alembert & Voltaire's correspondence. You know my ardent admiration of the latter ; but he is only second fiddle to the correspondent. Strong, firm, clear sense, enlivened by sterling wit, predominates ; tho' Voltaire is witty, lively, playful & gay, but yields the palm to the superior powers of D'Alembert. Talking last night upon those persons, led naturally to Prussia & la *Oursie,* as Voltaire calls Russia. Do you know anything about the history of the latter country ? I know little or nothing beyond Coxe & Ruhlière : but it is strange how the petticoats have prevailed in the Govt. Four Empresses (3 without rights) have ruled, with intervening Czars who appeared but to be murdered ; and the permanence of this Emperor, Alexander, may, the wags would say, arise from his being of a *dubious gender.*

Lady Holland wrote on November 24th : " I hear from Brighton the King is shut up in his harem, no egress or ingress ; not a mouse passes. The streets are dirty, the wind high, and all unpleasant. Lady Conyngham walks at 9 on the Cliff to maintain her health and beauty. Orloff and some foreigners are there with him, living à la *Ourse,* all in one room."

Thursday, November 29, [1821].

. . . The Cowpers have dined twice with the King, & he has persuaded them to stay another week. Luttrell was invited, & dined the last time. The King has given his picture with brilliants to Lady C., & seems cheerful & happy, & good humoured with all the world.

---

[1] From Ampthill.

The reign of the Loves & Graces is better than his former reign of
Terror ; for the Marchioness,[1] her predecessor, certainly ruled with
the instruments of inspiring him with hatred & suspicion of all about
him, not a good mechanism for a King's mistress.   Lord Lauderdale [2]
leaves town, I am sorry to say, tomorrow, but dines here today with
C. Greville, Ossulstons & Luttrell.

The duel to which reference is made in the next letter was between
Edward Bruce, 2nd Lord Kinloss, who was killed, and Sir Edward
Sackville, later 4th Earl of Dorset.   It took place at Bergen-op-Zoom
in 1613, on land purchased for the purpose.   The celebrated Lady
Venetia Stanley, afterwards wife of Sir Kenelm Digby, may have
been the cause.

Saturday, 26 January, [1822. Old Burlington St].

The day of the Fox dinner, my headache forced the transfer of
dining with my mother at her house to dining *here,* which she and
Sir Henry did ; & in due course left me to the study of *modern medals,*
which is now becoming a serious pursuit.   Lord Stowell [3] was very
entertaining, & will give *me* to give to the Antiquarian Society a
curious paper he has written upon the subject of the celebrated
Bruce & Sackville duel. When I withdrew, I hear the conversation was
enlivened by Mr Knight's [4] learning upon the Arts, sculpture, etc. Sir
Wm. then opened upon the Ladies' Statue, raised by subscription to
commemorate the victory of the Allies over France. A difficulty
had arisen ; & the artists had submitted to the female subscribers
whether this immense colossal figure should preserve its antique
nudity or be garnished with a fig leaf. It was carried for the leaf by
a majority. Sir Wm adds, the names of the *minority* have not transpired. It seems the great Bowl opposite the Horse Guards was
removed for the purpose of erecting this figure ; but the ground
was too rotten to support the weight, & a spot in front of the windows
of the Admiralty is selected.   Don't tell Dundas [5] I said it ; but Lord
Melville objects stoutly to such a gigantic proportioned figure before
his windows, & has at least begged that it may be a little turned from
a full view.

[1] Lady Hertford.
[2] James, 8th Earl (1759–1839), an old friend of the Hollands.
[3] Sir William Scott, lawyer (1745–1836). The figure mentioned below is
now in Hyde Park, the " Achilles." It is by Sir R. Westmacott.
[4] Richard Payne Knight (1750–1824), virtuoso.
[5] Lord Melville's son, Robert, a friend of Henry Fox.

The bridal party [1] are all to remove to Chiswick in about 10 days where the wedding will take place *privately*. The D. of D. is to fit up in D.H. an apartment for them, until Agar can suit himself with a house ; very good natured, as indeed he always is. Ld Jersey arrived last night. He came in the smoakey (*sic*), & does not like it at all. I saw him last night.

Sir Robert Wilson had been dismissed from the army in September, without explanation : and raised his own case from his seat in Parliament. His motion was defeated on the grounds of the prerogative of Government. A debate also took place in the Lords.

14 *February*, [1822].

. . . Sir R. Wilson produced a favorable impression on his audience last night by the plain, simple statement of his case. Several who went down determined to vote against him were convinced, Mr N. Calvert & several others. Lambton was injudicious, & did his utmost by unnecessary & offensive topics to do away the effect, such as *murder*, & *Parlty Reform*. Lord Londonderry mistated your Papa's speech in the Lords, & shewed a glorious jumble of ideas, or rather complete ignorance of language. He said, " He had a general *hydrophobia* for Martial Law," which shews that he thinks hydrophobia is a Greek word for *horror*.

March 12, 1822.

We dined at Lansdowne H. yesterday,[2] & in the evening there was a great assembly. Mrs Lennox was the *beauty*, & honestly ; but great great judges did not admire, such as Lds Morpeth & Grey. She is

---

[1] George James Agar Ellis (1797–1833), later created Baron Dover, was to marry Lady Georgina Howard, daughter of Lord Carlisle, and niece of the Duke of Devonshire. Charles Greville wrote, at the time of Lord Dover's death (*Memoirs*, ed. Strachey and Fulford, 1938, II, 390), that he was on his way to propose to the Duke of Beaufort's daughter, but, staying for a few nights at Castle Howard, proposed to his host's daughter. " There never was a less romantic attachment or a more businesslike engagement ; nor was there ever a more fortunate choice or a happier union."

[2] In connection with entertainments at Lansdowne House, Rogers's opinion, although a very personal one, dating from a year before, may be quoted : he came from dining at L. House, making fresh vows that he would never dine there again. " Nobody notices what I say ; it falls dead. At Spencer House all runs & is relished. At L. H. nobody smiles, nobody listens. Why do I go ? It is always so ; but they are charming people, I dare say."

rather scraggy & uncommonly ill-dressed.   Three Miss Edgeworths,[1] all disagreeable looking people . . . Fazakerley [2] is returned high in health & spirits, tho' somewhat thinner.   I think something might intervene to prevent the marriage.   In all probability he would not be sorry himself ; for these engagements entered into abroad, faute de mieux, are often unwillingly ratified at home.   Sydney Smith avers that marriages settled up in a country house ought to be considered as null & void when the parties meet in society.

March 13, [1822].

Our dinner was late, as the Lords took a chattering fit in the House ; but all the ladies came.   Some went to the Opera.   Ly Gwydyr staid late, & was very cheerful & agreeable as usual.   She is invited to go with the Morpeths on Saturday to the Pavilion.   There has been an idle report of the King coming to the Opera on Saturday. Whenever he does come, it will be the *Turco in Italia*, as he dislikes the Campanese's singing. . . .   The great royal pastime at the Tuilleries with the favorite is to take snuff from her shoulder.   Papa says he has heard of lovers putting the portraits of their mistresses on their snuff boxes, but never of their converting the lady into one.   I fear there will be much dishonesty about Napoleon's will, such as defeating his intentions & enabling Louis to get the money.   *Drouet*, who is one of the most respectable of Napoleon's adherents, has sent me a flatter-ing message, regretting that he is not personally acquainted with me.

Friday, March 15.

. . . Some of the Pavilion company came here, freshly returned. The mode of life is apparently pleasant & rational.   Lady C. has certainly the merit of inviting society befitting the King to see ; & there is a very moderate degree of form, great attention to expense, much abridgement in wax candles & fires ; the whole denoting an attention to economy.

[1] Lord Broughton (*Recollections*, ii, 185) wrote in May : " Dined at Ellice's, the celebrated Miss Edgeworth and her two sisters there.   She was not affected at all.   She is showing London and the world to her two sisters ; and they told me took incredible pains to go through the ceremony with them."   Henry Fox wrote in his *Journal* later in the month, " I was introduced to Miss E., who is collecting materials for a new novel among the gaieties of London."

[2] J. Nicholas Fazakerley, M.P. 1812–37.   He became engaged at Nice, and married Miss Montagu.

Monday, 20 *May* 1822, [Holland House].

. . . Our dear Jack [1] would have chuckled at the confusion & discomfort on Saturday from my unmethodical head. We were pressed & jammed, in consequence of an *unaccounted* number rushing in during dinner. Broglie [2] is very pleasant, & appears really much struck with this country, the institutions, wealth & universal ease. Jack would have scowled hearing me run off in my usual strain against public education to Staël, ignorant that he had timed his arrival so as to speak upon the general meeting for the advancement of knowledge all the world over. It was much such a bévue as Mr Bankes's, who wished Hyde Villiers joy upon Lord Francis's marriage being declared, supposing it was for Theresa Villiers.[3] When Ld Stafford first saw the young lady, he told her she was going to marry a very *poor* man. It seems that the D. of Bridgewater being a batchelor did not contemplate the marriage of any of his successors ; so there is no legal mode of making a settlement upon that property. However Lds Stafford & Gower can obviate this upon their property. Old Charles Greville talks disgustingly & not wisely, asserting that Ld Gower will never marry, but live long enough for two sons to be born before Ld F. becomes Marquis, which will secure the two properties being vested in Greville blood ! A pretty blood to be sure.

In the evening of Saturday, Mr Brougham came, to use a vulgar saying, *clipping the King's English*, having dined with a Scotch party. Yesterday, the oppressive heat made me languid & sick : truly hot atmosphere only known to that extent in the valley of the Thames, a steam exhaling from the spungy ground, stewing the poor mortals between the earth & the rays of the sun. Rogers made his entrée at breakfast, giving a most agreeable *prose* account of Italy : that in

---

[1] John Allen.

[2] Duc de Broglie, Achille Victor (1785–1870), later Foreign Secretary under Louis Philippe. He married Madame de Staël's daughter, Albertine. His brother-in-law Auguste de Staël was also dining.

[3] Hyde Villiers was brother to George, 4th Earl of Clarendon and Miss Theresa Villiers, later a flame of Henry Edward Fox. She married, in 1830, Thomas Henry Lister, and 2ndly Sir George Cornewall-Lewis.

Lord Francis Leveson-Gower (1800–57), 2nd son of George Granville, Marquess of Stafford, later Duke of Sutherland, had become engaged to, and married in June, Harriet, daughter of old Charles Greville and sister of the diarist. Lord Francis was created Earl of Ellesmere in 1846, and succeeded to the Duke of Bridgewater's estates.

Lady Holland wrote elsewhere, " The marriage was declared yesterday, and settled the night before at Almack's in the Tea Room."

verse I carefully avoided to touch upon.[1] He was very agreable, & seemed as usual in other respects. Lord Valletort writes to Ly Londonderry & others of his family the marriage of B. Baring to Ly Sandwich's daughter.[2] Mr B. gives them £5,000 pr. am. at present, & puts £25,000 pr. am. under settlement; jointure for her £3,000 a year. Lady S. is not much liked; so people do not much rejoice at this delightful young man being snapped up for her ugly daughter.

Rival balls were an excitement in society. There seem to have been two. The first was got up by Lady Hertford and the Dowager Duchess of Richmond. Then Lady Conyngham started another, with many of the same patronesses. To this the King of course went. "The Irish Ball," wrote Lady Holland elsewhere, "produces much malice and charity strongly blended. I avoid hearing the tittle tattle, but it is abundant."

Holland House, *May* 24, 1822.

. . . Lord Francis is to be married in a few days . . . I think there never was much danger of the young lady refusing. The Staffords have, I hear, behaved very well & kindly. Ld Liverpool mistook Sir Joseph Copley for old Charles Greville, & wished him joy. He was furious, & next day, retorted, by complimenting him upon his marriage with Miss Liddell.[3] B. Baring's marriage is postponed for a year, which gives his friends some hope that when he sees a little of the world & other faces, he may escape the clutches of Lady Sandwich. The D. of York's horse, Moses, won £7000 at Epsom; &, what I am very glad of, Punch won 3500, tho' the *Legs* (*sic*), with whom he betted, deny the debt; but it is to be hoped he will nevertheless get the better of their roguery. The Irish Ball does not fill as might have been expected. Tickets go off heavily; & there is a difficulty about Dukes of Gloucester & Sussex. The King will not allow them to be invited; & the D. of Devonshire dislikes the rudeness of not doing so. Lady Jersey, fortunately for the peace of the town, was invited to Carlton House last night. She knew the Princess of Denmark at Paris.

[1] Rogers's poem *Italy* was published anonymously.

[2] William Bingham Baring (1799–1864), son of Alexander Baring (later Lord Ashburton) and his successor in the title. His marriage to Lady Harriet Montagu took place in April 1823. Her mother was widow of the 6th Earl of Sandwich, and daughter of Armar, 1st Earl of Belmore.

[3] Lord Liverpool's second marriage, not to Miss Liddell, but to Miss Chester, Lord Bagot's niece, took place in September.

June 1st, 1822.

The little incidents of the Ball make topics : such as Lady Londonderry placing herself in the seat next the King, intended for Lady C. : said Lady C. looking dreadfully cross & askance.   Thereupon Mlle Le Vert, the handsome Parisian actress, placed herself directly under the King, ogled & caught his eye.   She never lost it, & there went on a most brisk œillade between them, which may perhaps lead to something.

Lord Londonderry committed suicide on August 12.   Canning succeeded him as Foreign Secretary.

Thursday, August 15, 1822.   Hd H.

. . . This shocking event quite stunned me.   We heard of it the day it happened.   Ld Egremont sent us an account from Petworth, to Woolbeding.   The speculations upon the consequences have not yet reached my ear ; but the few I have heard seem to mark Peel as likely to be supreme.   Some say it may have its effect upon Canning's Indian destination ; but he is neither popular with King, D. of York, Chancellor, Bathurst, etc : nor with the Country, nor with the Opposition.   Towards them & the Country, he has, by some rash & uncalled-for declarations against *Reform*, placed an insuperable barrier, & latterly by the line, unnecessarily active, upon the Scotch business indisposed several of our leading men personally against him ; but till H. M. returns we can know nothing.   Lord Gower, as you have heard, took George, with an intention of proceeding on to Edinburgh, but hearing this dreadful catastrophe, returned to see his friend Clanwilliam,[1] who is cruelly cut up by this blow ; but he will receive all the consolations friendship can offer.

25 *September*, 1822.   Hd H.

. . . The King in his first interview with Canning recommended Clanwilliam, whom he said was a legacy from Lord Londonderry. Accordingly he is to have a good German mission, Berlin, as soon as Mr Rose can be expelled.   Ld Howard[2] is precis writer, merely to put him into harness.   Some say it is infra dig. for a peer ; but in these enlightened, equalizing days that does not much signify.   India is still unsettled.   Mr Huskisson is to have something good, certainly

---

[1] Richard Charles Francis, 3rd Earl (1795-1879).   With Lord Castlereagh at Vienna in 1814.   George Howard was Lord Morpeth's son.

[2] Lord Howard de Walden, *see* p. 19.

not the C.ship of the Exchequer, as Ld Liverpool holds him as dear
as Miss Chester ; probably but little *difference* in their intimacy. Lady
Conyngham is just come to town. She has been staying at Denbighs.
Some think there is a coldness between the Lovers. There is Knighton
at hand to foment any difference between them.

Saturday, November 9th, [1822].

. . . Rogers seems to let his affections slip into new channels, &
has given us up. He is always with the Grenvilles, & trying, I suspect,
to get quite initiated into the Stafford concern at Richmond through
Mr Grenville. He is a strange man, & will throw off many friends
with whom he might have gone through life comfortably. It is
foolish at any age to give up established friends ; for sickness & old
age come on, & then old habits are valuable.

Monday, November 11.

Yesterday we had Fitzpatricks & Smiths, 2 Broughams, Campbell,
Heber, Ld Gower, etc. If infirmities were matters of mirth, one really
might have smiled yesterday, tho' poet Campbell [1] took it up in the
horrified strain. Mr Smith,[2] *loud sniffs* next to C. ; opposite, Vernon,
with twitches & convulsions, involuntary muscular motions ;
Brougham as usual ; & young William, his brother, with incipient
jerks & distortions. Four persons all making faces at each other,
à l'envi, certainly excite the risible faculties. Not mine, as it gives
me pain & disgust.

Saturday, Nov. 30.

Lord Spencer has told Mr Venables, his manager, house steward
& factotum, that it is necessary he should reduce his expenditures
£10,000 pr. am. If such persons feel, what must little ones do ;

---

[1] Thomas Campbell (1777–1824).

[2] Robert Percy Smith, best known as " Bobus " (1770–1845), elder brother
of Sydney Smith, married Caroline Vernon in 1797, one of the three Misses
Vernon celebrated in Horace Walpole's Correspondence, daughters of the
1st Countess of Upper Ossory, by her 2nd marriage with Richard Vernon.
She had found a home partly with Lord Lansdowne, who had married her half-
sister, Lady Louisa Fitzpatrick, as his 2nd wife, especially after the latter's death
in 1789. Her eldest brother, Vernon, was later created Lord Lyveden. Miss
Elizabeth Vernon, another of the trio, never married, and lived after 1804 with
Miss Caroline Fox, Lord Holland's sister, at Little Holland House. Lady
Holland usually in these letters refers to these two as " Our Ladies " ; whereas
" The Ladies " more often indicates the Ladies Anne and Gertrude Fitzpatrick,
daughters of the 2nd Earl of Upper Ossory.

especially in our case, where the *whole* of one branch of income is cut off totally & has been sometime, the West Indies, I mean. Watson Taylor's [1] books are upon sale, & his furniture will soon follow. His house is settled, so is not saleable.

When Judge Bayley was at Harrogate, after dinner he wrote a letter. Being puzzled about the orthography of the name of the place, he called the waiter, asked him if there was a W. in Harrogate. ' Yes, Sir, several, but we don't bring them to the Hotel.''

[1] The well-known collector.

CHAPTER II

1823–1824

Fox had spent December and January with his parents, and went off to the South of France and Italy in February with John Wortley.

10th March, [1823].

. . . I was much shocked & grieved at the death of my poor friend Kemble,[1] who was as estimable in private life as distinguished in his public career. It is a strange coincidence that his foolish but much attached friend Bob Heathcote died almost at the same time. Poor Kemble ! He was sincerely attached to me. Mrs Siddons was preparing for her journey to Lausanne to spend the summer with him. All these events have made me feel out of spirits. For God's sake & mine, dear Boy, be careful of your health, take opening physics & wrap yourself up well ; a Southern sun is not indifferent, & has always been inimical to your health.

March 13th, [1823. Burlington Street].

. . . I took Mary [2] to the Opera. The music is exquisite of the 1st act. The Ballet of *Alfred* has pretty dancing & graceful groupes ; but the violation of all regard to costume, & the want of all splendor of decoration, makes it very inferior to our Covent Garden spectacles in that respect. After all, an opera is a very moderate species of amusement to frequent habitually. In Italy, however, it does very well : it suits their manners. The boxes are spacious, & they have no drama. At Florence in old times the fling at the Tuscans was their parcimony, & which upon close calculation seemed to them that a box was cheaper than lights at home. They are a very frugal people, & I doubt not were correct in their estimates.

The D. of Devonshire likes rapid travelling. Today he went before the lark, to reach Chatsworth in the evening. He is arranging with Mr Wyatt his books, shifting them to another part of the house. I believe you were told that the silly game of Cardinal Poüffe has an equal run with écarté. Hundreds are won & lost at it after dinner. It was an importation from Bruxelles.

[1] John Philip Kemble, the actor (1757–1823). Mrs. Siddons was his sister.
[2] Hon. Mary Fox, her daughter.

16

Lady Jersey [1] is in town, more agreable than she has been for years, *talkative* as you must suppose, but not tedious in her politics. Indeed, we had none here except towards the close of the day ; & then she took a turn at the Tithes & Corn, but she was soon turned from these topics to some more feminine.

Direct to Hd H.   We leave this on Wednesday next.

21st March, 1823.   H. H.

We came last night to this venerable & beloved mansion. Of course the weather became *worse* the day we were to move ; a heavy fall of snow for some hours, but as it does not lie long at this season we fulfilled our plan.   Ly C. Lamb has published another novel, [2] in which Ld B. is represented as the *evil one*.   It is a strange rhapsody, from as much as I could read of it, apparently helped by Mr Bankes, who is a very intimate ally, in the Turkish & Oriental passages.   The dedication to Lydia White [3] is well imagined & literally executed ; but as there is some feeling expressed probably Wm Lamb worded it. There is Greek in the Motto, I believe.   The book is called *Ida* (*sic*) *Rees* or *Reis* ; but to say the truth, I could not wade through, & guessed the author very soon, & found was right upon enquiry.   Some one said of Ly Caroline, that her head was *red*, her heart *black*, her liver *white*.

It is cried out against the Ministers for giving something in the Marines to the amount of £4000 pr. am. to the D. of Clarence, considering how many naval men are reduced by the Peace & want some places of emolument : also in voting the monument to Ld St Vincent, which, by the bye, was suggested by Ld Althorp. [4]   That to Ld Duncan was added, in order to lessen the compliment.   Ld St Vincent for mental powers, science and knowledge of all sorts, was the *greatest* man this country has produced among his contemporaries, but he was stern & harsh & personally unpopular.   Ld Keith [5] has left his property much as it was rumoured he would, the

---

[1] Sarah Sophia, daughter of 10th Earl of Westmorland, married George, 5th Earl of Jersey.   She inherited the immense wealth of her grandfather, Robert Child, the banker, and took a leading part in society, with strong leaning to the anti-Whig side of politics.   She died in 1867.

[2] Wife of William Lamb, later Lord Melbourne.

[3] " Miss Diddle," of Lord Byron's *Blues*.   A wealthy Irish woman, who entertained profusely.   She died in 1827.

[4] Lord St. Vincent died on the 14th.   His monument is in St. Paul's.

[5] George Keith Elphinstone, Viscount Keith (1746–1823), Admiral.   His daughter Margaret (1788–1867), married the Comte de Flahault in 1817.

money & Scotch estates in trust for any son his daughter Margaret, now Ly Keith, may have ; in default of having one, to his second daughter.

March 25, 1823. Hd. H.

. . . We have not yet been able to move into the Library, but live in the winter Drawing Rooms ; the inner one with a small party only seems quite crowded.   Yesterday we had a pleasant one : 5 Morpeths,[1] George & Mrs Lamb, Ld Ashley & C. Ellis.   Ld A.[2] is improved in manner, less stiff.   He talked much to Allen, consulted about books, which appears always a good sign in a young man.   He is well looking ; tho' Ly Georgina observes truly enough, that he has a *Smith* look, which as far as it goes takes off from his beauty & agrémens.   Harriet Howard is a charming girl, full of vivacity with some mildness, & brilliancy of mind & wit.   The D. of D. has declined the Royal mandate, alleging a long-settled party at Chiswick.   The Theatricals are not abandoned, therefore.   The "Iron Chest"[3] is the play : Sir Edward, by Lord Normanby ; George Howard, Wilford ; Mrs Hope, Ly Normanby, & Theresa Villiers, the Ladies & Ly Tankerville.   The Morpeths & Granvilles go to the Pavilion for a few days. Ly C. Lamb's novel, in which Lord Byron is represented as the *old one*, the enemy of mankind, besides Mr Bankes's [4] pen was chiefly compounded by *Godwin*, the author of *Caleb Williams*, etc.   He is very poor, keeps a stationers' shop, & is ready to assist with his pen any distressed author or authoress.   It seems also that in her former writings she was assisted by Mr *Combe*,[5] the man who was known as the author of the *Diaboliad*, a satire on the Luttrell family.   Rogers has

---

[1] George, Viscount Morpeth (1773–1848), succeeded in 1825 as 6th Earl of Carlisle.   His wife was Lady Georgina Cavendish, daughter of William, 5th Duke of Devonshire.   Three of their daughters were with them.   Georgina, the second, as has been noted, married Agar Ellis : and Harriet, George Granville, Earl Gower, subsequently Marquis of Stafford and 2nd Duke of Sutherland.

[2] Anthony, Lord Ashley (1801–85), later 7th Earl of Shaftesbury, the philanthropist.   Lady Holland's account of him in early life is amusing : " Your friend, Ld Ashley, is going abroad for two years.   His absence will be a blessing to young ladies.   He is a male coquet, the cruellest of characters & the most cold hearted.   But he is very handsome and captivating ; & young ladies are willing to be deceived, & from their own vanity often exaggerate attentions. But if they fall in love, poor things, it is hard, let the fault be where it may."

[3] By William Godwin (1756–1836), the dramatised version of *Caleb Williams*. He was husband of Mary Wollstonecraft.   His shop failed in 1822.

[4] William John Bankes (*d.* 1855).   M.P. for Dorset, and traveller in the East

[5] William Combe (1741–1823), author of *Dr. Syntax*.

sprained his ancle. Charles [1] is safe at Dublin, well, & full of good advice to us on the advantage of keeping early hours. Mr Knight is publishing his epic poem called *Alfred* in 13 books. Foscolo [2] is giving lectures at 5 guineas a person on the Italian language & literature. They will be excellent ; but he will have many subscribers & no audience.

[*April* 1, 1823.]

. . . I went behind the scenes & heard Lady Tankerville rehearse. [3] It was very pretty, her accent & tones ; the whole was a scene of business & bustle, all gay, occupied & good humoured. George [4] accused of handling too roughly those he got in contact with : warned not to grasp the ladies with vehemence. The Duke has given up acting himself, being afraid from his deafness he may, by not catching the *cues*, put out the others : but to show his zeal, he delivers the Prologue. Lady C. Greville, [5] by her caprice & almost ill-breeding, has caused delay. She rehearsed & acted well, but owing to Punch's interference, threw up her part, which has been suppressed in the play. None of the Grevilles were to be invited ; but George begged so much for Ly Francis, who was so eager to go, that she has been indulged in consequence of her condition. Lord Francis has become a daily visitor at Murray's, where he is going to publish translations from *Faust*. Those who have seen his verses say they are admirable.

Mr Wortley [6] was captivated by H. Majesty's graciousness at the Pavilion, patting his shoulder & giving snuff & various attentions irrestible when from Majesty. Sydney [7] is as joyous as ever, making us laugh beyond all measure. You never saw a person enjoy his jokes more than Ld Howard, [8] who, strange to say, had never heard of him

[1] Charles Richard Fox, the Hollands' eldest son. Originally in the Navy, he was now an Army captain.

[2] Ugo Foscolo (1778–1827), Italian patriot. In England after 1815 : a protégé of the Hollands.

[3] In the "Iron Chest." Corise Armandine, daughter of Antoine, Duc de Gramont, wife of Charles, 5th Earl. Her sister married Marshal Sebastiani.

[4] George William Frederick Howard (1802–64), succeeded as 7th Earl of Carlisle in 1848, son of Lord Morpeth (6th Earl).

[5] Lady Charlotte Greville, "Punch" Greville's mother, wife of old Charles Greville, and daughter of 3rd Duke of Portland.

[6] James Archibald Stuart-Wortley (1776–1845), M.P. for Yorkshire. Created Lord Wharncliffe in 1826. Father of John Wortley, with whom Fox was travelling.

[7] Rev. Sydney Smith.

[8] Charles Augustus Ellis, 6th Lord Howard de Walden from 1803 (1799–1868), succeeded his father, Charles Rose Ellis, 1st Lord Seaford, in 1845.

before ; it was a wonderful surprize. Rogers has been confined by a sprained ancle which he fancies requires great nursing, so we have been deprived of him sometime.

April 18, 1823.

. . . On Wednesday, St George's Day, Mary will be presented to His Majesty by Lady Lansdowne. Then she will be fairly *out*, a *bill upon the door*, to say she *is to be had*. Lord Byron has written to Mr Moore an account of you, very pretty & complimentary : you shall see it, as I could not resist taking a copy, tho' the alliance with such a man is not desirable & creditable beyond distant admiration.[1]

There was last night an unpleasant affair between Messrs Brougham & Canning,[2] in which the latter quite lost his temper, crying out, " *That is false* " ; but it was made up by the House & the Speaker, so I hope there will not be any suite. Your friends the Peels [3] dine here today. Henry Greville has not been to see me tho' staying in town. I always told you, we were not *fine* enough or exquisite enough for him. Harriet Howard is the admiration of all London : she is lovely & captivating.

The mischief to Canning has been incalculable. He has ceased to inspire any reverence among his followers. His voice no longer imposes silence, or summons them to his standard. He has been in a minority. B. has acquired great control over the House by his judgment & temper. If he can hold this hitherto even tenor, he will be the greatest man there ; but he has always erred in the moment of victory, become intoxicated & offensive. The night of the Foreign Papers, C. advised Marcellus [4] not to go the House, as he might hear expressions injurious to his Court. However he went, & certainly heard abundantly in that strain. C. on going out saw him, & said, " Tu l'a voulu, tu l'a voulu, George Dandin," proud probably at being able to quote a scrap of French. Marcellus out of vengeance wrote to his Court that B. was a thorough " *Radicale*, aucunement dans la bonne compagnie." James Brougham is coming into Parliament for one of Ld Darlington's boro's ; also Mr Alderson—this is of course all out of compliment to B. himself.

Ld Byron's *Age of Bronze* makes little or no sensation. What it does, is not favourable : I have not read it. He writes too much. The prettiest thing of his that I have seen is his description of you :

---

[1] For the letter to the poet, see *Journal of Henry Edward Fox*, p. 165.
[2] In the debate on the Catholic Claims. (Compare *Creevey*, ii. 67–8.)
[3] Laurence Peel, younger brother of Sir Robert, married Lady Jane Lennox.
[4] Comte de Marcellus, French diplomat.

there is *more* poetry than in any of his later productions, tho' I think more *truth* than poetry. At least my heart feels it as gospel light.

27th [April, 1823].

. . . We went to the ball at D. H., where Lady Lansdowne undertook the charge of Mary. Said Mary looked very pretty & was much admired. Her dancing, as you may believe, was not excellent, but your friend Ld Ashley was very anxious & kind in assisting to keep her right. The comical event was that her début in dancing was with Marcellus. The whole room were diverted, & ascribed it to a joke of Ly Tankerville's. It was odd, considering that so few hours had elapsed since Papa had been pretty sharp on *his* Court. I was very well satisfied with the result of her first appearance. I hope she will continue to look as well at Esterhazy's, etc. Almack's from what I hear is declining in fashion. Écarté has died a natural death. As Mary is *out*, I think it will be better policy to keep her in the eye of the batchelors. As you know, my opinion is that her charms consist much in the beauté du diable ; & I wish for your assistance to introduce some good épouseurs to her notice. Prince Leopold says she is as fresh as Hebe ! Accordingly she admires said heavy Prince, who is beginning to play a part as future Regent to the future Queen, his niece.

Hd. H. *Monday*, 5th May.

. . . I added to the body of Papa's letter a few words, to apprize you of the brilliant event in the Howard family.[1] It was a surprize to all ; as Ly Augusta Hervey was the person George & others believed Ld Gower was disposed to offer to. Dear George will be extremely happy, as he is very fond of Ld G., & agrees with me in the same partiality on account of many traits of resemblance to Lord Morpeth ; tho' of course there is much superiority in Ld M., both in natural powers & acquirement, but the morale is alike. Harriet is a lucky person, as I really do not know a blemish in the character of the futur, & I sincerely hope she will make him happy. The Greville family will, I trust, be speedily baffled in their expectation of having *their* dependants heirs of the Stafford & Bridgewater properties. It is lucky for Ly Charlotte she has no more daughters, else the viper tongue of your friend Hy Greville would keep away all suitors ; as nothing is more injurious than a mauvaise langue in a family to the young ladies.

[1] Lady Harriet Howard's engagement to her cousin, Earl Gower.

Joanna Baillie's [1] *Poems*, of which she is the editor for a charitable purpose & has obtained contributions of verses from various poets, is published. It has answered her benevolent view, but is a flimsy, dull collection. With the exception of *Macduff's Cross*, by Sir Walter, there is little to praise. By the bye Sir Walter is become a member of the Roxburghe Club, in quality of author of *Waverly*. He accepted by saying he would represent the author. [2] Capt Franklin's Journey to the Coppermine river & Polar Sea is an interesting narrative, written with great simplicity & feeling. [3] Indeed it is so well executed, that one does not think of the style & manner in the least, which is the best test of merit in such compositions. Ld Wm Gordon, six hours before he expired, sent his old servant with a message of good will to Lord Egremont, to tell him he was going the long journey, & wished him happiness. Ld E. was a good deal affected. Ld Glenbervie is dead. [4] Poor old man, he never felt much for others, so cannot expect great sympathy for himself. He had, however, one gift which was pleasant, & he retained it to the last, great eagerness of mind in any pursuit in which he engaged : & he always had a pursuit, to the moment of his death even. He was busy in writing a Life of Ld North ; & the proof sheets were with him to the last.

H. H. *12th May* [1823].

. . . We dined at the Cotton King's [5] yesterday, always a huge concern, especially as Sydney was not there to dispel the gloom. We avoided calicoes & cotton twist, as carefully as one should *la corde* in a maison de pendu ; for I believe, now they are so wealthy and senatorial, all allusion to the shop is dropped. After our dinner we went for half an hour to Ly Jersey, who is by way of being in devotion on Sunday, i.e., only dining out, but not going to an assembly, but receiving all the town at her own house. Being early we only found a few. Mrs Hope [6] came in from a dinner at Ly Sandwich's, where she met

---

[1] Scottish dramatist and poetess (1762–1851).

[2] *Waverley* was published anonymously. *See ante*, p. 2 *n*.

[3] Sir John Franklin, the explorer (1786–1847).

[4] Sylvester Douglas, Lord Glenbervie, born in 1743. An Irish peer.

[5] Samuel Boddington, M.P. for Tralee. Henry Webster, Lady Holland's second son by her 1st marriage, married his daughter Grace in 1824, after some strenuous opposition from her parent.

[6] Louisa Beresford, youngest daughter of William, Lord Decies, Archbishop of Tuam, married William Hope, of Deepdene, the collector. They were caricatured as " Beauty and the Beast."

Mrs Baring,[1] whom she described as looking quite mortified & wretched. Ly H. Baring bounced forth in favor of foreign countries, society, manners, climate, etc., & *her* intention of going speedily. Upon being asked how her bridegroom liked that plan, she replied, " He is but a boy just out of College. What can he know, or what can he like ? " She is just 17. One might have acquiesced in her opinion as to his unformed & unsound taste in choosing her.

Ampthill. 18*th*, 19*th*, *May*, [1823].

. . . You are wrong in ascribing such an absurd opinion, as my doubting the competence of a person under 40 being capable of forming an opinion. I may have thought a mature opinion better than a raw one of a lad. You will make painful discoveries every year of the fleeting charms of beauties, even those in your youth whom you admired ! Beauty, alas ! is a transient ornament, as all life is too much so ; but Mrs Alfred's eyes I dare say speak pretty things still. We grieve over your smoking practice. Not that I mind the fumes as others do ; but the breath, digestion & teeth are its victims, & the brilliant tints of your complexion will go rapidly & make you as pale as your companion, & sodden as Ld Francis.

I am not surprised at the disgust you feel upon reading Rousseau's *Confessions.* One abhors the man ; not even the magic of the style covers the atrocity of his mind. Naturally suspicious & selfish, he confirmed the latter propensity by thinking & writing eternally of *self, self.* No habit so pernicious & sure of producing conceit & selfishness as writing Confessions or Memoirs ; unless the writer has been engaged in public life, & describes men & events he has witnessed & shared in, whom from his station he has been thrown with. And even then he must avoid thrusting himself too forward as the hero of the tale he describes.

We came on Thursday, found this pretty place in great beauty ; the tender greens of the foliage, the blossoms & the gay population of birds, squirrels, game, etc., render it cheerful. The only visitors are Wm Rose & Rogers, both agreable ; the latter in his best style. Tomorrow, the Ords ; Thursday, Woburn for 2 nights ; & on Saturday, Hey ! for Hd H. Mary goes Wednesday for the ball at D. H. on Friday. She will go, I trust, under the wing of Lady Georgiana.[2] The D. of D. surprised his numerous guests with a

---

[1] Anne Louisa, daughter of William Bingham of Philadelphia, wife of Alexander Baring, afterwards Lord Ashburton. For her son, Bingham Baring's marriage to Lady Harriet Montagu, *see* p. 12.

[2] Morpeth.

magnificent supper after the Opera on Friday. They were gratified,
which does not happen often when people try to please the public ;
& the Duke is such an object of envy that he is viewed with especial
jealousy ; but his genuine good-nature & sincere desire to please
seems to conquer the bad, envious passions of the beau-monde. The
Eton Montem is today : many are gone. Lord Sefton, who has a
ferme ornée at Stoke, near Windsor, has a party, of which Ly Jersey,
Mr Brougham, Luttrell, & others make a part : perhaps also the
Cowpers, as Frederick is still at school.

I rather enjoy the retired tranquillity of this place, having been
able to read *de longue haleine*, without interruptions, which at Hd H.
is rather difficult, unless one shuts the doors to all comers. W.
Scott's novel from the extracts in the Journals seems to be out. From
them it is not promising.[1] He should never cross the Tweed : he
rarely has done so with impunity, tho' *Ivanhoe* is all countries, being
I suspect the manners of no one. Allen is teazed with lumbago, &
quite overwhelmed with Anglo-Saxon & *Norse* learning.

Ampthill, 22nd May, [1823].

. . . Ld Melbourne [2] was hustled at Montem & had his pocket
picked. There has been a great fight at Andover. Old Ld Lynedoch [3]
took the stage coach to himself, & went 60 miles for that purpose.
What a wonderful man, at his age to be so eager, & to have such
powers of doing what he likes. His poverty is his only arrogance ;
& that arises from having squandered his substance upon Ly Asgill
& her sisters.

I hear Miss Canning [4] is beset by Marcellus & all the young
foreigners ; but that is ascribed to political ruse, to get a footing
with Canning in quality of Foreign Secretary. *Quintin Durwood* is
rather heavy. It has no original character . . . You had better
wait till you get home to read it.

Henry Fox returned from his trip abroad in June 1823, and remained
in England for over a year. Afterwards he first went to Paris, and
then on to Switzerland and Italy, the chief reason for his departure
being his attachment to Miss Theresa Villiers, which for several reasons
his parents did not view with approval.

[1] *Quentin Durward.*

[2] Peniston Lamb, 1st Viscount, died 1829 : father of the Prime Minister.

[3] Thomas Graham, 1st Baron (1748–1843), General.

[4] Miss Harriet Canning, to whom Henry Fox was making up in 1822. George
Canning's daughter. She married Ulick, 14th Earl and later 1st Marquis of
Clanricarde.

26 January, 1824.

. . . You do well to work, you will be both a better & happier man, & also give yourself a chance of being great & useful. You have power for *anything*, a singularly clear head ; which will, if you exert yourself, that is if you will persevere, enable you to conquer all the ruggedness of learning.

We had to dinner yesterday, Villa Real, Binda & Macintosh,[1] & sat for the first time in the drawing rooms. Mac. is staying here : he is better, thank Heaven, & of course agreable. How full & ready he is with his knowledge.

Ly Westmorland [2] visited Lady Tankerville at Paris. Her head was adorned with a circle of stuffed humming birds & parraquitts. She has a watch with an alarum which begins humming at the hour fixed, a signal to finish her visit. Alas ! when she visited me she had no such monitor. Lady Downshire, when she left Paris was accompanied by a physician of the name of Morrison, an English freemason. The Neapolitan Govt had notice of this, & gave orders to arrest him on the frontier & prevent his entering their territory. At Florence Morrison was detained by some business ; so she only approached the Kingdom of Naples with Mr Reid, who was instantly seized, stripped, his body examined to ascertain whether he had any cabalistic marks, & admission absolutely refused, as nothing would persuade the people *he* was not Dr Morrison.

Henry Fox was at Brighton at this time.

Hd House. *Feb.* 7, 1824.

. . . I have not myself seen the articles against Ly Conyngham ; they are in the evening papers. It is explained by Knighton [3] having withdrawn from the editors the large sums hitherto given for hush money upon all Royal matters. It is but fair *he* should be involved in the abuse. It is reported that his Majesty will almost immediately come to Windsor for change of air. Is this so ? Lord Tichfield [4] has relapsed. He had been so well as to be restored to mutton chops & Cobbett, coarse fare ! He then went out, & exposed himself im-

---

[1] Sir James Mackintosh (1765–1832).

[2] Jane, 2nd wife of John, 10th Earl, and daughter of Dr. Saunders. She died in 1857.

[3] Sir William Knighton (1776–1836), Physician, Private Secretary and Privy Purse to George IV.

[4] William Henry Cavendish-Bentinck, Marquis of Titchfield, eldest son of 4th Duke of Portland, died in March.

prudently to a cold Club room without fire, & is thrown again upon his couch. I am really sorry. He is one of the few young men who are not very frivolous. I am sorry to hear écarté is becoming such a game, even in the country. 50 guineas were lost in a moment at Middleton. Papa dines today at C. Ellis's to meet the W. Indians, a necessary, but in this stage of the business fruitless duty, as your friend Ld Bathurst,[1] by delay, has brought the Colonies to the brink of destruction. Your Papa told me a story against you that is good, I hope not quite true, that a lady, upon hearing you kept a diary & drew characters, said, "It ought to be called 'Fox's Martyrs'." Is this true, & who was the jester?

The Duke of Bedford was taken seriously ill in the summer of 1822, but lived until 1839. He acquired the adjoining property to Holland House on Campden Hill in the summer of 1823, the house being known as Bedford Lodge, and subsequently as Argyle Lodge and Cam House.

April 21 [1824], Woburn Abbey.

The Duke of Bedford passed a better night than usual. His cheerfulness & equanimity of temper is delightful. Agar is all astonishment and admiration of this practical philosophy. He could not, without having witnessed it, have believed such benevolence co-existent with such a state of suffering and threatening; for one cannot disguise to oneself that Damocles could not have had a more precarious tenure. The Sculpture Gallery is a great amusement & resource to him. It really contains some very choice & curious things. Some of the modern rubbish, which was only left by way of fill up or stop gaps, will be removed. We have been looking over some very fine sketches of Flaxman's for two bas-reliefs from Milton; some of the number are very spirited & good.

The Ministers objected to Lord Francis's[2] marriage in Carlton House, so it is to be at The Cottage. The King has purchased Hollygrove in Windsor Park for him; & they are to live in Warwick House[3] in London. The jewels are very splendid, *donations* from an old relation in N. Ireland, who is in retirement; the same good body who gives the £20,000.

[1] Henry, 3rd Earl. He was Secretary for War and the Colonies.

[2] Lord Francis Conyngham (1797–1876), whose elder brother, Earl of Mount Charles, died in December 1824. He succeeded his father, as 2nd Marquis of Conyngham, in 1832, having married Lord Anglesey's daughter, Lady Jane Paget.

[3] No doubt Princess Charlotte's house in West Street, Cockspur Street

Holland House. *9th July.*

On Wednesday I spent a most agreable day at Campden Hill. Eliza [1] dined to meet Mary. Papa at G. Byng's, where he met & admired Ly J. Thynne. Mr Tierney came down to sleep here, & joined me at the Duke's. He keeps perfectly well : defies even punch & turtle. We dined here yesterday with Tavistocks, Ld Grey, Lauderdale, Alvanley. With the latter I dine today, & go afterwards *probably* to San Antonio's concert to hear Rossini . . .

I have got an invitation to Cassiobury for Dumont.[2] It is a place every foreigner should see, to know the perfections of keeping gardens & grounds. The Duchess of Beaufort has had an amiable interview with Ld Worcester,[3] & invited Ly W. to England. Her religious scruples have taken this turn ; but the marriage is still liable to be dissolved any day by any ill-natured person. Lord W. is of such an amiable nature that he is sure of winning the affections of all ; so open & free from every species of conceit, perhaps too humble in his own opinion.

Charles Richard Fox married Mary FitzClarence, the Duke of Clarence's daughter by Mrs. Jordan, on June 19 ; and on the 28th, Henry Fox left England for Paris.

Hd. H. 16*th July,* [1824].

. . . Your Papa was pleased with his dinner ; Canning in his very gayest mood. The ladies of his family very agreable ; the young one is in great beauty. Ly Westmorland the night she arrived preferred staying at the Hotel in Thames Street to proceeding to the West end of the town. She is now at Nerot's (?), where she intercepts those who go to bathe, by *imagining* their visit is to her. Thus she caught Lord Cowper for some hours. At Cassiobury we had hardly any company ; but the day I left the Duke, many of Lord Essex's ragamuffins arrived, Sharp (?), Nicholson, wife, etc.

The silly Bishop Pelham married Lord de Dunstanville & Miss Lemon.[4] The little he had to do he did ill throughout ; & to the consternation of the Clerk closed the Ceremony by saying, " You are now God & Man," instead of " Man & Wife."

[1] Lady Georgina Elizabeth Russell.

[2] Pierre Etienne Dumont, Swiss professor, who was a habitué at Bowood and Lansdowne House before returning to Switzerland in 1814. He died in 1829.

[3] Henry, Earl of Worcester, and subsequently 7th Duke of Beaufort (1792–1853), married his 1st wife's half-sister, Emily Frances Smith.

[4] Lord de Dunstanville's 2nd wife was a daughter of Sir William Lemon.

We have had little Moore [1] to breakfast this morning. He confirms
what I before told you of there not being a line in the suppressed
portion of Memoirs by Lord Byron, not a line as far as my memory
extends. I forgot whether you read his own account of the
marriage. I send the vile thing. By the bye I hear there is great
abuse of me in *John Bull*. Lord Essex was much insensed at it being
sent to him last Sunday, which he says was done because it was known
I was at Cassiobury. I never have seen it, so cannot tell to what it
alludes ; probably connected with Hy Webster's business. I agree
that a fit of the gout would be opportune, if it prevented La Fayette
from going to U. States. [2] He is too old to move his household gods.
Should he be well enough to return to La Grange, I hope you will
make him a visit there.

[Undated. End of July ?] *Tuesday* [1824].

Your charming letter did me good. It not only amused but
gratified me. The tone is so natural to your own heart, so unlike
the coarse or knowing slang of London beaus & belles : so pretty &
feeling, without palaver & sentiment about Souza & La Fayette. Dear
boy, you must be most agreable to them. Mrs Charles Fox has been
able to drive out. She is, I fear, a sickly subject. I was in hopes the
roturier blood of the mother might have mitigated the Royal con-
stitutions. Charles fidgets up here, often ending his days in London,
& hurrying back in a hack chaise too late for stage coaches.

Mr Petre [3] was to give a breakfast, to which Miss Villiers was to
invite ; but Ly Morley told me he could not for love or money get
an acre of ground near London, but was still trying. He even tried
at Twickenham ; but Eliza or Ly Jane Peel told me last night it was
renounced. The Peels go in a few days, via Brussels, to Switzerland.
They dined yesterday, & were agreable & good hearted. I like
both uncommonly.

[Undated. Probably July or August.]
   . . . Canning is behaving admirably, but he will never get the
Court or, I fear much, the public. His early vacillation, or as
some would say defection, sticks like a bar to his reputation. Ly C.
Lamb was so outrageous at the Horse Guards, to force her way

---

[1] Thomas Moore, the poet (1779–1852). He destroyed the Memoir and later
wrote a *Life* of Lord Byron.

[2] He took only his son with him (*see Journal of H. E. Fox*, p. 191).

[3] Hon. Robert Edward Petre, son of 9th Baron. Well-known on the Turf
and in society.

through at eleven at night, challenging to fight the Sergeant on duty, that a mob assembled, abused her ; when a gentleman very properly apprized them at Melbourne House of the scene. Wm Lamb & servants took her by force ; she was intoxicated to a degree of fury. She attempted to kill some of them. The violence continued ; & she is now attended by two women from a mad doctor. William Lamb is going abroad, the son is put to Mr Trimmer, & she is to remain confined at Brocket. All this is brought on by immoderate drinking on a violent, ungovernable temper. It will be a relief to William, as the physician declared he could not answer for the lives of those about her. She is kept low, which means being limited to one bottle of sherry daily. There is something horrid in such a termination to a person one has known so intimately from infancy ; but she never had a particle of good in her whole composition.[1]

Hd H. *31st August*, [1824].

. . . We are excessively overcome here by heavy fogs, augmented by the East winds & smoke of London ; not above 4 hours in 24 clear. This heavy atmosphere oppresses us all extremely, but nothing seriously amiss. Ly C. Ashley's[2] marriage is declared with Mr Lister ; he is well spoken of, but is not rich enough to have a lovely wife out of a great house, & have a hunting establishment besides. He has only £3000 pr am. L. Smith,[3] *alias* Moloch, has been cured of his love some months, so looks upon the affair with indifference, adding that had he not been cured, the choice of such a suitor would have done it. He says they are an insipid pair. What says Ld Ashley ? The D. of York dined here on Sunday, & was in tiptop spirits, excellent health, & much more agreable than he was ever known to be. He was very obliging to Charles, but merely distantly civil to Mrs Charles, who is a nice person & deserved more partiality. Our party was gay & pleasant. I asked Henry Webster, who is going on very oddly in his amour ; but by discreet & respectful behaviour he will ultimately succeed, I hope, as he wishes it, with the father. All *I*

---

[1] Lady Holland wrote on September 6 : " Wm Lamb seems in better spirits, tho' Ly C. is again turned loose. The physicians will not sign to her being mad enough to be confined. They say she is only wicked from temper & brandy. So you see Allen's saying was quite just, that ' if madness was a disease of the heart & not of the head, she was mad, not otherwise.' "

[2] Lady Charlotte Ashley, daughter of 6th Earl of Shaftesbury, married Henry Lyster, of Rowton Castle, Shropshire.

[3] Leveson Smith, " Bobus " Smith's younger son, who died in 1827.

inculcate is to avoid any appearance of clandestine proceeding, to
act openly in all he does, & on no account to marry without the
consent of the family, as old Boddington has all in his power, and
would either re-marry or adopt his nephew ; & poverty would not
suit either Miss B. or Hy W.[1]

Dear Charles is very well in health, but getting into his usual restless
way.   He wants to fly for shooting into Sussex, because he cannot
go to Ampthill till the 7th ; & is half angry at Ld Lansdowne for
not receiving him when they are quite alone, he & Ly L.   In that
yesterday he was in one of *his ways* : got out of bed the wrong side.
He does not like the notion of three days at Bushey, where she naturally
likes to be.[2]   When he has been in harness a few months longer, he
will bear the restraint better.   En attendant, tho' fond of her, he only
considers her as an auxiliary to his medals & other possessions, not
as a principal.   But it will all do well ; as she is very winning, & very
firm, & sincerely fond of him.   Ld Ellenboro'[3] has at last succeeded
in getting a young wife, a poor girl who has not seen anything of the
world.   He could only snap up such a one, Miss Digby, a daughter
of Capt. Digby & Ly Andover.   She is grand-daughter to Mr Coke,[4]
who has *another son*.

4th November, Brighton.

. . . We came yesterday in *one day*, which is at all times an effort,
but in this season & none of us very strong, was a miracle.   The
moon was our friend latterly.   We are lodged, en attendant our own
house being vacant, in this most disagreable gîte, York Hotel ; but
in the small rooms adjoining, which is better than the great *Tavern*,
for such it is.   We have as yet only the D. of Devon., Ly Jersey &
Tierney.   The town is immensely enlarged.   Kemp Town at the top
of the East Cliff is to cut out old Brighton.   Already £800,000 have
been expended : hanging terraces to the sea, parks, & what not.
The Steyne is much injured by a huge mass built at the opening to

[1] Henry Webster was married in October.   Mr. Boddington became quite
reconciled to the match, gave his daughter away, and made " all suitable
settlements."

[2] The Duke of Clarence lived at Bushey.   Charles Fox's collection of medals
and coins was purchased at his death for Berlin.

[3] Edward Law, 2nd Baron (created Earl in 1844).   His second wife, many
years younger than him, was Jane, daughter of Admiral Sir Henry Digby.   She
was divorced in 1830, and married, 2ndly, Baron de Venningen, Prime Minister
of Bavaria ; and 3rdly, Sheik Medjwal el Misrab.   Lord Ellenborough was
Governor-General of India 1841-4.

[4] Thomas William Coke, " of Norfolk " (1752-1842), created Earl of Leicester.

the sea, which obscures the walk, & keeps off the sun & sea breezes. Also near the Pavilion are some frightful houses, which will overlook the *menus plaisirs* of his Majesty.

The Apponis [1] are much mortified at having been foiled in their English Embassy. They say Mde de Lieven is rejoiced, as she was jealous of her coming. There is a report of Ld Wellesley coming here to high office, & Lord Bristol succeeding him at Dublin ; but it is a mere street story. Ly C. Lamb is busy with Hobhouse about printing Ld Byron's letters. She is determined to shew the world how much he loved her. Hobhouse says in justification of Ld B., he will in that case publish *hers* ; but advises very sensibly to burn the whole correspondence. It is pleasant for Wm Lamb to have the degree & extent of Ld Byron's love for his wife discussed by the public.

At Lambton Races there were two incidents. [2] Ly Londonderry in a passion beat her maid till the poor woman fell into hysterics ; & Lambton himself fell upon his butler with a stick. The man threatened to return the blows. Odd that he did not. Do not mention this last story. They are both *true*. Mary is very tolerably well. She is to begin riding tomorrow, and is deep in *Anglo-Saxon* ; a very good study for her, both for English & German, & will please Allen whom she means to surprize with her learning.

18 *November,* [1824].

I find Hobhouse's pamphlet, which I possessed when I wrote last, is to be suppressed ; it was recalled from our possession. This measure is by the advice of Burdett & Brougham. Hobhouse could hardly be brought to acquiesce. I know not the reasons which were urged, but admired the warm, generous feelings which impelled H. to vindicate his friend from the misstatements of Medwin. Ly C. Lamb has failed in pressing Murray to publish a selection of Ld B.'s most passionate letters, to prove that he was in love with her. [3] Therefore she has lithographed & circulates at least one, which a person I know has seen. Mrs Leigh dined here the other day ; I used to know her

[1] Count Anton Apponyi, Austrian Ambassador in Paris for many years.

[2] Creevey (ii. 82–3) confirms both these stories. *See* also Hobhouse (*Lord Broughton's Memoirs*, iii. 80), who formed a very poor opinion of Creevey's manners there, while being in no doubts as to his abilities. Of Lady Londonderry, he wrote, "The Marchioness looks like a young Lady Holland without her talents." Frances Anne, daughter of Sir Henry Vane-Tempest, was 2nd wife of Charles William, 3rd Marquis. She died in 1865.

[3] No doubt the articles for the *Quarterly Review*, which Murray accepted, and then refused to publish. Mrs. Leigh was Byron's half-sister.

formerly. In consequence of some communication since Ld B.'s death, we have been thrown together. She is very plain, yet with a strong likeness or caricature of the Howards, Ly Julia especially. She seems amiable, & desirous that her brother's memory should be spared, alike from friends & foes.

Parliament is certainly to meet on 5th Feb. Ly Stanhope [1] is very amusing, gay & original, *not of the best polish*, but still very sprightly ; I like her much. She has the advantages of voice over Ly Morley, [2] but is as strong & *highly* coloured in her stories, tho' not quite so coarse. They are both good tempered, & a pinch of them suffices for occasionally, not for every day ; yet Ly S. has less effort about her.

22nd November, [1824].

. . . You would be surprized at seeing how much we are all won with Ly Stanhope. Her liveliness & cleverness is very bewitching, but her extreme good nature & kindness is quite delightful. Tho' very open in her opinions of people & droll, she never says anything sarcastic or ill-natured. We like her much ; & she has been very soothing to me by enlivening & at times doing me good. Miss Rogers is here with some of her family. She is a most sensible, thoroughly amiable woman. You are severe upon my friend, [3] yet there is truth too much in your observations, but not to the full extent you push them. He is not quite a safe inmate, because he observes too minutely every action, & often puts his own constructions which are frequently wide of the reality ; but he is not intentionally mischievous. He narrates domestic occurrences, more out of a silly vanity to prove he knows them, than with an intent to injure. That he ever spoke slightingly of Papa, I do not believe ; unless it was an indirect slap at me or others of the family.

6th December, [1824. Brighton].

. . . From all I have heard of Ly Bute, [4] I suspect when you get

[1] Catherine Lucy, daughter of Robert, Lord Carrington, who married 4th Earl Stanhope in 1809. She died in 1843.

[2] Frances, daughter of Thomas Talbot, of Gonville, Norfolk, 2nd wife of John, 1st Earl.

[3] Rogers.

[4] Frances, daughter of Thomas Coutts, the banker, by his 1st wife. She became John, 1st Marquis of Bute's 2nd wife, and died in 1832. Henry Fox wrote :

" Lady Bute's manner is peculiar, and at last wins one. I feel myself growing to like her better than I did before," thus fulfilling Lady Holland's prognostications. Her son, Lord Dudley Stuart, became one of his greatest friends.

acquainted with her she will captivate you beyond your expectations.
Her manner is insinuating & thoroughly winning. In extenuation
of her selfishness, this must be considered. She was the favorite
child of a doting, indulgent father. Educated for a high station, to
be obtained by marrying some old noble, she was destined to relieve
the mortgages on old Ld Lansdown's estates. Mrs Smith [1] making
that fail, she was given to an equally old Marquis, who, fond of her
beauty & character, indulged & humoured every wish. This naturally
produced whims & vagaries ; but her nature is good. All concur
is praising Ld D. Stuart; Wrio. says he is universally beloved at
Cambridge. I long to know him.

The Aberdeens [2] are come. She is nervous at the prospect of a
solitary Continental journey, yet of course cannot bear the separation.
She will go after Xmas. Robert Gordon [3] has been here for a few
days. He is one of Lord Dudley's [4] bêtes noirs. They did not speak
since Vienna ; but the matter was adjusted here, & a hollow reconcilia-
tion has taken place. Ld D. is very vindictive. Mr G.'s only offence
was sending a verbal invitation to dinner, which he assured Ld D.
was the usual fashion in Vienna. He & Rogers have met frequently,
but neither like the other ; nor has Medwin's *Conversations* [5] tended
to allay the wrath ; indeed by printing the epigram, it has rekindled
the embers of latent hatred. Medwin is a very incorrect narrator.
The famous story of a bout of rudeness between Rogers & Kinnaird
is only half told. The former remarked at dinner, " We are thirteen."
K. said, " The observer may remedy the evil." R. retorted, " The
physician may take his own prescription." Neither were civil nor
witty ; yet so the dialogue passed. You are too hard upon Rogers,
as you only dwell upon the notorious blemishes, without accepting
the qualifications of sound sense & generous upright principle &
real benevolence of heart. His tongue is viperish to be sure : but
many times it is darted without intended mischief, & inflicts perhaps
pain upon those who are too sensitive.

[1] Mrs. " Bobus " Smith. *See ante*, p. 14.

[2] George, 4th Earl of Aberdeen (1784–1860) married, 2ndly, Harriet, daughter
of Hon. James Douglas, and widow of James, Viscount Hamilton. Her son
became 1st Duke of Abercorn. She was at this time going abroad with an
ailing daughter.

[3] Sir Robert Gordon (1791–1847), plenipotentiary in Vienna, 1815, 1817
and 1821.

[4] John William Ward, Viscount Dudley (*see ante*, p. 4). He was abroad on
the Continent 1814–22.

[5] Captain Thomas Medwin's *Conversations of Lord Byron*.

The Granvilles [1] are delighted with Paris and the house belonging to the Embassy. It is doubtful if it will be kept as such. Great offers are made for the ground for building small houses & a street ; but this probably will be decided when Canning goes, which he is to do shortly, to visit the Granvilles. Entre-nous, the outcry is not small at the report of his going. A Secy of State ! All the Holy Alliance & diplomats are in an uproar, & see nothing but deep schemes in what appears a very simple action, of visiting in December an old friend whom he was to have visited at the Hague in August.

13th December, [1824].

. . . Of Ly Davy's [2] merits, *you* know I have very long been aware. She has more heart, talents, quickness of parts, & other excellent qualities, than almost anybody. I really *love* her, & I shall soon importune her with a letter when I am in better plight. Kinnaird's [3] delightful little wife is much beloved in Scotland : she is truly a gay, amiable person, & will sustain his interest in the world admirably. I have a letter from Wortley, 7th November, Philadelphia. The whole tone of the letter shews good feeling & that they have been pleased with mankind in the strange & various shapes in which they have seen them.[4] Mrs & Miss Canning go next week to visit the Granvilles. An apartment is preparing for them. Mr C. has for the present abandoned his trip : but will fetch them home, I dare say, as he has a fancy for Paris.

I went last night to see the old play revived, of a *Woman Never Vexed.* It has not much interest, but as a picture of times & manners it is interesting enough. *Rowley* is the writer, an author subsequent to Shakespeare, from whom he has taken largely, particularly from the *Merchant of Venice.* Young C. Kemble, Miss Chester, do their best ; & Cooper is improving daily. Macready apparently is the Chief at D. Lane ; therefore my visits to that theatre will be scanty. Ly Wm is as ladies like to be. This is fortunate, as it will give her an occupation when she must part with Hastings, & reconcile her to being quiet

---

[1] Granville Leveson-Gower, Viscount, and later Earl Granville (1773–1846), Ambassador in Paris 1824–8 and 1830–41. Lady Granville was daughter of 5th Duke of Devonshire.

[2] Jane Kerr (1780–1855), after the death of her 1st husband, Sir Shuckburgh Apreece, married Sir Humphry Davy (1778–1829), the celebrated natural philosopher.

[3] Lady Olivia Fitzgerald, daughter of 2nd Duke of Leinster, wife of Charles, 8th Baron Kinnaird, who died in 1826.

[4] " We have been everywhere well received, and at Boston, where we staid 3 weeks, nothing could exceed the hospitality of the inhabitants."

for a few months in Dorchester.[1] Ld Wm has made acquaintance with Ly Susan O'Brien,[2] with whom he is quite enchanted. Her cheerful conversation so full of anecdote & agrémens of all sorts. She has suffered from the alarm occasioned by the violence of the storm, which seems to have been as great on the coast of Dorset as we had it at Brighton. Ld Ilchester has lost his decoy or swannery entirely. The embankment gave way, & the whole is filled with sea & shingles.[3] The house at Abbotsbury was filled with wretched shipwrecked mariners of all nations. Happy for them to meet with shelter & hospitality.

December 16th, [1824].

. . . You do not mention the studies of the young foreign artists. What are Gibson, Campbell, Westmacott? They all have reputation.[4] The latter is very promising, & will, I hope, succeed. His father has just been defeated, by a Scotch job, of getting the order for Lord Hopetoun's statue intended for the town of Edinburgh. The order is sent to Rome to Campbell, who has not yet cast anything in bronze. I am sorry the Marble Gallery at Petworth has been enlarged considerably, so as to be capable of holding much sculpture. Already Ld Egremont has a large collection, & by fresh orders will augment it greatly.

The K. & Ly C. are represented as quarrelling. Ld C. has reduced the splendor & excellence of the table down to meanness ; & H.M. complains of mauvaise chère. The good cooks are dismissed ; & the dinner is supplied for each guest at so much par tête, which certainly is a miserable way for any decent house. I believe in truth there is some diminution of love between the venerable lovers.

[1] Elizabeth Anne, daughter of Hon. J. Rawdon, married Lord George William Russell (1790–1846), son of the Duke of Bedford's 1st marriage. She died in 1874. Francis Charles Hastings Russell became 9th Duke of Bedford. Lord William was a soldier, but later became distinguished in diplomacy.

[2] Lady Susan O'Brien, daughter of Stephen, 1st Earl of Ilchester, was living at Stinsford House near Dorchester, and died there in 1827. " She is a prodigy," Lord William wrote, " and a most pleasing prodigy."

[3] This description of the great storm of November 23, 1824 was somewhat exaggerated : though the height of the sea, which had been forced over the Chesil Beach by the violence of the waves, was 22 feet 8 inches above the ground, at the entrance to the Swannery. It is recorded that 38 pheasants were picked up drowned, besides " hares, rabbits, rats, mice, etc. innumerable."

[4] All sculptors. John Gibson (1790–1866), R.A. 1838 : Thomas Campbell (1790–1858), of humble origin : Richard Westmacott (1799–1872), eldest son of Sir R. Westmacott.

CHAPTER III

1825–1826

10th January, [1825].

. . . Douglas Kinnaird has had a very satisfactory acct of his brother's amended health. He appears to have been very ill. I cannot help hoping he will return to enjoy his large income with his charming wife, fine family, spacious mansion & numerous society of friends. This would be more creditable, &, as he is no longer in the very bustle of youth, more happy than continuing his Bedouin life, sans foyer sans racine, neither loved nor of course much respected. Campbell, the sculptor, has been on a visit at Dunbar [1] & Woburn. He continues in England until he has made busts of the King & the D. of Wellington. His chisel is very classical : his dialect & manners homely. To whom did you wish to sit ? Not to this one, as he is here ?

17th January, [1825].

We are mightily pleased with the appearance of Mr Abercrombie. [2] He has certainly *turned the* corner. However it will be expedient that he should be careful. The House of Commons business, added to his professional labors, must be taken in a very mitigated dose. Fortunately *that* is likely to be less, because the two great questions, Ireland & the Railways, are to be in Committees, which do not, I believe, run into late nights.

People are beginning to prepare for town, tho' as yet it is scantily filled. Lady Jersey, most gaily & gallantly, after Woburn, is to go to Chatsworth. Lady Cowper has had & has great parties. Luttrell [3] rather grumbles at the change of society there, many new faces, &

---

[1] Lord Lauderdale's house.

[2] James Abercromby (1776–1858), Speaker of the House of Commons 1835–9 : later created Baron Dunfermline.

[3] Henry Luttrell (1765 ?–1851), the celebrated wit, a natural son of 2nd Lord Carhampton. Lady Holland, writing in 1821, said of him, " We still have Mr. Luttrell, who, as you know, is brilliant as lightning & sharp as a Toledo when excited by a large audience ; but in a small coterie he is ditch water, as flat, yawny and sleepy as possible. How unlike most of my other worthies, such as Papa, Brougham, Tierney, poor Romilly, Fitzpatrick & a long list of others."

an overflow of foreigners & diplomats. She is quite right to shift
the scenes to fresh decorations & faces ; even for the policy of enjoying
old friends, it is good to vary & mingle. At Woburn they have been
acting ; Wrio. very well, the part of Jerry Sneak,[1] or I believe
Sturgeon. Miss Tree alas ! within these 5 days consents to become
Mrs Bradshaw.[2] The offers were so splendid, they could not be
resisted—a foolish acquiescence on her part. She will be poorer, &
miss the excitement & gratification of her present occupation ; as
these unequal marriages never succeed, unless the rank & station are
so powerful from wealth & family that they are carried down per
force. Miss Love, who at present belongs to Lord Harborough, has
succeeded Miss Foote in Col. B.'s[3] penurious favor. In her he will
meet his match in all ways.

Ly Aberdeen took leave of me yesterday. She goes tomorrow in
a most uncomfortable way, without any servant of her *own*, only
the courier, one loaded carriage for herself, brother-in-law & daughter,
a little caretta (*sic*) for her maids : & thus all is told. This for a
delicate, sick woman, quite pampered with every ease & luxury, and
never having been out of the island or from the region of physicians.
I think Ld A[bercorn] will be vexed when he hears of this discomfort
for her. Great changes are making at Cassiobury, reduced establishment, & less open for the world at large.[4] He is grown very much
occupied in écarté, building, planting, etc., & likes to have a more
permanent set staying in the house.

Our accounts of, from, & about Charles are highly gratifying.
His wife appears to be a delightful person ; & Charles himself is so
popular, beloved & esteemed. Indeed I feel persuaded he will be
a very distinguished person whenever a fair career is open to him,
which will happen sooner or later. Walter Scott's second son is to
marry Miss Jobson, a young lady with £90,000 for her fortune.[5] His
novel is not out. Sydney Smith quits us today for Yorkshire. It is a
great loss in the house.

[1] The volunteer Major, Sturgeon, made love to Mrs. Jerry Sneak, in Samuel
Foot's *Mayor of Garratt*.
[2] " We shall, it is dreaded, lose Miss Tree. Mr Bradshaw has made every
offer ; & his family are preparing to reconcile their minds to the connexion,
to which there can be no objection personally, to the captivating little being."
December 21st, 1824.
[3] Colonel Berkeley, subsequently Earl Fitzhardinge.
[4] George, 5th Earl of Essex (1757–1839), who was a friend of the Hollands
of very long standing, lived at Cassiobury. He was separated from his wife.
[5] Miss Jobson actually married Walter, the elder son.

7th February, [1825].

. . . Fred. Ponsonby marries wretchedly.[1] When he wrote to me to announce it, I could only say I knew he had met with good temper, & that was the most valuable ingredient for happiness. When Ld Bathurst was asked by the Bessboro' family for the name of his solicitor, he said he had forgot it. Shabby man, he will do nothing. She has only £4000 in the world. I suspect your friend Hy Greville has had the luxury of bringing about this marriage.

They will have with places & appointments about £1400 pr am, besides the douceurs of official houses, horses, etc. They are neither of them good œconomists. Ld B.'s joke, of no instance of a female Bathurst ever marrying, is now destroyed.

We had enquiries without end this morning, it being reported Hd House was burnt down. There was a tremendous fire, which demolished the large house where is the overflowing well on the Uxbridge Road. It is very tormenting to the poor people. It is inhabited by an East Indian family, who were carousing till a late hour. The flakes of fire reached our stables.

18th February, [1825].

. . . Mary has entirely recovered her health. She really looked beautiful last night, rich glowing tints & her pretty black crop.[2] She was extraordinarily admired. There is some vague suspicion of Dissolution in the autumn ; because Ministers are hurrying on very much the Parlty business. The quarrel is quite made up between the old lovers. The King will now leave his bed ; & they are to enjoy love in a cottage at Windsor next week. *She* has been away almost a month, & only been to him twice ; upon which he took to his bed & starved—his old practices when lovesick. He once had a vein opened, & would not let the blood be staunched till Mrs Fitzherbert came to him. She lived in Grafton Street ; & there was the utmost difficulty in getting her down to him before he fainted too much.

The Duke of Northumberland (Hugh, 3rd Duke, 1785–1847) was

[1] Hon. Frederick Ponsonby (1783–1837), 2nd son of 3rd Earl of Bessborough, Major-General and K.C.B. He was marrying Lady Emily Bathurst, daughter of Henry, 3rd Earl Bathurst.

[2] Lady Holland wrote in March, " Her head is not quite to my taste. In a short time her hair can be turned up in the pole, which will give her a dégagée air."

sent to France as Ambassador Extraordinary at the Coronation of
Charles X : and himself bore the expense of the Embassy.

25 February, [1825].

The Duke of Northumberland takes many young men, besides
those named by Canning : Lords Hervey, Pelham, etc. ; £8000 of
diamonds are to be added to the already splendid family necklace ;
20 carriages ; fêtes at Paris ; £3000 for house rent. The misfortune
is that his Grace is a very bad Frenchman, & cannot utter many words.
Ld Granville's carriage is very fine, cost £1600. Ld Apsley is to
marry that lovely Miss Forrester ! the young, pretty one ; an alliance
of hunting families. A great love of a coronet, as, tho' I like him
best of his family, yet he is not beau à voir, nor clean nor wholesome-
looking.[1] Polignac after all *did* go to the diplomatic dinner, & was
uncommonly civil to Alava.[2] People abuse Ld Clanricarde, both his
looks, manners & habits.[3] I hope he will behave well to her, for I
cannot but have a good will to her & her family, as they behaved so
very well in your love affair ; tho' she is herself a little in the style
of your flippant misses, tho' less so than any of them.

Mde de Bourke is coming to London.[4] She is busy in marrying
her nephew, upon whom she is going to settle the bulk of her fortune.
She has given him three ladies to choose among. Campbell has made
a very fine bust of the D. of York. I think he is going over to Rome
directly to finish. He is a very fine sculptor. Ld Macclesfield[5] is to
marry the rich Miss Wycombe, the heiress whom the D. of Clarence
wanted to marry some years ago.

4th March, [1825].

. . . Wortley, it is reported, will go on to S. A. when his companions return from U. States. I am sorry, as the climate is very
hazardous ; & his loss would be dreadful to family & friends. I should
hope it may not take place, as travellers vary their plans wisely enough
according to circumstances. Ld Apsley is to live with the Bathursts

---

[1] The marriage did not come off. Lord Apsley, who succeeded as 4th Earl
Bathurst, died unmarried in 1866. " The Bathursts fear he will never marry
after this disappointment."

[2] Don Miguel Alava had fled from Spain after opposing Ferdinand VII in 1822.
He was later Spanish Ambassador in London. Polignac was French Ambassador.

[3] Miss Harriet Canning had become engaged to Lord Clanricarde.

[4] Count de Bourke, a Dane, was Minister in Spain, where the Hollands first
met them. He died in 1821, Madame in 1844.

[5] Lord Macclesfield's 1st wife died in 1823. He did not marry again.

as they cannot make up a separate income. They are all good-tempered people & like the marriage, so that it will do well. London has not yet begun its gaieties. Mary is invited to a splendid dinner at D.H. tomorrow : she takes Mr Ellis's place, & goes with Ly Georgiana [Morpeth]. I wish the Duke would give something of a party ; tho' the young world are going back to their hunting again. Ld F. Leveson is worried to death by these railways. He says he would willingly renounce his contingent prospect of £120,000 pr am for a *secure* £10,000. The uncertainty must be very harassing. Ld Grey has played at whist with me. I cannot always get my party, tho' it really does me good.

18 *March* [1825].

Fred. Ponsonby was married the day before yesterday. At the altar he could not find the ring. After 20 ! minutes search, it was at the bottom of his pantaloon pocket. They were to dine on the road, & reach Cirencester for the hymeneal rites. Mary is looking quite beautiful, & is considered so. I wish there were any sparks who would shew their admiration ; but it seems odd none do.[1] Ly Georgiana Morpeth's trip to Paris is very unlucky for her. She is without exception the best chaperon, from knowing so well all the young men, & their being at their ease with her, which is rarely the case. George [Howard] will apparently come in without difficulty for Yorkshire. Ld Fitzwilliam is very friendly. His heart & soul is in politics, tho' écarté carries it off in the evening occasionally. I hope he will marry his namesake, the heiress of one of the family who has an estate of £8000 pr am in Nottinghamshire. Rogers has hurt his head by striking it against a marble chimney : he did not feel the pain for 10 days. It then came on keenly ; Brodie confined him to his bed, cupped & blistered him ; & in a few days he will be downstairs. Henry Greville is better. He has renounced going to Paris.

---

[1] A letter from Lady Granville to her sister, Lady Carlisle, "Paris, May 1826," a year later, perhaps explains Lady Holland's complaints. "What I meant about Mary Fox is, that by nature a little gummy, she is so tied by the leg, watched by the eye, so regulated, so tamed, so not to say this, not to do that, not to go there, not to stay here, to cut this man, to avoid that girl, that she has lost all effect in society but that of being gêned herself & a gêne to others. Her very beauty suffers from it. She has no spirits, no opinion, no expression, no conversation. Yet she is not low, she is not grave, she is not foolish. She sits by the side of our ladies, & answers very prettily when spoken to. I never saw so many advantages thrown away. Ibby has as much chance of a lover as she has" (*Letters of Harriet, Lady Granville*, i, 384).

He is very, very handsome. It is distressing to see so much illness about him. We move on Monday to St James's Square. How very kind in them.[1] The thought was really the dear little Duchess's herself.

Before the period of the next letter which we print, a bombshell had exploded in family circles. A misdirected letter had brought it home to the Hollands that Miss Theresa Villiers (*see ante*) still occupied a large place in their son's thoughts, if not in his heart—a flirtation which they had fondly imagined had come to an end with his departure from England in 1824. A somewhat frank and heated correspondence ensued ; but the wise advice of Miss Caroline Fox, always the peace-maker on such occasions, prevailed ; and by July the breach was closed, at least to all outward appearances.

The Hollands went to Paris early in September, and remained until the late spring of 1826. Henry Fox joined them there, but not till March.

24th December, 1825. Rue Grange Batelière. No. 1. Paris.

. . . I can hardly think people were serious in describing this house among *the gay ones* of Paris. No ball, fêtes or soirées, which are what constitute gaiety. Being much at home I see many people certainly of all sorts, conditions & parties. Yet I doubt if any one evening would be agreable to a regular dandy. A new novel called *Granby* has appeared ; the hero is a sort of Brummel, only with more cleverness than Brummel ever showed. There is nothing that marks much genius in the author.[2] It is evidently by a man who has seen London society, tho' he talks of a person as *gentlemanly*. It is mixed up with bad religious stuff, & a strange discourse, which I had not patience to read, on suicide. *Matilda* is very clever, especially the *dinner*, that shews much wit & observation. Some of the facetious parts are not so good as the Judge family, always excepting the Manchester —— Pelisse, which is an admirable stroke of humour & sagacity.

[1] To the Duke of Bedford's house.
[2] By T. H. Lister, who later married Miss Villiers. Of *Matilda*, Lady Holland wrote, " It is for the first 50 pages full of wit and observation upon manners and society, and then becomes commonplace and like any trashy, sentimental novel. It is ascribed to Luttrell (falsely), Sneyd, Galley Knight, Cradock, Chas. Moore and others ; but I doubt any of these. Some say Ld Normanby. John Russell is the father of stray books, but it is not his I think." Actually Lord Normanby was the author.

. . . The Embassy is a pleasant, & to us a most friendly house. My friend C. Ellis is come,[1] which is a great pleasure to me. He gives but an indifferent account of Lord Howard's health which annoys me. Ld Ponsonby is to go to Columbia as Envoy.[2] Very kind of his former *bonne amie* to think of him, but he deserves nothing from his family nor indeed from anybody ; & his despatches may be classed with those of Ld Strangford but with less talent, but an equal absence of truth.

The Hollands returned from Paris in the early days of June, Fox preceding them in May at his father's urgent request, but only remained five weeks. He left London on July 3.

Hd H. *Tuesday, July* 4, [1826].

. . . We dined at Rogers', an agreable party : Sir Thos, T. Grenville, Cary the translator of Dante, Mr Ottley a great connoisseur & virtuoso, Kenney the lively dramatist, Johnny [Russell] from the Priory, & Miss Rogers. The house is quite beautiful, freshly ornamented, & enriched by new pictures & pretty little bits of art. His mode of lighting the rooms is admirable, taken from the method of lighting the statue of Voltaire " Aux Français," adopted by the D. of Devonshire for shewing his " Endymion," & now by Rogers, & I hear also by Lord Francis L.-Gower. It throws light abundantly, & spares the eyes. Mary, having a little cough, sent her excuses to Esterhazy. The ball was, I hear, very gay & splendid. Lambton has been wise enough to fight a duel with Beaumont,[3] the only way of getting out of the unpleasant reflections about a white feather. He was bruised in his arm, but no blood drawn. D. of B. is at St Ann's.[4] We cannot go there for a week, as Mrs Fox has a party who stay with her for some days. We dine at the Ladies Fitzpatrick today.

[1] Charles Rose Ellis (1771–1845) created Baron Seaford in 1826. He was father of Lord Howard de Walden. A very old friend of Lady Holland, for whom, when Lady Webster, he had at Nice given a coming-of-age party.

[2] John, 2nd Lord Ponsonby, who died in 1855. Minister Plenipotentiary at Buenos Ayres, 1826–8. Probably the reference is to Lady Conyngham. Canning is said to have sent him abroad at the King's request.

[3] The duel between J. G. Lambton (later Earl of Durham) and Thomas Wentworth Beaumont (1782–1848), M.P. for Northumberland, was occasioned by incidents in the election, in which the latter lost his seat. It took place on Bamburgh Sands. Mr. Beaumont had challenged Lord Grey in 1823 on most insufficient grounds.

[4] Mrs. Charles James Fox's, near Chertsey.

July 5, [1826].

. . . We dined yesterday at the Ladies'. Company, B. & Bss
Robeck, G. Robinson, Col. Gordon, Arbuthnot, Ld Euston, Pony
Barham, H. Webster. A very good dinner, tho' a very hot room.
A party in the evening, from which I fled to visit Sir James [Mack-
intosh], leaving Papa at cribbage. Sir James has been most kindly
invited by Staël[1] to go with all his family to Coppet. This tempts him,
but the journey in his state of health is arduous. He means to go, if
he goes at all, by water to Rotterdam, from thence to Antwerp, &
then join the Rhine & proceed to Basle. He looks forward with
delight to the banks of the Rhine, which must indeed be very refreshing. I found him reading Mrs Radcliffe's tour on that very route,
which is very well written, less loaded with fine language, & more
substantial than descriptive. It seems, however, that Lady Mac.'s
going is rather a drawback to the pleasure of the party, but will not
I hope be an impediment to his going. He appears better, but is
still tremulously alive to any symptom that denotes a change in health
or sensations.

Lord Chichester [2] is dead. He was a very old friend of mine ; &
there was a period in his life, for several years, that he would have
sacrificed that life & all he held dear for me. But tho' I esteemed
him, I never could return his devotion. He was a mixed character,
& perhaps had as many enemies as friends. I have had latterly very
little intercourse with him ; as his wife disliked his coming, or in any
way communicating with me.

Sunday, [*July* 9, 1826].

We went yesterday to Cheam,[3] where we dined & passed a very
agreable day. Only the family, our Ladies. My mother dined with
the Ladies Fitzpatrick ; Allen at Dulwich. Mr Smith seems to enjoy
his country residence extremely. It is a good house enough. He
ought to like it, as certainly his life has been improved by the complete
restoration of his health . . . On our return we found the Duke
of Montebello,[4] who is delighted with all had seen on his tournée.
The contests in Westmoreland & at Preston delighted him. He is

---

[1] Auguste de Staël, son of Madame de Staël.

[2] Thomas Pelham, 2nd Earl (1756–1826), often mentioned in her *Journal*,
which was published in 1908.

[3] Bobus Smith's house.

[4] No doubt son of Lannes, 1st Duke, Napoleon's Marshal (1803–72).

eager & intelligent, full of manly pursuits, & will, I am persuaded, distinguish himself & be a happy man. Mary had no chaperon for Mr Petre's party, so could not go. Our dinner at Lady Barbara's [1] was remarkably pleasant. Gowers for the last time : they were to go yesterday. I was more pleased with her than ever. She spoke with so much judgment, good nature & sense about the individuals of her husband's family, that she is much raised in my estimation. About your favorites Ld & Ly Francis, she spoke admirably, & I believe justly : all seems to go on comfortably. I cannot believe Lord Francis will be all you expect of him. He has not the genius ; & when he gets older, the world & he will make the discovery ; & he will end in being no bad thing, a very good sort of man.

We found a few very pleasant people at Lady Jersey's, Ly Euston, etc. : a good deal of merriment. Some comical stories about Ld & Ly Southampton [2] too long to write : all the schemes & artifices to bring the marriage to bear, & her folly & coquetry before & since with Punch Greville. He seems to be a perfect Cymon, without the polish his love, if such it can be called, ought to produce. They are in Germany, travelling about near or on the Rhine. Lady C. Powlett [3] is full of life & cleverness. Her first abord both of voice & looks surmounted, makes it intelligible how she can turn heads as she has done & still does. I liked her prodigiously ; yet she is Lord Milton in *short* female attire. *Alla Giornata* is written by Lady Charlotte Bury. I have not read it, tho' it is said to be better than her former publication. It had need be so, to be worth anything.

I hear Mr Canning has been fretted about the Irish election in Galway, on acct of the immense expense to Lord Clanricarde, & also the improper use the over eager Paddies have made with his name to obtain votes. Indeed he has been compelled to cause a letter to be read on the hustings to disavow the use of his name. This is very provoking, & I am sorry for it, as anything to teaze a gouty man is pernicious.

[1] Lady Barbara Ponsonby, heiress through her mother to the Barony of Mauley, and daughter of Anthony, 5th Earl of Shaftesbury. She married William Francis Spencer Ponsonby, 3rd son of Frederick, 3rd Earl of Bessborough in 1814, who was created Baron de Mauley in 1838. She died in 1844.

[2] Charles, 3rd Lord Southampton (1804–72) married, in 1826, Harriet, daughter of Hon. Henry Stanhope. She died in 1860.

[3] Lady Caroline Lowther, daughter of 1st Earl of Lonsdale, married William John Frederick Powlett (1792–1864), who became 3rd Duke of Cleveland for a few months. She died in 1883.

Thursday, [July 13, 1826].

. . . Yesterday we dined at Campden Hill ; only Westmacott & some of the family. The Duchess has given, intended for a birthday gift for the Duke, a beautifully executed sort of Register of her children. It is richly illuminated & emblematically decorated ; the 2 sailors & the soldier appropriate ornaments to their professions, all admirably executed, a pretty thought. It is not finished, as her confinement occurred in the midst of her occupation. The Duke, Wm Adam & his 2 girls go off on Saturday to Devonshire. I wish him well back. He is never well there . . .

The state of the country is very alarming. The manufactories are comparatively vacant ; & the hay-harvest has fallen so short & made itself, that few hands were employed. No orders given for goods. In short, the next ten months, it is expected, will be worse than the last. The wheat crops are injured. Mr Byng has a tenant who has already lost £2000 of wheat. The hail cut off the ears entirely. This makes people tremble for their rents ; all agree the agricultural distress will now have its turn, as the manufacturing & financial had last year. God knows what we shall do. Poor Mrs Sheridan [1] has lost her son, a boy in the Navy. He fell from the mast, & was killed on the spot. Her daughters are admired. One is to marry Mr Norton, a brother of Ld Grantley's. They are both young & exceedingly in love ; but not much means of subsistence. I hope the King or D. of York will do something, poor girl.

H. H. *17th July*, 1826.

We spent a very pleasant day at St Ann's. It was looking quite beautiful. Mrs Fox has placed a vase in the corner of the garden where Mr Fox used to sit & listen to the birds. His favorite lines from the *Flower & the Leaf* are inscribed, & some very pretty verses, full of feeling, by Adair, to tell the story. The vase is very plain & simple ; the whole is quite lovely & charming, & does credit to her taste & tenderness. On Sunday we went to see Windsor Castle. Jeffrey Wyatville [2] did the honors of his magnificent work ; for his it is, as nothing could be more paltry & bad than Charles II & George

[1] Caroline Henrietta Callander (1779–1851), wife of Tom Sheridan, R. B. Sheridan's son, and mother of the three beauties, Lady Dufferin, Duchess of Somerset and Mrs. Norton. The last named married Hon. George Norton, son of Lord Grantley, in June 1827.

[2] (1766–1840). Nephew of James Wyatt. He took the name Wyatville. His friends were Thomas Phillips (1770–1845), the portrait painter, and Richard Collins (1755–1831), miniature painter.

III's share in the building. We had three artists, Wyatt's friends &
guests, Westmacott, Phillips, Collins. The structure is noble ; the
private apartment has all the comfort & compactness of a small
mansion. The State rooms, I suspect, he has been cramped about,
as they are not spacious enough nor sufficiently numerous. The
glory of the architecture is great ; & the view of the Long Walk
through the archway really fine. The King came whilst we were
there. He sent for Wyatville, but on hearing he was with us bid
him return with civil messages. The little architect went to him a
second time, & told me he had said to the King what I had criticised
about the road in the Long Walk being *too narrow* seen from under
the Archway. The King said I was right, & it should be widened.
I believe we ought to have gone down to the King, but I am always
for hanging back, not seeking. I think you would admire the edifice.

Cassiobury. *Wednesday night*, [*July* 19, 1826].

We left home yesterday. Found a very small party. I felt ill in
a most provoking way, from the exertion & fatigue of seeing Windsor
Castle, which I did not feel at the time. All my unpleasant old pains
are returned, & I have been confined entirely to my great chair,
literally not moving . . . Lord Aberdeen has been over to see me
twice. He wants Mary to go & pay them a visit at the Priory to
meet Ld Liverpool, Peel & Robinson. I wish she could go ; but
even if she could, she is shy at going alone, & dislikes it naturally
enough. Papa has caught a magnificent trout & one fair pike. He
is enchanted. He says he thought he never should get another, the
gout being an enemy to all sports.

Ampthill, 24th [*July*, 1826].

. . . I should be glad were Ld & Ly Dudley to come here.[1] She
succeeds admirably, which of course must give him satisfaction.
Indeed tacte seems strongly in her character ; a desire to please with
so much power must succeed. Her voice is so winning, that it adds
a charm to all she says, & prepossesses her hearers. I believe you
have heard me say Napoleon's voice was inimitable : so melodious
that no heart could resist. She described the society of Mde Murat
at Trieste as delightful. Shall you not be tempted to try it ? It will
make a variety in your road either to Italy or to Vienna. . . Ld Clan-

---

[1] Lord Dudley Stuart (1803–54), son of 1st Marquis of Bute, by his 2nd wife,
Frances Coutts. His wife was Christine, daughter of Lucien Bonaparte, by
his 1st wife, Christine Boyer. Lady Dudley's first marriage with the Comte
de Possé had been dissolved shortly before this time.

william shewed so much feeling at the time of Ld Londonderry's death, that I have esteemed him much ever since. He is very quick & has much talent. His enemies say his defect is a want of accuracy ; but I cannot say I ever detected him in any such offence against sense & honor.

Ampthill, 7th August.

. . . The King is building at the Virginia Water a Fishing House, in the Chinese taste, full of gilt dragons for ornaments : rather too expensive, *on dit*, considering Windsor, Buckingham House, York House, & the state of the country. York House [1] is taken by the Govt off the Duke's hands, & is to be kept as a residence for the next heir to the Crown. The reports vary of the D. of York's health, such as it is. The physicians do not allow him to think of Belvoir. Your Papa has offered him this place for shooting in the middle of September. It is delightful for game, & the manors are near the house, & so well stocked. I know not whether he accepts or not. General Burton (Lord Conyngham's brother) is to be the successor of the D. of Manchester in Jamaica ; & Lord Maryboro' is to release the Buckhounds by returning to [his] old office, Master of the Mint, upon Mr Wallace's death, which the greedy calculate cannot be long delayed. The C. family get on pretty well in life, I think, at least in the pelf line.

Ampthill, 9th August.

. . . Lord Aberdeen left us yesterday to go for a consultation about Nice, whether Ly A. is to go or not. He is very much out of spirits about his daughter, tho' she is not worse. Ly Harriet (Ly A.'s daughter) [2] is grown so rapidly that her height is upwards of 6 feet, rather alarming in a family where there is such a want of stamina. Wrio. [Russell] complains of the extreme dulness of St Petersburgh, & of the uncertainty which prevails as to the period of the Coronation, to say nothing of the expense, which is enormous to the young attachés, as they do not live with the D. of D., but are on their own.[3] All who have seen the Pss Royal of Sweden are enamoured, her beauty & grace & captivating manners. Such smiles & voice. Wrio. is very much struck with Lord F. Leveson. He likes him mightily, so pleasant to live with & good natured. I am like a fish out of water

---

[1] Later Stafford House, now the London Museum.

[2] Her Abercorn daughter (*see ante.* p. 33, *n.*).

[3] The Duke of Devonshire was representing the King at the Coronation of Nicholas I. His mission was said to have cost him £50,000.

when Allen is absent, which is the case at this moment; being at Dulwich but returns tomorrow.[1]

Ampthill, 14th August, [1826].

. . . We have had our house quite overflowing, & obliged to put up a bed in the large Library for Mr Whishaw.[2] We have had Frere,[3] who is very pleasant, tho' too drowsy after dinner for our agrémens & his own health. He talks of Malta; but his family push him to get Lady Erroll to join him here, especially as climate, her physicians say, is of no service to her complaints. She is lost to all when there, & even to himself. In consequence of your wishes about Cradock,[4] your Papa wrote to ask him to take us chemin faisant to those hateful Doncaster Races. I expect the Carlisles [5] next week, as they leave Paris today. He writes very cheerfully, as if he had been pleased with his séjour there. You cannot imagine what very gossiping, ill-natured stories about Lord Granville come from Paris. I do *not* credit them; indeed I fancy I *knew* they are not true. But they are very current; everybody repeats them. It seems to me an act of benevolence, almost of charity, is perverted into scandal. The weather is become much cooler. I have put on a blanket for the first time on my bed since Paris. Lord Wm Lennox fought Lord Glengall at Cowes, upon an accusation of writing in the *Age*.[6] They exchanged two shots; & when the strife was over, would not shake hands. Many of Ld Wm's officers suspect him of knowing more than he ought of that infamous publication, & consequently shun him.

The case of the D. of York is quite desperate. I have too good reason to believe he is beyond human skill to save. He is to go to Brighton for a week, & return to the Duke of Rutland's house in

[1] Dr. Allen was Master of Dulwich College.

[2] James Whishaw was a regular correspondent of Lady Holland's, and at other times a constant guest.

[3] J. Hookham Frere (1769–1846), diplomatist, who after his retirement lived almost entirely in Malta. He married, in 1812, Jemima, Dowager Countess of Erroll.

[4] J. Cradock (1799–1873), who took the name of Caradoc, later 2nd Lord Howden. Known as "le beau Caradoc." He married, in 1830, Catherine, Princess Bagration. Lady Holland wrote of him a month earlier: "He is doubtless very quick; but I am not sure his abilities are as remarkable as they appear. He dazzles, but does not enlighten."

[5] George, Viscount Morpeth, succeeded his father as 6th Earl in 1825. His wife was sister to Countess Granville.

[6] Son of Charles, 4th Duke of Richmond. Richard Butler, 2nd Lord Glengall (1799–1831). C. M. Westmacott was editor of the *Age*.

Arlington Street. He has taken an aversion to his own house in Audley Street. The King is ill : he caught cold fishing, & kept his bed. He fancies, without any reason Halford says, that his disorder is similar to his brothers'. However he is no danger ; unless one of his inflammatory attacks on the chest should come on.

Flaxman is going to make sketches for Bunyan's *Pilgrim's Progress*, in the style of the horses he did for *Homer* & *Dante*. He is full of genius ; but I wish he had chosen a better subject than this allegory of " the Slough of Despair," etc. *He* is a little dominated (?) with the belief of good & evil spirits, very mystical & obscure in his faith.

21 *August*, 1826. Ampthill.

. . . Frere has prolonged his 24 hours to 10 days, & does not seem to contemplate departure. The only drawback upon his society is his terrible propensity to sleep ; he frequently spends the *whole* evening in a great chair sleeping soundly & even noisily, until we are all gone to bed. Mackintosh has met with the utmost courtesy from these foreign Courts, as to their official correspondence during the period he is employed upon.[1] Even Metternich has exceeded all expectation & offers to send the originals of the Venetian dispatches, the Court of Turin also for the Genoese, & Florence for the documents of the Medici. This will assist him much. He has been disconcerted by information from Rome, being warned not to publish until he sees the documents from the Vatican ; because the Stuart family held papistical principles which would throw quite a new light upon their characters ; & that our *Protestant* Martyr, Charles, was a staunch Roman Catholic, as can be proved by papers. I am sorry he has heard this, as it will make him dissatisfied with the already copious materials he possesses ; & from the activity of the Jesuits any publication from thence would inspire distrust, as they are very capable of falsifying their extracts to answer the purpose of the moment ; & to obtain inspection by a trustworthy person of what they term their " Monumenti " would be impracticable. So we must be content to take the record as they give it themselves.

It is said that Lingard [2] will reply next spring to Allen's review ; & many archives in Europe will be ransacked for a refutation. Poor Mackintosh is so irresolute even in his plans. He varies again, & talks of Edinburgh ; Ghent & Geneva have long been renounced. It is

[1] His *History of the Revolution in England*, published in 1834.
[2] Allen wrote two reviews on Lingard's *History of England*. The latter replied in a *Vindication*.

now between Tenby & the neighbourhood of London, a sad state of vacillation ; to have so many schemes across his mind [is] to unhinge him for any.   He is a wonderful man, such a store of learning, so accurate, with such clear distinct views of the different subjects he discusses.   His conversations upon history, pleaded with acute & profound observation, are most admirable to hear.

Coxe is coming out with an historical work, drawn from the Pelham papers, in reply to Walpole's *Memoirs*, intended to be a justification of Newcastle's Ministry.[1]   Ld Chichester once promised Mac. a view of the papers, but then retracted his offer : he considers them as very curious.   Lord Bute has some, which I understand from Mr Tierney the late Lord said might be seen when George III died.   Ask Lady Bute if that was not his intention ; if so, perhaps they might be brought to light some day.   Ask who possesses them, whether the present Lord or the Executors ?

Mary is really a very surprizing German scholar I am told, & from her correspondence with her masters & the facility with which she translates, it really appears to be so.   She is a very excellent person, so steady & well judging, & full of every right & honorable feeling. She is become quite a comfort to us all ; & I begin to dread that encreasing, so as to make it a pang whenever she marries.   Yet one cannot be so selfish, with all her beauty, modesty, innocence & charms, to wish to keep her from the comforts of a family of her own ; but it will now be a cruel loss to us, dear girl.

The account I have of the D. of York is frightful. . . .   His case resembles very much that of Mr Fox.   The King has erysipelas in his leg, but nothing serious.

Ampthill.   *Thursday,* 31st *August,* [1826].

. . . Most of what you say is just about Lady Westmorland. She has a noble spirit which soars far above real life, too much exalta-tion of head ; but her excesses of sentiment all depart from right feelings however impracticable to be realised.   Yet she has a little mixture of passions of baser alloy ; but upon the whole she means well.   It is a pity she has torments about her servants.   I heard of a visitor finding her clad in deep mourning for Ld Bessboro', who happily is enjoying most perfect health.   She believed an election paragraph was genuine of his death in Italy, where he has not been these 5 years.

[1] W. Coxe's last work, *Memoirs of the Administrations of Henry Pelham*, published posthumously in 1829.

I am glad you like Lord John.[1] It is a victory, as you never did
him justice. He is essentially excellent, & a model for any one to
follow. All is sound & right about him, with great talents & ambition
to distinguish himself in all that is laudable. Indeed I hope he will
come into Parliament : & have very little doubt, as all must yield
to him that matter, however one might wish for others. The D. of
Bedford is in Scotland ; he made a visit to Kinnaird & found him
worse, very feeble, the victim of his insidious disorder.

The distress at Glasgow, Paisley & Manchester, etc. is terrible, with
no prospect of mending. The difficulties of the agricultural interest
will come with the approaching winter. Papa has most kindly,
almost one might say charitably, relieved Mackintosh from the state
of vacillation under which he was suffering, by letting him live here
for six months *certain*, perhaps more. He will take possession immediately upon our removal, & fill the large Library with his books, &
pursue his historical labors.

Calcott brings a deplorable account of the health of Wilkie.[2] It
is all over with him, I fear ; he was at Vienna. He has let his house
at Kensington. In addition to his misfortune of health, he has suffered
pecuniary distress by the bankruptcy of a brother in trade, & the
failure of Hurst & Robinson, who were engaged with him in the sale
of his engravings : a very melancholy condition altogether.

4th September, 1826.

We have the Wm Russells & their delightful children. As to
Hastings he is without exception the most pleasing, promising child
I ever saw, full of *sense* besides his acquirements, with all his father's
courage, manliness & gentleness : not in the least spoiled, well behaved
& tractable.

The meeting of Parliament has little other object in view before
Christmas than to pass a Bill of Indemnity to Ministers for opening
the ports. It is comical enough that all the noise last session was
about an Act to enable Govt to dispense with the law respecting the
importation of grain, if it should be found necessary ; & now that
the necessity arises, the Act turns out to be so worded that it will
not meet the case, & Ministers are driven to the very course they
took so much pains to steer clear of.

[1] Lord John Russell sat for Bandon, 1826–30. He was at Geneva at this time,
where Henry Fox was staying.
[2] Sir David Wilkie (1785–1841), recovered sufficiently to be painting again
by the summer of 1827 in Rome. Augustus Callcott (1779–1844) was elected
R.A. in 1810.

Walter Scott's creditors allow him £2000 a year from his places & property, trusting for the payment of his debts to the produce of his pen. This is most liberal on their part. He is busily employed upon the life of Napoleon, which from him will only be a libellous romance, as he has not the materials or candid qualities to be the historian of so recent a period.

I do not think the D. of D.'s friends are pleased at a caricature of his landing at Petersburgh, rowed from his ship by ladies ; & the vessel in the offing manned by *women*. There are some good caricatures upon Ld Wm Lennox's duel. The enclosed is some good nonsense of Sydney's. There is another on " Mustard."

Ampthill. *6th September,* [1826].

Your delightful letter, my dearest child, reached me yesterday. If my letters please, it must be only that you love us dearly ; as God knows they are flat as ditch water in the way of agrémens. You saucy rogue, in construing my being amused by my *Town* friends into my believing it was to be a love of rural life. I am not under any such delusion for myself, yet can imagine persons with occupations connected with county employments being satisfied. When the weather was fine, so as to enable me to be out many hours to enjoy the views, shade and air, it was delightful, & the inspecting improvements, & the *real* use one is to the poor is a pleasure. The reverse of the medal is now in full force, heavy rain, cold raw East wind, diminished party.

We have on Allen's account delayed our departure to the 9th. 8th, being *Friday*, was impossible.[1] This we have done to pacify his mind. He dreaded being left, & was in a state of agitation at the annoyance to us of finding H. H. disordered without him, which it would be.

I cannot agree in " being more sorry for the King than the D. of York," tho' for old acquaintance sake & believing he has some good qualities, I might lament the King. Yet, for the D. of York, I feel almost affection & certainly great esteem & respect. He is a man of principle, probity & truth. Ly Westmorland must by this time have exhausted your patience ; for tho' flattery well directed may be long administered without palling the appetite, yet she is not skilful in her doses. However, she is a high minded woman, yet full of imagination more than reason, even in her tastes. They say, " Beauty is the Lover's gift." She endows those she prefers with most moral gifts ; &, when

[1] Lady Holland was far too superstitious to commence a journey on a Friday.

attached to Ward, certainly the qualities she gave him were imaginary, & were none that he coveted, being much too sublime for any hero short of an Amadis or Oroondates. How strange her love was, tho' sublime and, she imagined, purified from all grosser passions. Does she still cling to the fond remembrance ?

18 *September*, 1826. Hd. H.

We are once more within these walls that have witnessed much of the felicity of my life. The sight of them when ill, always makes me melancholy, to contrast past pleasures with actual suffering. Some writers observe the difference between the passion of Love & Friendship is, that one is from the imagination & heated passions from hope & fancy : the other from recollections & the handy habits of intercourse, where every object recalls a tender reminiscence, an intercourse bound up with existence & every circumstance & event of life. The remark is somewhere upon Petrarch's fanciful love for Laura. There is a good deal of truth in it. Thus the grief for a very young child is agony ; but time assuages it, as there are so few events that come into the daily habits & recollections, so many hours that nothing is brought back of the intercourse. So in love, unless between a married pair or contracted lovers who live entirely for years together.

The death of John VI of Portugal had brought many difficulties to his Country. The heir apparent, Dom Pedro, was already Emperor of Brazil : and abdicated in Portugal in favour of his daughter, Doña Maria da Gloria, aged 7, to take effect when she married her uncle, Dom Miguel, then 23. The latter was proclaimed Regent in July 1827, but soon afterwards usurped the throne. Subsequently the little Queen took refuge in England. Long before this, however, at the end of 1826, a military revolution had broken out, the rebels being based upon Spanish territory. The Regent and Cortes applied to Britain for assistance ; and a Resolution was moved in the House of Commons on December 11, for the immediate despatch of a British Expeditionary Force. Five thousand men were sent under Sir William Clinton ; and the first ship cast anchor in the Tagus on Christmas Day.

New Burlington Street. *December 15th*, [1826].

Here we are in this spacious house. The journey was painful from the roughness of the roads, which had been newly strewn with large unbroken stones. This in my state is most painful. You cannot imagine, my dear Child, how very uncomfortable my whole daily life is, from the total inability under which I labor, not only of getting out, but moving *at all* in the house, always wheeled from dressing room to bed. My spirits naturally sink ; so that with your absence, my condition & our pecuniary affairs, my existence is sad. Your Papa made a very good speech the other day upon the King's Message regarding Portugal.

Woolryche[1] is head of the Medical Board for Portugal, & sails on Monday. Many officers are already gone : numbers volunteered. Charles is foolishly wild to go. Lady Wm [Russell] has been longing for a war in Peninsula, just to be la grande Dame de garnison.[2] She is to be here a maîtresse femme dominante au logis. Somebody asked Mde de Lieven if Lady Wm was not very clever. She said, " Y-e-s fairlly," adding, " but I will tell you who has 10 times more ésprit, & that is Lord Wm. . . ."

Hd H. *Friday* [*December*, 1826].

The D. of Y. was certainly cupped on Friday sé'nnight. He is fully aware of his state, but clings fondly to life, determined " to die with harness on his back " : as he signs & regulates all his business, as if he was well. He sees no persons except Sir H. Taylor,[3] not even his favorite sister, Pss Sophia. It is a mournful state for a high spirited man.

The King has contrived his Palaces so ill, that he has not a place to sleep in, & has promised for two years the apartments of the Duke of Cumberland at St James's.

The Charles's are to live in a very pretty house in Addison Road. They are much pleased at it, she for her garden, he for arranging his books. Allen says, he will be perfectly happy for a month, when all his matters are placed, medals, etc., but she will enjoy it permanently. She is a very pleasing, complying person, without any assumption. I wish they had children, as it seems to prey upon her spirits ; besides it would be an amusement to us in our old age.[4] Lady Cowper goes to Paris today for a few weeks. She is in tip top spirits thereat : expects to find Lady Jersey, who has been detained uncomfortably on her road from Vienna by illness of her own & servants. It makes my mouth water to hear of abroad ; we have no chance till next

---

[1] One of Lady Holland's many doctors.

[2] Ld. William was in command of the 8th Hussars at this time.

[3] Lieut.-Gen. Sir Herbert Taylor was Military Secretary at the Horse Guards.

[4] Lady Holland wrote about this time : " Charles & his wife will take Mary's place. His face will amuse Papa, & her unassuming, yet cheerful ways will be agreable as an inmate. She is very attentive & considerate to me, & when quite at her ease amusing, but only en très petit comité."

year. We have got Lord Braybrooke's house in Savile Row, next door to the Smiths ; but we shall not give up the good air of Brighton entirely ; as the Bedfords, Aberdeens, etc. will be there, besides the delicious, invigorating breezes.

CHAPTER IV

1827

2d January, 1827.

. . . The poor Duke of York is still alive. Yesterday he was sensible enough to have the despatches from Lisbon read to him. He sinks into fainting fits which have the appearance of death. When he revives, he says, " What still here." The King has the gout, & he is of course agitated & ill otherwise. The poor Pss Sophia is perfectly wretched. For upwards of 40 years they have been in the daily habit, when he has been in or about London, of meeting. He had the greatest affection & confidence in her. Never was there more general regret for any man, all classes & descriptions. Such is the tribute to integrity & truth, for he certainly never broke a promise nor deserted a friend. Great magnanimity also towards those who went against him in private & delicate matters. No officer suffered in his promotion for supporting Mr Windham's plan of limited service or voting upon Mrs Clarke's business.[1] As to his political prejudices, they are at least sincere. I am excessively grieved myself, having for many years had a personal attachment founded upon his great kindness to me & mine.

I am sorry say the prejudices are very great against the D. of Clarence ; & I hope & believe in many points unfounded. The rock he will split upon will be over favor to his family. Some are already, I fear, very indiscreet in their language. I of course know nothing.

Savile Row, 12 *January,* [1827].

. . . You would be astonished at the vast unpopularity of the appointment of the C. in C.[2] Much as the poor Duke of York is lamented for his excellent qualities, yet this nomination adds greatly to the universal regret. *On dit,* it has been a battle with Canning in which he was beat. Ministers are quarrelling together openly, but in all probability as usual will adjust their differences by the meeting

---

[1] The peculations of his mistress became a public scandal in 1809.

[2] The Duke of Wellington succeeded the Duke of York as Commander-in-Chief. The latter died on January 5. He held anti-Whig sentiments.

of Parliament. Much is expected from your friends Denison [1] & Ashley. Of the former I have little doubt ; the latter is enthusiastic for Canning, & laments his promise to his constituents at Woodstock about the Catholics. What will Lord Shaftesbury say of him if he revolts ? It will be one of the few cases I should be for son against father ; for father in the kind sense he has never been to him. Ly C. Ashley [2] has been living for months with Lady Warwick at the Castle. I did not know they had been such friends.

I am very sorry for Punch Greville, who will be completely ruined by this calamity. He did everything for the Duke, Privy Purse & Stud, & did it well. He is a sensible man, &, tho' without affections, did his duty towards his master.

23d January.

The Pageant was very shabby, & people were much vexed & disappointed. Yet the regret is universal & undiminished for the poor Duke. His successor is perfectly abhorred ; it is strange what he can have done to be so odious.

The " General orders " to the Horse Guards announcing the D. of York's death & the appointment of the Duke of W., is strange, undignified, not unlike addresses from Corporations upon the death of one King & the accession of another, condolence & rejoicing. Very scurvy performance. King is getting well of his shingles : bathing & shampooing at Brighton.

[January 30th, 1827.]

The approaching meeting of Parlt. already brings monde. The party at Chatsworth breaks up on 30th, to be transferred for a few days to Hardwick. Poor Palmella is in a perplexed state, in consequence of a strange unexpected accident during his absence at Brighton. M. de Abrantes, the defeated leader of an insurgent party & foe to P., fled to England. Having business at the Embassy, he went to the office to speak to a Secretary. He was seized with a dreadful paralysis which deprived him of power of limb & speech. Of course he was lifted to a bed, & ordered by physicians there to continue. Thus, when P. & his family returned to their house, he found it in possession of his enemy, a man of the worst character, convicted of being the

---

[1] John Evelyn Denison (1800–73) ; Speaker 1857–72, and created Viscount Ossington.

[2] Lady Caroline Ashley, who married Joseph Neeld, of Grittleton in 1831, daughter of Cropley, 6th Earl of Shaftesbury (1768–1851).

confederate of Don Miguel in the murder of M. de Lotti, a transaction accompanied with circumstances of treachery & atrocity worthy of the days of Caesar Borgia. So poor Palmella is likely to be suspected by his own party of harbouring a traitor ; & by the other of dispatching a foe. Canning begins to be sick of the intense adulation of Me de Lieven, quite satiated by her toadyism. . . .

Your poor friend Lydia White died Tuesday, in consequence of an injury from a blow from the corner of her sofa. She had grown most unwieldy, & she is supposed to have burst the inward tumour. Her life was harmless. I had frequently been your representative in supplying game & our famous turkeys. She was very grateful, and of course felt that it was to *you* she owed the attentions.

I went last night for the first time to Drury Lane. Nothing could be worse than Kean's [1] performance of Macbeth. He is grown large, bloated & vulgar ; but his voice is not worse. I was fatigued & could not stay the Harlequin farce.

Sir James is making great progress in his History ; but his health is feeble, & he will not attend Parliament on any but the Catholic Question. Papa is well. Allen has been very kind about you. A letter would not be ill bestowed, especially on *church* matters. [2]

2d February, 1827.

. . . The D. of Clarence dined yesterday. [3] He certainly is one of the best tempered & best natured man I ever knew. He has become very prudent, & has much approved [? improved]. If he has any judicious, sincere friends, they will advise him to keep quiet, & not alter his mode of proceeding from his change of station. If he errs, it will be from the wrong-headedness of some of his children & their rapacity. I shall be sorry if they render him unpopular, as he seems to have many of the requisites to make a good King of this country.

Canning is ill, confined to bed by cold & severe lumbago, for which Sir Matthew [4] has cupped him twice. He is at Brighton. This good news from Portugal will be a cordial & revive him. He is in a precarious state politically, as the war rages openly between him & the D. of W. The latter has the Royal ear.

" The King was very angry, when he heard how miserably the ceremony had been performed," wrote Charles Greville, who cor-

---

[1] Edmund Kean (1787–1833).

[2] Allen was a confirmed atheist.

[3] The party consisted of the Duke and his son Colonel FitzClarence, Tierney, Abercromby, Scarlett, Rogers, Luttrell and the Charles Foxes.

[4] Sir Matthew Tierney.

roborated the illnesses resulting from the funeral. The Duke of Montrose recovered.

9th February.

The D. of York's funeral will, & has already produced many more. The Bishop of Lincoln is dead in consequence of a chill. D. of Montrose not likely to recover : three servants of the Royal Household from cold. The D. of Wellington very near dying, & several others. You will be shocked to hear great alarm is felt at Mr Canning's illness. At a late hour last night the accounts were very unsatisfactory ; he is at Brighton. You would be agreably surprized at the alteration for the better in George Howard.[1] He is less full & swelled in his features, & tho' not slim yet his figure is less clumsy. He is very busy in reading about Corn, & seems to understand the subject. All my friends are now come to town, so I shall try to collect matter to make out better letters.

13th February [1827].

We expect our Ladies [2] next week. It will be a delight to Mary, as she has really had no amusement. Tonight Ly Gwydyr kindly takes her to the Opera. *She* is one of the very few I like to allow Mary to go about with. Mr. Denison has been full of kindness about you. He is a sincere man, & would not express regard unless he felt it, nor approval of any whom he did not esteem. Mackintosh is just come up from Ampthill, & is actually in the room. He has worked hard this winter, & is doubtless making progress in his History.

Mr Canning is out of danger. The discipline he has undergone has been severe, & must, I fear, impair his health. However, he has written to say he shall be able to take the field in favor of the Catholics on 2d March. The D. of Devon. is less deaf than he was before he went to Russia. He is busy in arranging an apartment for Lord & Lady Granville, whom he can no longer lodge in an upper story, but means to sacrifice a portion of the ground apartments for their use. Indeed, after the noble house they have been accustomed to enjoying at Paris, I do not think any but D.H. could accommodate them. Ld. G. comes to take his seat, to qualify for C. Question. I shall much rejoice at seeing them again ; they were so essentially kind to me at Paris, & they are always agreable.

The new Juliet, Miss Jarman,[3] is graceful, but whines. Kean draws

---

[1] He had become Viscount Morpeth, on his grandfather's death in 1825.
[2] Miss Fox and Miss Vernon.
[3] Frances Eleanor Jarman (1803 ?–73), later Mrs. Ternan.

full houses, but reverts to his toping habits. He was, I heard, quite tipsy last night in *Richard*.

Monday, 6th March, [1827].

The whole town was in a ferment yesterday in consequence of the outrageous behaviour of Mr Raikes [1] to Mr Brougham in the public Club room of Brooks's. It arose out of the trial of the *Age* for a libel. Mr B. was on the defendant's side. The accusation chiefly was the ugliness of Mr Raikes, which Mr B. with drollery commented upon, but in no way whatever injurious to his character, only to his personal want of beauty. Mr R. burst into the Club, where Mr B., with about 8 other persons, was quietly sipping his broth. He began by saying his abuse had provoked him, & that he had gone to the utmost verge of the protection his profession afforded. I will not attempt the words ; suffice it to say they were very offensive. Brougham got up, & replied that if Mr R. was offended *that* was neither the place nor the mode of obtaining redress : something to that effect. Spring Rice, who was one of the 8, hurried to Bow Street : & the two gentlemen were bound to keep the peace. B. sent a challenge by Sir Robt Wilson ; as yet nothing has transpired of the reply. The Club are indignant, & the profession also. Probably it will end without any very disagreable issue ; but in these cases one cannot but be anxious. Some ladies are suspected of having goaded on the business. I will not mention names ; only one is the active Irish Countess who always meddles & not for good objects.

Tuesday. I had several accounts spontaneously sent from the House during the debate, to give an account of George Howard's admirable speech.[2] All concur in its being the speech of the most complete success for a maiden speech ever heard. His poor mother was overcome to stupefaction after the speech. Ld C[arlisle] was there. How delightful for them all ; & how sincerely glad I am for his & their sakes. Hardly anything has given more universal satisfaction.

Tonight is the crise (?) for the Catholic Q. Entre-nous, the result is rather doubtful ; & the majority, if any, will be slender. The King has taken a more decided part than his father ever did, so that the division will be much influenced. Mr C.'s fate as a statesman

[1] Thomas ("Dandy") Raikes (1777–1848). *See Creevey*, ii. 106–9. Lady Glengall was the Countess in question. Raikes was forced by "Brooks's parliament" to apologise to the Club.

[2] On Sir Francis Burdett's motion for the relief of the Roman Catholics from their disabilities. The motion was defeated next day by 4 votes.

is hanging upon it.   Mr. Huskisson is in a bad state of health, enough
to alarm his friends.   Maton attends him only.   Mr Villiers Stewart [1]
is much praised among the young speakers ;   Stanley still holds his
ground.   There is much new talent among the young ones.   At Ch.
Church, Ld Villiers [2] is praised, not only for his acquirements but for
steadiness & changing the effeminate system, as he gives the ton of
that society & is followed by all the young ones. . . .

The winter of 1826–7 had proved to be a period of successive
shocks to Henry Fox's parents.   In January, without any previous
intimation to them, he had written to the Duke of Norfolk, whom
Holland had persuaded to find a seat for his son in Parliament at Horsham, to announce his resignation before he had even signed the Roll,
as he had made up his mind to remain abroad.   Two months later,
having announced in December that he had renounced all further
thought of marriage with Miss Villiers, he suddenly informed them
of his engagement to Mademoiselle Natalie Potocka, and asked their
consent.   The young lady in question was of excellent family,
daughter of Count Alexandre Potocki and his ex-wife, by then
Madame de Wonsovicz ;   but the match was hardly likely to conform
to the desire of the Hollands to attract their errant son to come home
and stay at home.   However, consent was not refused ;   but the
engagement hung fire until August, when the lady broke it off.

Tuesday, [?*March* 20, 1827].
You will have received by the last courier a full letter from your
Papa & one from me.   In that I told you your communication had
so puzzled & confounded me, that I really did not know how to reply.
Still I am in the same state.   Tho' certainly to see you established
would be a comfort, yet remember that comfort is founded solely
upon enjoying of your society ;   for absence & remote residence must
inevitably break in time even the strongest links, & you ought to feel
very sure of the extent & depth of an attachment that would endanger
the snapping of those.
A foreigner is a guess, & a Catholic foreigner !, whose habits &
opinions must be so dissonant with those of all your connexions.   Look
round & see what examples there are to be comforted with.   Lady
Pembroke,[3] *born* & educated entirely in this country.   Lady Laving-

---

[1] Henry Villiers Stuart, of Dromana, co. Waterford.
[2] George Augustus Frederick, Viscount Villiers (1808–59), died 3 weeks after
succeeding his father as 6th Earl of Jersey.
[3] Catherine, only daughter of Simon, Count Woronzov, married, in 1808,
as his 2nd wife, George Augustus, 11th Earl.

ton [1] was a lovely Bohemian of low family, rescued by Ld. L. from
the tyranny of her aunt at Prague, & knew no connexions but those
she formed in this country. Lord Herbert [2] with a wife & no wife,
the laws of Sicily preventing her enjoying her dower out of the
country. Polish ladies have the great advantage of legally breaking
their marriages ; but the contracting party, if an Englishman, has
not the same facility. Behold Mr. King, who is bound, tho' his wife
has had two husbands since him. I think any foreign connexion is to
be deplored ; but Laurette or Mlle Bertrand [3] passe (*sic*) encore, as they
know the value of English sterling importance & would not despise
us ; but most other foreigners from ignorance hold cheap advantages
they cannot attain. In short, my Love, I am all *abroad*, as the vulgars
say, & know nothing specific.

The parties are beginning at D. H. There has been a suite of
immense dinners for the Granvilles. We dine there shortly ; & *they*
have prolonged their stay one day to dine with us. Mr C[anning]
is better. This relapse was merely owing to a ride in a cold Easterly
wind, a vapour bath afterwards, & the fatigue of the H. of Commons.
All this produced rheumatism & lumbago ; he is well again. Political
affairs are in a very strange state ; nothing will probably be known
till Easter. Even the D. of Wellington is not quite well.

March 23d, [1827].

The Granvilles almost long to return. The life of bustle is too
fatiguing & unlike their tranquil mode of living at Paris. The D. of
D. made a programme before they arrived, & which consisted of
large dinners of 30 & 40, with soirées numerously attended ending
with a supper. Tonight there is to be a concert, supper, ball. Mary
goes with Lady Jane Peel. I am not equal to the exertions : Papa
would have gone faute de mieux. We all dine there tomorrow.
Lord Hertford [4] takes the Garter to the Emp. Nicholas. It is considered as a piece of address in Canning to get Lord Hertford in any
way, as it has never been usual to employ a nobleman upon such

[1] Frances, daughter of Henry, Baron Kolbel, of the Holy Roman Empire,
married Ralph Payne, created Baron Lavington in 1795. She was born at
Dresden, and became a member of Queen Charlotte's suite. She died in 1830
at Hampton Court.

[2] Princess Octavia Spinelli, daughter of the Duca di Laurino and widow of the
Sicilian Prince Buttera de Rubari, married, in 1814, Robert Henry,Lord Herbert,
who succeeded as 12th Earl of Pembroke in 1827.

[3] Perhaps a daughter of General Bertrand.

[4] Francis Charles Seymour Conway, 3rd Marquis (1777-1842), who succeeded
in 1822. The "Marquis of Steyne" in Thackeray's *Vanity Fair*.

service ; a man from the Heralds' Office being the usual bearer of the insignia to invest him properly. For the first time Sir Chas Stuart [1] & Ly Elizabeth are invited to the Cottage. They go today, not a little pleased at it, as much as he was mortified at the delay.

30th March.

. . . People are shocked at the immense charges brought to Parlt for our diplomacy ; & Rogers is full of jokes upon the conduct of it. In the first instance we sent a deaf man to Nicholas (D. of Wellington). Then we sent a *deafer* (D. of D.). Then we emptied the infirmary & sent a lame one (Ld Hertford), who can hardly stand. Then it was a Duke to get a Garter, D. of D. Now it is a Garter to get a Dukedom. In short, he is full of epigrams on the subject.

Lord Grey had no belief in Canning's desire or power to push the Catholic Question, when the latter formed his Cabinet in April : and refused to take a hand. Holland felt himself bound to follow his leader, and refused office ; though in view of Lord Lansdowne's inclusion in the Government, he promised his support. Lady Holland also wrote on June 26 :—" I am quite grieved at Papa's not being in the *boat* with his friends. One of his chief objections arose from Ld Grey, and thinking that by remaining out he might mollify and reconcile him. But you see how ineffectual all that has proved." The position is fully set out in the editor's *Chronicles of Holland House*, pp. 77–9.

25th May.

Here there are marriages enough. Mr. Denison has happily obtained the consent of the Duke of Portland to marry Lady Charlotte Bentinck when she comes of age. The only objection was the profusion of brothers & sisters and mother-in-law all living with him. Perhaps that is to be altered ; besides they were not reckoned agreable & comfortable inmates at all. Ly Augusta Brudenell, very pretty, but fickle & coquetish, marries the son of Henry Baring . . .[2]

All you say of politics is perfect. I rejoice at Lambton being so right, & really wish he had come ; for he might have prevented much ill blood from Lord Grey to his old friends, & done him service too, as he has not distinguished himself respectably or amiably. I never cease regretting Papa's delicacy towards him in declining office. He

---

[1] Created Lord Stuart de Rothesay in 1828 (1779–1845). Ambassador in Paris 1815–24, and again in 1827–30. He married a daughter of Philip, 3rd Earl of Hardwicke.

[2] Henry Bingham Baring (1804–69), M.P. 1832–68. Lady Augusta was daughter of Robert, 6th Earl of Cardigan.

would have been of the utmost use to his friends & their cause by being in the Cabinet. However, in the chapter of accidents he may perhaps change, & if anything occurs he may be again urged. Hitherto Mr Canning has behaved with the utmost frankness to his new allies.

Lady Jersey [1] has been meddling sadly. I only care as far as it affects the D. of B[edford] : but she has done mischief between him, his sons & brother. Her conduct has been much like what she did about the Queen. She fancied all the ladies of London would have followed her ; she had not one. And now she imagined the men who went to her house were her followers, & that she was the oracle of politics. Failing in this, she has become a pattern of filial duty, & speaks with romantic fondness of the *noble* conduct of her father, & indeed of all who have resigned.

Holland House. *29th May.* " *The Restoration*, not a day of joy to Allen." [2]

. . . At the dinner of Westminster electors for purity of elections, there was a riot, broken chairs, etc. The Tavern keeper sent in his bill. A gentleman replied that *reformers* never paid for their *seats*. A good joke enough.

June 8th, Friday.

. . . Brougham has taken his patent of Precedence,[3] but this will not be sufficient to keep him straight long. He is a man of towering ambition, & looks to the highest rank his profession can yield. Two Lords of the Bedchamber have resigned, in consequence of voting against the Government, Erroll & De la Warr. The King has given carte blanche to Canning to dispose as he pleases of places to secure a support to his Govt. The list of those who are admitted to the Royal Stand at Ascot is submitted always to the King. He scratched out the name of the D. of Wellington & substituted Canning's. Lord Grey has not acted at all becomingly with his former conduct &

---

[1] Sarah Sophia, daughter of John, 10th Earl of Westmorland, married George, 5th Earl in 1804, and died in 1867. " A virago in these political strifes," Lady Holland elsewhere calls her. She had strong Tory leanings.

[2] The anniversary of Charles II's entry into London. Allen was anti-Monarchy.

[3] He had been unable to obtain preferment owing to the King's spite against him. Canning had offered him the post of Lord Chief Baron, hoping, no doubt, to rid himself of his interference in the Commons while retaining his support. But this Brougham had refused.

principles by making a most factious & inconsistent opposition. Lambton is mightily improved in sense & understanding by his foreign journey. The absence from his toadies & principality has been of service to his head & heart. I am afraid his affairs are not so flourishing, as since his union with Ly Londonderry's Colleries he has made a speculation against which all combine ; so his coals have not their usual sale. But this will soon come right again.

19th June, [1827].

My dear Child,

Papa's cold is somewhat, indeed greatly, better. We both went to the fine concert at L[ansdowne] H. last night. It was really as splendid as anything anywhere, house, company & voices included. Many very pretty young women. Miss Doyle from Paris, fresh : & a daughter of Lord Pembroke's. Two beauties I have not seen are Misses Gold & Bailey.

Mrs Coutts is finally married.[1] The ceremony went off very decorously. The Duke in returning thanks at the health of D. & Duchess being drunk spoke very properly, better than he could have done de son chef ; so it must have been prepared. The King, in reply to all Mrs C.'s communications upon the subject of the marriage, wrote a civil reply, which was read at breakfast. Before the ceremony Mrs C.'s servants wore the Coutts livery ; immediately after, they appeared in the St. Albans yellow & black stockings. Sir Francis Burdett was not of the party, rather silly & ill-tempered ; but Butes & Guilfords were in abundance. She has given the Duke £30,000 of her savings, & an estate value £26,000 in Essex. In return, all his unsettled property is answerable to the Bank for any claims upon it.

July 3d. Hd. H.

I had a visit this morning from the lovely sister of Lord Dudley S[tuart].[2] She came with Ld Sandon. Indeed she is a beautiful woman, more like a Grecian statue than a being of these regions. To maintain her beauty she ought to resemble the stillness of the statue, as much of the spell is broken when she smiles. However, she is a handsome person anyway. Her *toilette* is not one of much recherche, not enough for the usual style of young women.

---

[1] Harriet Mellon, widow of Thomas Coutts, married William Aubrey de Vere Beauclerck, 9th Duke of St. Albans. Coutts's daughters were Lady Burdett, Lady Bute and Dow. Countess of Guilford. She died in 1837. Creevey's unsavoury description of her in 1828 (*Life and Times*, p. 266) is worth noting.

[2] Lady Frances Stuart married Lord Sandon (2nd Earl of Harrowby) in 1823.

Mary will herself write an acct of the fête at Boyle Farm,[1] which was perfect in all its parts, & has given universal satisfaction to those present, & produced much sarcasm & ill-natured remarks by those not invited. Neither Rogers nor Sir Joseph Copley [2] were admitted, excluded by acclamation. It was hard on the daughters of the latter. It is a great relief to Ministers that Parlt is over. It closed today.

10th July.

Ld Stafford [3] has attained the great object of being possessor of York House, a most magnificent residence. It is not settled how it is to be called, whether Godolphin House, the name it bears in the lease, or Stafford House ; not being a freehold the latter might be reckoned improper. Ld S. intends coming at the end of the summer to establish in London, in order to superintend the preparations, furnishing, etc., so as to be ready for their reception at Easter. Ld F. Leveson has his father's permission to occupy Cleveland House.[4] To do so with comfort, he must encrease the allowance to Ld F. ; otherwise he will not be able to warm & light such a palace. I am rejoiced at the Gowers having such a residence in perspective, as I have a very warm affection for Ld G., who has been invariably kind & friendly to me at all times. Mr Canning dressed & dined here on Sunday. He is feeble, but not as ill as I was led to suppose. The D. of D. has offered him Chiswick for a month. Were I Mr C. I would feel superstitious, on account of the catastrophe there in 1806 when your poor uncle died ; to say nothing of the spot being unwholesome from stagnant water & low, damp situation. . . .

Canning died at Chiswick on August 8, in the same room which had witnessed Fox's death. The King then sent for Lord Goderich, not the Duke of Wellington, as had been generally expected.

[About *August* 10, 1827.]

Your Papa has been confined some days, & suffering from pain in his hand & wrist, occasionally shifting to the foot. His illness was

---

[1] The property of Lady de Ros, at Thames Ditton.

[2] 3rd Bart., of Sprotborough (1769–1838). He married the divorced wife of 1st Marquis of Abercorn.

[3] George Granville, 2nd Marquis (1758–1833), later created Duke of Sutherland. He married Elizabeth, Countess of Sutherland ; and was father of Earl Gower and Ld. F. Leveson-Gower. The house was built on crown land for the Duke of York, partly on the site of a Library built by Queen Caroline, and partly on that of Godolphin House.

[4] Originally Berkshire House, it was purchased by Barbara, Duchess of Cleveland ; and was later altered to the present Bridgewater House.

much aggravated by the sad tragedy at Chiswick. Indeed it has overwhelmed & affected everybody, as you may imagine, who has any good feelings. Our departure is delayed for an indefinite period.

Henry Fox was clearly beginning to find time hanging heavily on his hands, and, looking about for some occupation which would keep him abroad, he began to covet a diplomatic post. He seems to have asked his mother to help him, in the belief that the change of Government might make the moment opportune.

12th Sept., Holland House.

. . . You are mistaken when you say, " Now the Whigs are in power." They are not in power. The few that are in are viewed with jealousy & distrust, & have little or no patronage. The principle upon which the Administration is founded is that there must be a mixture. You cannot call the Premier a Whig, Chancellor, or indeed the majority of them. As I told you at first, I never expect nor ask for a favour however small. Should circumstances arise that might make an alteration, that of course would be different. As to the Greys, the estrangement is entirely on his side, if any there is. Yr Papa smiled at yr recommendation as to Ly Grey; for he says he wrote to beg you to communicate with her & testify your affection. They have given in to a very different set of connexions, Bathursts, Londonderrys etc. You will, I fear, never see Lord Guilford again. . . .[1] He is a good natured, friendly, clever man; his loss will be deplored & felt by a very extensive range of friends & dependents.

You are too hard upon young Stanley,[2] tho' he has not proved himself all that was expected. He has talents, & a great name backed by a princely fortune, which tells in this country prodigiously. F. Lamb[3] is returned looking, I hear, thin. He has no fancy to go to diplomacy again. Alvanley says of him, " He hates half mankind, & wishes the other half dead." A culprit was reprieved. Alvanley said in a whisper, " How shall we break it to Frederick?" Ld

---

[1] Frederick, 5th Earl (1766–1827), brother of the 3rd Earl, who married Miss Coutts.

[2] Edward George Stanley, who succeeded as 14th Earl of Derby in 1851 (1799–1869). His success during a long period in the Commons, gained for him the name of " the Rupert of Debate " (Lord Lytton). Under-Secretary for the Colonies under Canning and Goderich.

[3] Frederick Lamb (1782–1853), 3rd son of 1st Viscount Melbourne; diplomatist. Created Baron Beauvale in 1839, and succeeded his brother as 3rd Viscount Melbourne in 1848.

Melbourne is so weak that he is never allowed to go out of the house : with care he may last a year or two. It is important he should, as it may be doubtful whether a proper Secretary can be appointed to succeed Wm Lamb in Ireland.

The Cowpers are just returned from a brilliant party at Chatsworth, where they sat down 33 daily to dinner. This will be succeeded by another equally numerous, of which Ly E. Vernon & John & the Grevilles will be. John Russell has written a work, or rather made a compilation from Oriental writers, of the history of the settlement of the Turks in Europe. Lord Normanby [1] was very agreable indeed. The only day I saw him here at dinner, very clear & lively. He is a pleasant man. I think they have had enough of *abroad*, & are looking forward to settling here with pleasure.

Ampthill. *27th September.*

. . . We have had much too large a party for pleasure or agrémens of any sort. Indeed, since the Tierneys have left us, we have not had a pleasant day ; tho' many elements form good & witty society. Sydney is still here. The Smiths & Falcks [2] are gone : Johnny also, who talks of Paris ; I hear no more of Genoa. The world say Ly E. Vernon,[3] who has occupied him at Ryde all the summer, is the attraction. How odd that all the Russell family should have been in love in succession with her. Lady Bute, I understand, is not going back [abroad] with Lord Dudley. She is now at Southampton. I cannot give any account of their reception from the great Duchess. Ld Chesterfield [4] has spent upwards of one hundred thousand pounds this last year, & is going on in the same style. He is very well spoken of by all people who know him. It is only the folly of a young man with bad entourage, unhappily without parents : but he is good au fond.

Not one line have I read of W. Scott, tho' I have reason to believe the anonymous copy I received from Edinburgh was from him. It is not approved at all by the French or even English public.[5] The

[1] Constantine Henry Phipps, Viscount Normanby (1797–1863), the author of *Matilda* (*see ante*, p. 41). Succeeded as 2nd Earl of Mulgrave in 1831, and was created Marquis of Normanby in 1838. He married, in 1818, Maria, daughter of 1st Lord Ravensworth.

[2] Bobus Smiths. Baron Anton de Falck (1776–1843), Dutch Minister.

[3] Lady Elizabeth Bingham, daughter of 2nd Earl of Lucan, married, in 1815, George Vernon, who added Harcourt to his name. She died in 1838.

[4] George, 6th Earl (1805–66).

[5] His *Life of Napoleon.*

Doncaster Races were very brilliant. Yr friend Petre won £20,000 :
Ld Normanby £1500, & Mr Foley same ; but many were losers,
poor Chas Greville a heavy one I fear.

Ampthill. 1st October, [1827].

. . . You accuse me of not mentioning politics. At this distance
what can one say ? If a speculation is afloat, perhaps before the
following post it is overset ; & strictures upon individuals always
seem harsher when written than spoken. I hope & believe the Govt
will stand. The K. seems very sincere & friendly : & will find by
the honorable conduct of the few Whigs he has employed, that they
are not so awful & worthless as he has been taught by his former
Ministers to suspect. The loss of Canning has been a severe blow
to the Country, both for abroad & home ; for what you wrote from
Rome last winter of the change produced on public opinion abroad
in favor of this Country, in consequence of his spirit & firmness, was
corroborated in all quarters. His poor wife is so altered that to
common acquaintances she would not be known.[1] From her daughter
& C. she meets with every tenderness ; and they have hired the house
Ld Mandeville lived in near Huntingdon, in order to live with her
entirely. She is left in a very poor way. Canning was quite destitute,
& her fortune was diminished ; & what she has goes to pay his debts.
A pension from the King will be given, but that is very limited, &
I hardly know whether an application to Parlt will be hazarded.

Young Kean[2] is pitted against his father, who I am sorry to find we
have at C. Garden. Not that it will much signify to me, as I am too
nervous to return at night from the theatres ; &, as I told you, we shall
not afford a London house this winter.

[October] 15th.

We yesterday dined at Melbourne House.[3] The poor old man has
fallen into a deplorable state of caducity. He appears at table, but
hardly sees & cannot move. . . . He retains the spirit of hospitality,
urging his guests to eat & drink. He knew us & was pleased. This
hopeless state is made less cruel from the attention of his family. He
is never without one or more in his house, & they are careful &
contribute all they can to his comfort. The Cowpers are inmates,
as they are enlarging & building their own house, which will not

[1] Joan, daughter of Major-General John Scott, married George Canning, in
1800, with a dowry of £100,000. She died in 1837.
[2] Charles John (1811 ?–68), son of Edmund Kean. Married Miss Ellen Tree.
[3] In Whitehall. After Lord Melbourne's death, it became Dover House.

for months be ready. The G. Lambs also ; & Frederick, who is looking well, but greatly altered from what he was, or what from his age he ought to be : but he has tried his constitution with every excess. Wm. Lamb is reckoned to be doing well in Ireland. Emily [1] is lovely, reported as very clever. Already two swains are *poorly* (?), a young Wortley & a Talbot ; but being of the *detrimental* class, they may sigh away in vain.

Lady Davy like a good wife has renounced Paris & its attractions, to devote six weeks change of air & scene to Sir Humphrey, who is in an unpleasant state of health. She is all in all at the Foreign Office, [2] where her empire is only shared with the Chancellor*ess*, a handsome woman, [3] very Portuguese in her appearance. At Chatsworth they all were gay, acted charades & ran races. Lord Chichester was victorious ; but the bets ran high upon Morpeth, who is really become slim & active. Knighton is gone to Berlin about young Prince of Cumberland, [4] who is destined to be our future sovereign by marrying Victoria. They are both fine children ; but these matters remind me of the story of Malherbe (the French poet), who saw a courtier affecting sorrow for the death of a young prince. He said, " Monsieur, Monsieur, celà ne vous doit point affliger ; vous ne manquerez jamais de maître." So whether it is one Prince or another, we are sure of a master. The Chancellor & his handsome brunette wife dined here. He is very good humoured. She is odd & clever. He has made Mrs Fox very happy by giving a living to a protégé of her's & of Mr Fox's in the neighbourhood of St. Ann's. It must be pleasant to oblige in this way so many people, as this small donation has.

22d October.

There is a good caricature, that, but for postage, I would send you. It is a large pair of scales : on each is seated Walter Scott & Tommy Moore. One holds his 9 vols of the *Life of Napoleon*, the other is single, little one of the *Epicurean*. Moore of course sinks ; the other kicks the beam. It is called, *The Ballance of Public Favor*. The like-

[1] Lady Emily Cowper, daughter of the Cowpers. She married Lord Ashley in 1830. William Lamb was Secretary for Ireland.

[2] Viscount Dudley was Foreign Secretary under Lord Goderich.

[3] John Singleton Copley, Lord Lyndhurst (1772–1863) son of the painter, was Lord Chancellor in the same Government. He married a widow, Sarah, daughter of Charles Brunsden, in 1819.

[4] Prince George of Cumberland (1819–78), better known later as the blind King of Hanover.

nesses are very strong & good ; the joyous air of Moore is very well
represented. What did you think of the work ? The Banquet scene
appeared to me very well executed and striking. Lady Jersey has
been making an effort to alter the days of the Newmarket meeting,
in order to prevent travelling on *Sunday* ; but Ld Sefton made good
fun & proved it impossible, as the distances many come would
throw [out] the Sunday for others, tho' it might it save Ld Jersey's *soul*.
This idle stuff has made a noise ; but it is better than her political
clamour, & less mischievous or productive of wrath & dislikes among
old friends. She is to lie in next March.

The battle of Navarino had been fought on October, where the
English, French and Russians destroyed the Turkish fleet.

Brighton. *Nov. 27th.*

. . . I saw for the first time today the Duke of St. Albans. He is
rather melancholy . . ., a handsome face with features quite im-
moveable, no sort of expression. A large handsome, dark, fixed,
glazed eye. She affected to be very joyous, but I think her gaiety
all assumed. It is a strange alliance. Sir F. Burdett came to make
her a visit. They are outwardly (?) friends. She says he only came
to borrow boxes for Miss Calcraft. Lord Melville has had a bad fall
from his horse in Scotland. You do not mention Wilkie. Is he in
Rome ? Hayter [1] has lost some of his best friends by his unfeeling
conduct to the woman who lived with him, at least in their esteem.
If you should see Mr Callcott, remember I shall feel obliged by any
civilities you can shew him. He is a clever, agreable man, & lives
very intimately at Hd H. We are surprised at the little sensation the
news of Navarino has made upon you, you who were such a warm
Greek. Is it not cheered & hailed as the harbinger of Christian liberty
in those countries ? Mrs Tierney is here, rather discomposed at his
being detained for news from Stratford Canning. As yet the Ministers
have not the official account of how the Turks decide after their
Council in the Divan ; so it is still not without anxiety. Rogers is
very kindly come to visit me for a few days. He has not his sister,
so will not take a house, which I regret, as it might tempt him to stay
longer. He came from the Deepdene, [2] where there has been a large
party of *Malignants*, [3] as they are called. You must have found a

---

[1] George Hayter, the painter. Henry Fox gives details of this unpleasant
episode in his *Journal*, p. 235.

[2] Thomas Hope's house.

[3] The Whigs who had become estranged from the rest of their party.

great improvement in Lord Howick,[1] both as to manner & every thing else. He is quick, clear & well informed ; & when softened down by intercourse with the world will be a useful man, &, as he is already, a great comfort to his family. I hear Mr. Hallam [2] longs for the bracing air of the North, tho' mightily satisfied with his journey. It is said his book will be severely handled by Southey in the next *Quarterly* ; but he is not a formidable opponent upon those subjects, they say. The Dudley Stuarts have probably joined you by this time. She is very lively & pleasant ; & he is all you think.

Don Miguel is expected on the 9th.[3] The Ministers & wives are kept in town, as the King is to give him a splendid dinner, a concert, & two days chasse, one au cerf, the other shooting. As he is acknowledged, he will be treated royally. Fred. Lamb goes to Lisbon with him, by which he gets the rank of Ambassador.

December 12th. Brighton.

It would gratify Lord Egremont, could he ever know the sensation produced by his danger among all classes : many from his admirable talents & agrémens, sound, shrewd wit, all from his benevolence & great qualities of mind. He just gave £1000 to Sir Wm Beechey, who was at Petworth retouching one of his own pictures. He saw he had a large family, as they were all invited to Petworth, & knew he had been defrauded of his legacy from Nollekens ; so he made him this splendid present. These are acts of kindness & generosity he is doing perpetually. He lives like a Patriarch. At this moment, without including the stable men, he has 68 souls under his roof. Lady Aberdeen looks very lovely, notwithstanding her watchful nights.[4] Mrs Tierney lives next door but one. He has, unluckily for himself and us, been constantly detained in town expecting news from S. Canning. He comes at all events tomorrow. I have been as useful to her as I could be, in giving her dinners & lending the new books. The Fazakerleys are here living in a *sheltered* spot beyond the Pavilion. They both dislike the roar of the sea & howl of the wind. . . . She is an amiable person, & has a charm to me of being, I believe, attached to you.

[1] Henry George, Lord Howick, succeeded as 3rd Earl Grey in 1845. He married, in 1832, Maria, daughter of Sir Joseph Copley.

[2] Henry Hallam (1777–1859). His *Constitutional History of England* had just been published.

[3] Dom Miguel was proclaimed Regent in July, but afterwards ousted his niece, Doña Maria, from the throne. Greville wrote : " He went out stag-hunting in red coat & full hunting costume, & rode over fences like anybody else."

[4] Her son by her first marriage, Lord Abercorn, had recently been desperately ill.

CHAPTER V

1828

The Hollands, seeing that their son was determined to remain out of England, had acquiesced in his desire for a diplomatic career. All such appointments at that time were dependent upon the Government of the day; and even the juniors who were in the course of learning their profession were therefore liable to find themselves turned adrift. Frederick Lamb was just starting for Lisbon as Minister; and Lady Holland's remarks are worthy of note on one under whom Fox was destined to serve for some years at Vienna in the not far distant future.

New Year's Day, 1828.

. . . You are very sensible in wishing for occupation. A life of désoeuvrement must be dreadful, &, with your talents especially for writing, quite mortifying. It is in this precarious state of the Govt advisable to *secure* something; tho' it may only be made the means of barter & exchange. Lisbon is now made up, & sails next week. The personal character of the *Chef* is not such as would make him pleasant to you; & the whole concern is rather repugnant. That for which we hope to attain,[1] Sir Wm A'Court, will be just what you wish as a school to learn your business. He is by far the first man in his line. I should myself have wished Vienna; but your Papa says you particularly dislike the Austrians, & besides it is overrun with Wellesleys in the Chancellerie, who view others with jealousy. You would find Sir Chas & Ly Bagot very agreable. Sir Chas was reckoned by Canning by far his cleverest man. Munich is not a bad place. Brooke Taylor is the brother of Sir Herbert & much liked for Berlin; but be assured the crack thing for acquirement & real business is A'Court. Stockholm is very disagreable & inferior in all ways. Madrid has only young Bosanquet; Mr Gordon not being yet moving from Rio. Otherwise *that* would have been pleasant, barring that the climate kills. I only do hope now you have engaged in this career, you will continue & not give the world the appearance of such fickleness as is always a discredit. Having made your election, abide by it, my Love.

Lord Goderich resigned at the end of 1827, but early in January

---

[1] A post in Russia, where Sir William, later Lord Heytesbury, was Ambassador.

changed his mind. The life of his Ministry, however, was not long
extended by this volte-face ; for Huskisson and Herries, two of its
mainstays, came to blows on finance, and by the end of the month
Wellington and the Tories were installed in office, with a number of
Canning's followers who had been found willing to be included.

18*th January*. Berkeley Square.

As yet nothing has transpired, who is to be the Minister.   Certainly
the D. of W. cannot make a pure Tory Govt.   Mr Peel declines,
unless Mr Huskisson will agree to form part of the arrangement.   It
is said H. stipulates for the measures with which he is identified,
Free Trade & Foreign policy : as a pledge for the last that Lord
Dudley should retain his present office, not to be under Mr Peel : &
Herries to be out of the Exchequer.   It seems odd that the result
of Mr Huskisson's personal quarrel, in which he was supported by
many members of the Cabinet against Mr Herries, should be that the
two belligerents should remain in office, & those who sided with
Huskisson be dismissed.   These are such odd shuffles in politics, that
common people who only judge of right & wrong from feelings of
honor & justice cannot understand ; nor to say the truth, for one,
if such is the upshot, do I want to know.   However, the thing is
not yet done.   The King has written with his own hand most urgently
to the D. of D. to remain ; but he, as he always does upon essential
points, behaves honorably ; & in a long interview yesterday, when
the King tried to coax & cajole him, firmly declined, & resigned
as Lord Lansdowne had not been applied to to remain.   Knighton,
Herries, Rothschild, Nash, Hill, are the real ministers in the interior
closet, who pull the strings of their puppets.   Hill is a Clerk in the
Treasury ; Nash,[1] the architect, who has sums uncounted for the
expenditure in buildings, etc., not supposed to be all appropriated to
those purposes.[2]

Charles is with a large party at Woburn, where Ld Grey is to join
them on Sunday.   Now he has none of his old friends to attack, his
violence will be lessened in Parlt probably.   I hope Lord Howick
will distinguish himself & do well, which I daresay he will.   We

---

[1] John Nash (1752–1835).

[2] Lady Holland wrote on February 22 : " The disgraceful scenes in the House
of Commons are sad.   Last night Mr. Herries was completely exposed ; & the
connexion with the Jew & the Doctor seems almost established by his silence.
A high Tory was expressing dissatisfaction to the D. of Wellington that he had
kept Huskisson in the Govt.   His reply was, that he was a good bridge for rats
to run over."

dine today at Lambton's.[1] He will by the time of (*illeg.*) be Lord *Wearmouth*. He has been odd & fantastic about his titles. He wanted to be Lord D'Arcy, then Lord Durham. The Duke of Leeds objected, & then the Bishop.

22d January, [1828].

There is a hitch in the Ministerial arrangements, one concludes, as the *Gazette* has them not yet. The chiefs have imitated in their deeds Octavius, Lepidus & Anthony, each sacrificing their best friends & gracious supporters to divide among themselves the spoil—Eldon, Westmorland & the high-flying Tories ; those abandoned on the other side need not be named. The D. of D. has been urged by word & letter from the King : & again pressed by another attempt through the D. of W. to remain, has replied that he must follow Ld L[ansdowne] as his political connexion, at all events, but that to him it was doubly incumbent, as he had been chiefly instrumental in bringing about the junction. He behaved with great firmness & honor, as he is sure always of doing upon great occasions. Young Stanley was pleased with the business of his office,[2] & liked Mr. Huskisson personally very much : but he has properly given in his resignation, as he came in politically from Ld L.'s connexion. He is very ambitious, & will exert himself this session. But he is far from popular with his young associates, tho' they all acknowledge his brilliant talents, & expect much from him. I believe Denison has again changed his mind, & is returned from Plymouth. One is sorry such an amiable man should be so unsteady, as it gives an appearance of vacillation always discreditable to a man.

[February 12.]

. . . It was most unfortunate that one of the days when Lord Hd was so *very* ill, he should have had the ill luck to get yr sneering letter. He was low from fever & pain. The effect was most distressing, as he was quite nervous & hysterical. Let this be a warning not to write sharp letters at any time, but more especially at a distance, when you may be ignorant of the state in which a person is when they receive it. Indeed, to *such* a man & such a parent, I cannot conceive how a feeling of asperity towards him could ever arise. I hope, however,

---

[1] John George Lambton (1792–1840), successively Baron, Viscount and Earl of Durham. He married Lord Grey's daughter, Louisa Elizabeth, as his 2nd wife, in 1816.

[2] Under-Secretary for the Colonies.

for your own sake in future, you will regulate both conduct & expressions in a soothing manner.

I dined quite *alone* on Saturday. Allen was at Dulwich ; Papa in bed. I felt childless, friendless, deserted. It quite overcame me. I had asked Morpeth & Howick to dine with me tomorrow to meet " Anacreon " Moore,[1] but they each have in my eyes the justifiable and amiable apology of being desired by their fathers to dine at home, as there is a party at dinner. They are, I believe, both very amiable in their family. The former loves home dearly, parents, sisters, brothers.

February 25th.

. . . I rejoice at Ld Seymour having escaped the toils of that veteran coquette.[2] I was afraid he might have got into an entanglement with her, as poor Ld Archibald [Hamilton] did with mother (?), which grievously affected his whole life, & kept him from marrying another. He is a person to be very happy with, & might with good connexions become something remarkable ; but it will depend upon the characters of the persons he is allied with. London is beginning to be very gay, Mrs Hope's first ball, which is said to be for Miss Fitzclarence. Those who overlooked the family formerly are very forward in attentions to the daughter of the Lord High Admiral. Not that I mean Mrs Hope, for she was always attentive and civil to them.

George Morpeth has made a very excellent speech on these disgraceful affairs. He is a delightful person, & does his utmost to make his family happy. Frederick[3] is full of good qualities & active benevolence & gratitude : he is odd, but not deficient. Ld Howick is much flattered at being put on the Finance Committee, which is

[1] Thomas Moore, so named by Lord Byron. He published a translation of the *Odes* in 1800.

[2] Edward Adolphus, Lord Seymour (1804–85), succeeded his father as 12th Duke of Somerset in 1855, his mother being a daughter of 9th Duke of Hamilton. He married, in 1830, Tom Sheridan's youngest daughter, sister of Lady Dufferin and Mrs. Norton. Henry Fox wrote to his aunt, Miss Fox, in January : " Lord Seymour has escaped from the clutches of Lady Sandwich, only however to fall into those of Miss d'Este, very much frying-pan fire-like. She is a brazen, hoydenish, old rouged coquette, and neither her manners or conversation are those of a demoiselle à marier. She is also about 10 years older than him. The success seems still uncertain ; but he seems so facile and gentle that I think she will bully him into marrying her." Miss d'Este was daughter of the Duke of Sussex and his 1st wife, Lady Augusta Murray.

[3] Frederick George Howard (1805–34), brother of Lord Morpeth.

done to please Ld Grey. He is a clever young man, but his ugliness prevents one from doing justice to the qualities he has. Ly Grey is well, but very thin. We see Ld G. very often.

29th February. Hd H.

As to Clubs, the Travellers' & Brooks's should seem enough. The Travellers' is very popular & pleasant; great difficulties to get chosen. Anthony Maitland has been black balled; as indeed has every body almost this season: Henry Greville & various others at White's. Crockford [1] does not seem to flourish at all. The expenses have been enormous of fitting up & decorating the house. Ld Stafford has at length completed the purchase of the late D. of York's house. It is a palace, & fit for them.

Mde Wyse, who styles herself Dona Letitia Bonaparte Wyse, is here. [2] She called, but I was too ill to see her. Her husband has written to say she left him without his consent. The *on dit*, but don't say it I beg, is that she is under the protection of Villiers Stuart. She is very much in Lady Charleville's society & taken notice of.

March 10th [1828].

. . . There is a general feeling that the Catholic Question must ultimately be carried, altho' the K. works himself up into a fury when the subject is named to him. The K. is not well. His knee is become a cause of serious apprehension. There is a mystery as to the disease, but it is not gout. Some think it is a white swelling from the scrofula which is in them all, but it is agreed & admitted that he will never walk again. I am rather sorry, altho' were he to live 20 years I should probably never see him. Yet personally I have a good will to him, partly from old acquaintance sake & partly from believing there is more good in him than falls to the lot of most Princes; and had he not been one, he would, I am persuaded, have been a most amiable man. I went with the D. of B. last night to the Opera, *dissipation* being recommended; & in that instance the remedy was agreable. Pasta sang divinely; but *Othello* is more painful, when so well acted, even than the prose. Yet the story is to me always disagreable to hear. Critics think Pasta runs about to avoid the uplifted arm of the Moor & makes too great a scuffle before she is stabbed. It is certainly true, as Charles remarked, that the resemblance between

[1] Crockford's, a house now remodelled as the Devonshire Club, was built in 1827; the decoration being said to have cost £94,000. Crockford himself died in 1844.

[2] Lucien Bonaparte's eldest daughter by his 2nd wife, Alexandrine de Bleschamp.

Pasta & Louisa Fitzmaurice [1] is very strong, tho' the beauty is not equal.

Ld Chesterfield was introduced to me the other night. He called the next morning. I say he has profited by the lessons of his great uncle in good breeding ; as young men of this age are not apt to be so well bred. He is not handsome, but his countenance is very pleasing & winning. He is going abroad immediately, being tired, he says, of hunting & shooting. It is regretted he has such an entanglement, as he seems to deserve better. She will, I dare say, keep a firm hold & follow him abroad.

You cannot think how much Ld Normanby is improved. He is quite amiable : so eager, gay, pleasant & good humoured. His only foible is the passion for acting, & that is very harmless. Mrs Norton, late Miss Sheridan, is much the subject of conversation. She is showy & clever, but too strange. Her poems are to be published, I believe, immediately, with her name. Tonight appears Ld Porchester's [2] Tragedy, with all that scenery, music & decorations can do ; but the actors & still more actresses are wretched for tragedy, & the public taste is also against the doleful. His father is nervous & anxiously alive to ill success.

18th March.

The King is better. His knee will not be so serious a complaint, I hope ; tho' he lies in bed all day, & only gets up to a dinner where he carouses till past midnight, & is much *overtaken* by his festive turn.

The Govt is not popular nor respected. Much disappointment at the D. of W. He is also nettled & sour at finding he can do so little. The H. of Commons is not manageable. The K. is not satisfied, & talks in all directions how much he liked Lord Lansdowne, that he was the only *gentleman*, & Lord Carlisle, he has ever had : in short, expressing all sorts of regrets at the loss of him, which he said arose from his own illness & great blunders of Ld Goderich. This I believe ; as it certainly never was the King's intention to have the D. of W. Some say the Govt will not last long in its present form. The K. says it is enough to cast ridicule and contempt upon any Govt, to have such a man as Ld Ellenboro' belonging to it : he protests the sight of him makes him *sick*, he is so absurd & contemptible in his appearance.

---

[1] Lord Lansdowne's daughter. Lady Holland wrote in March 1832, " She is a charming girl, full of conversation, and not at all like a *Miss*. Her face is really very pretty ; all she wants in figure is height."

[2] Henry George James Herbert, later 3rd Earl of Carnarvon (1800–49).

In going last night to the French play with Allen & Mary, we escaped a sad accident by a miracle going down Regent Street. We heard loud shouts & great clatter, & galloping of horses & carriage. This was from the Gloster mail ; the coachman was thrown off his box & killed within a few yards of us. The horses without guidance were within an ace of running straight upon us ; something caught the reins—a lamp post, & turned them into Charles Street, which saved us, & stopped the coach by throwing down the leaders. Two women, one outside & one within, were all belonging to the concern. The poor man's brains were shattered, & he was dead in an instant. It is a most dangerous way, to entrust to one driver only 4 spirited horses through such streets as the Strand, Fleet St, Piccadilly, etc. Accidents are become much more frequent within these few years. We were all shocked & alarmed, tho' till afterwards did not know our personal danger.

Cooper,[1] the author of the American novels is in London. As yet I have not seen him. He must be a man of considerable ability from his writings. He is always better *afloat* than on shore. He began life in a very humble station before the mast, as a common seaman.

21st March. Hd H.

We are here for a little change of air ; when perversely it took to raining, but not cold, nor does it prevent the before breakfast walks of Luttrell, Rogers, Mackintosh. Poor Tierney is very far from well, . . . & cannot bear much exertion ; even the sitting at table with our few inmates is painful & fatiguing. I do not wonder at the uneasiness of his family, as I am not myself free from apprehension about him. But we must hope that the belle saison which is approaching may be of material service to the restoration of his health. Miss Rogers also here with her brother. She is very amiable & sensible. I like her very much. Tomorrow the *Red Rover* is to dine here. So of him anon, when I can report from personal knowledge. As yet I only know his Works, & Rogers's very excellent stories, which he repeats so well—one of a whaler, & a chase from a pirate, etc., etc.

Don Miguel has played us false.[2] However, it does not appear

---

[1] James Fenimore Cooper, of whom Miss Fox wrote as " The Red Rover " (the name of the novel which he had just published), " the lion of the season, kept and exhibited by Rogers." Of this book, Lady Holland had written in December : " There is an admirable work by Cooper, the American, who wrote The Spy, Pilot, etc. This is superior ; tho' the moral in a Court of honour is very dubious, to say the least. The interest is *intense*. The sea seems admirably described. The author has read Scott & Byron evidently."

[2] *See ante*, p. 53.

that the Govt had such implicit confidence to him, as the money was not trusted to him but very properly consigned to our Ambassador, who of course was guided by the wisdom & experience of Lord Heytesbury. So it is almost all rescued ; & Rothschild, to whom we were *garants* for the payment, will have it restored, & we save our pence. One can hardly foresee how the business will terminate, tho' the other matters of Greece & Russia are the most urgent & important.

There prevails a general notion of want of stability in the Govt. People are disappointed in D. of W. ; & *he* surprized that his colleagues & H. of Commons are not as tractable as his military staff & councils of war used to be to his will. Ly E. Vernon is going to spend the winter at Florence. She sets off tomorrow to remain at Paris & north of Italy till winter season. She is in great beauty, & her absence will be most ridiculously painful to some members of the Russell family, more than one I suspect. The Miss Berry's go to the Rhine & Paris early in April.

Holland's speech, to which Lady Holland refers on April 18, introduced the Bill for the repeal of the Test and Corporation Acts in the House of Lords. It had already passed the Commons. Lord Eldon opposed the Second Reading, but the Bill became law in due course.

South Street.   Lady Affleck's.   *April* 17.

Sir W. Scott is in town. He has seen the *Red Rover*. I suppose they do not like each other ; but I know nothing of their feelings, only suppose jalousie de métier would interfere & prevent much liking between authors in the same line. Cooper is very Yankee in his feelings ; an utter abhorrence of this country, & very open to the flattery which is bestowed on them by French & Russians. I rejoiced at seeing your letter to that abominable Crockford. It did seem impossible, after you had told us that you had withdrawn your name & was sure that it would please us, but you were again re-elected.

April 18th.

Your Papa is reported on all sides to have made an admirable & impressive speech last night, full of knowledge, ability & talent. He is even satisfied with himself. He was very nervous, & afterwards could not sleep a wink. You must surmount your aversion to serious subjects connected with politics & read his speech. It is execrably given, he says ; but the outline will give you a notion of the matter. He is half afraid Ld Eldon, with his ingenuity & subtlety, will try to defeat the measure in the Committee ; & Newmarket on Monday carries off 12 or more votes. I hope the yielding this, what used to be called *Bulwark* of the Church, is only the prelude to the great question of Catholic liberty being carried. But that is quite another thing. You will be diverted to hear we slept in this pigmy, lilliputian house ; but you know I can squeeze my two trunks into a very small compass, always provided the female part of the suite are in good humour & trim.

April 25th.

. . . Lady Compton [1] is charming, & likes you much ; but do you think it nothing to her to have a young man of your qualifications & station attached, & to a degree belonging to her ? To speak openly, all these sort of friendships are but holiday affairs ; the solid are in connexions where the interest is so deep. I do not confine that to *mere* relationship, but to hereditary attachments & family ties, from habit long established, or begun at school or college. I look round, & see only such among my own friends but of that sort. The others are evanescent & local ; when each party, as they get on in life, revert to the solid links of connexion. I cannot feel much admiration for that poor visionary Ly W[estmorland]. I know her thoroughly ; she is devoid of affection & just principle. Inordinate vanity & self-conceit swallow every natural feeling. She has great volubility, & a sort of second-rate eloquence ; but there is nothing *sound* about her mind & heart. But you do quite right to keep on good terms with her, as she has a tongue & pen equally active where she dislikes. People are full of stories about Ly Blessington, Ly M. Ross, [2] D'Orsay, & sad trashy squabbles, quite contemptible. I wish you well out of such low din & squabbles ; & must trust your native good sense & taste have precluded your taking any share in the turmoil.

I did not send you Ld John Russell's book. It is a mere compilation of extracts from other books. I was sorry to see his name to it for 5 shillings. He ought to have sent it to some newspaper gratis. It was infra dignitatem for him to levy such a contribution ; & I would not buy it—at least I think I did not send it. He, poor fellow, is

[1] Margaret, daughter of Gen. Clephane. Earl Compton (1790–1851) succeeded as 2nd Marquis of Northampton in 1828. She was a devoted friend of Henry Fox. " A gigantic, well-informed, hard-headed, blue Scotchwoman," was his description in 1824. She died in 1830, to his great grief.

[2] Lady Mary Ross, daughter of Robert, 2nd Duke of Leinster. The Blessington clique were in Italy at this time. Actually Henry Fox had allowed himself, very contrary to his wishes, to become involved in the consequences of a libel by D'Orsay on Lady Westmorland, and almost became implicated in a duel.

looking like the famous " Lazarus " of Sebastiano del Piombo, quite
as livid.   I fear he will not do well ; as he has no care of his health.

Your own dear Papa is very well, but so dreadfully worried &
anxious about this Bill for the Dissenters, that he can think of nothing
else in any way : the more so as there has been a hitch in the progress
of it.   Some suspect the D. of Cumberland & Lord Eldon are full
of plots & evil designs.   End as it may, your Papa has done himself
great honor.   Yesterday, for the first time, I dined in company at
Argyll House [1] with Ld Goderich.   What a man to have been Prime
Minister.   No wonder a Govt melted away under his guidance.
How could it do otherwise ?   Mary looked beautiful at the Drawing
Room, & subsequently at Almack's.   She is a good girl indeed.

I have seen the new building at the Museum.   It is very spacious
& handsome ; but one always has some criticism to make, & Smirke
is too great a lover of the simple, plain style, without the sublime of
the grandiose.[2]   How many books do they say there are in the
Library at the Vatican ?   The Bib. du Roi contains 400,000 ;   ours
at Museum 200,000.   But the Vatican must exceed the two together
in numbers.   I hope you have seen all the curious MSS. there.

28th April.   Hd H.

The marriage of Lord Carmarthen & Ly Hervey has taken place.[3]
The D. of Leeds bears it quietly on account of the Dss, for whom he
dreads agitation.   He is, however, deeply mortified ; & his friends
have no consolation to offer but the improbability of her having any
children. . . .   The second son is a very fine young man, & just
what such a father would be proud of ; so if these consolations are
valid, all will be right.   They say Lady Hervey wanted six qualifications, youth, beauty, character, fortune, birth, sense.   She is nine
years older than Ld C., & has only assurance for sense.

I have only once seen Walter Scott.   He is in affliction.   The favorite
grand-child, for whom he wrote the little history, is dying.[4]   He is a
promising child, full of precocity of genius.   He desired me to thank
you for having brought a picture from or of Lady Compton, of

---

[1] With Lord Aberdeen.

[2] Robert Smirke was at work on the rebuilding of the British Museum from
1823 to 1847.

[3] Frances Godolphin Osborne, Marquis of Carmarthen (1798–1859), succeeded
as 7th Duke of Leeds in 1838.   His wife was Louisa Caton, of Maryland, and
widow of Sir Felton Bathurst Hervey.   His brother, Conyers, was accidentally
killed at Oxford, and the titles devolved on his nephew.

[4] " Hugh Littlejohn " Lockhart.

whom he spoke of as an old friend. He said when she married, he had something to do with the arrangements ; & a gentleman asked what sort of person she was. He replied, " I will say with *Tom Pipes* (*Peregrine Pickle*), she can steer & reef & sail with any sailor in the Isles." When she married, he said, she was most beautiful, but that I could not judge of her beauty now from her bulk, which, he said, startled him last year. Nevertheless I thought her face very fine. It reminded me of Lady Hamilton's, tho' she wants height ; which Ly H. had, altho' latterly she became almost unwieldy. Walter Scott looks well, nay better than he did when last in town ; but his infirmity is increasing, & he walks with difficulty. Rheumatism also aggravates his natural weakness in his limb. His Novel is not only written but printed, not published yet. It is called *The Fair Maid of Perth*. He surprized me by saying that when he wrote the *siege* in Ivanhoe, he was confined to his bed writhing from acute pain, & even in some danger, from an inflammation in his bowels ; but tho' hardly able to dictate from the difficulty of uttering, he did so to his patient amanuensis, & composed that beautiful scene with Rebecca.

I myself, I am going tonight with Mary to a ball at Ly Tankerville's, & to some gaiety on Thursday at Ly E. Belgrave's ; as Lady L. is ill & unable to take the office of chaperon, and Ly Carlisle does not go out tonight. Mr Smith's rich Nabob brother, Mr Courtenay Smith, is just arrived from India. He left this country when only 17, & returns at 50 with an immense fortune. It will be an occupation to amuse & keep him from forming any matrimonial engagement, which our good aunt will try, & Sydney, who arrives today, will by overdoing mar.

This house is filled in the morning with Jews & Dissenters ; people of all persuasions, even up to the Archbishop of York, to whom I sent Mary in the Library to amuse him until Papa got off some of the Sectaries. Today, thank Heaven, is the last day in the H. of Lords for that question. I can hardly bring myself to doubt its being carried ; tho' there are foolish rumours of the King's intention to put a negative to the Bill—a violent proceeding never ventured by any of this dynasty. The last instance was Wm III, but he was obliged to retract, from the violent petition from House of Commons.

The chit-chat of the day is about the young Prince of Cumberland, the supposed *futur* of our young Queen Victoria. He is a lively, pretty boy ; & if he says half the witty things attributed to him, he must be a remarkable child. He is remarkably inquisitive about the state of the Royal family, the succession, etc. The Dss of Kent, who has brought up her daughter in total ignorance of her *high destiny*, is alarmed at his spirit of investigation, as she apprehends his telling the child what is her situation. The boy was at the Drawing Room, & admired the beauties, especially Emily Cowper. He wanted her to be placed near him. His German education made him laugh outright at the deaf Sir . . . Shepherd, who put a trumpet to his ear. The child wondered he did not put it to his mouth to play. The D. of Gloster from absurd pomp does not allow the Dss to live on the first floor, in order to have a state! bedchamber. The folly of the man, in a London street house ! So she lives high up. When the boy got there, they said, " Is it not a Paradise ? " He looked up at the sky, & said, " Yes, & very near it too." This is sharp, if genuine ; but I am a great doubter of infantile bon mots.

Yesterday for the first time we sat in the Library, the Gwydyrs, Gowers, Luttrell, Sneyd, Kinnaird, & a few others, a pleasant party. And today I have been listening with delight to the nightingales & hailing the tender green leaves & flowers. You cannot think how much the garden is improved ; it is now quite beautiful. The D. of B. has had a very severe stroke, but is, I trust, recovering.

9th May.

I am sorry the squabbles occupy you at all. Of course here they are not of much interest. I had heard the story some weeks ago, before I left London, with the addition of the name of Lady Mary Ross ; and you mentioned Ly W.'s profane wild speech, about God Almighty fighting his own battles, etc. I am sorry, as no party can get well out of a quarrel where violent language is used on both sides. But why will Lady W. in a foreign country be the *Custodian* of the morals of the town ? They say we ladies like to cause duels ; but in this case I hope none will ensue. I have had a good will to Lady Blessington ever since she lodged, tended & nursed you so kindly when you had your fall ; & you then, I thought, praised her & D'Orsay for qualities beyond their deserts. He was not esteemed in this country at all. I hope you have not meddled in the affair ; as believe me anywhere women's quarrels are ridiculous, & if made a serious matter by appealing to high authorities are only laughed at. Why should people who only go for health, economy or amusement destroy their pleasure by getting into hot water & wrangling ?

16th May.

. . . Dear boy, how you are beloved ! Had I ever such advantages in my youth, what a different & more amiable person I should have been. But I have few relations in the world, never had a young associate, & only a father & mother who did not always agree with each other, & never agreed about me. The warm, ingenuous affections of youth were never drawn out, but blunted & repressed ; in that my adolescence & youth was gloomy, uncheered by any tender kindred feeling. I was solitary ; & till 13 years old, no mortal seemed to think of me beyond the necessaries of life, till an old friend of my father's, struck by my looks or my character, to a degree adopted me & became my tutor. The little I knew was from him, a man you have heard me name, *Anthony Storer* [1] ; but he was an invalid sinking fast under disease, & could only when in an interval of ease sketch out what I should learn. Such as it was, he was my mental benefactor, & gave a turn to my mind better than under the paternal roof I would have had otherwise. When I look back & recollect the weeks, the days, in which all the hours, except those for meals, were spent by me in *total* solitude in a back room in a London house in the dingiest situation, I cannot but make the contrast at our pains, taken to prevent Mary being *left* perhaps for 3 hours before her bedtime merely with a dull companion, such as Thérèse. Yet I am afraid it is only those who have been abandoned to themselves, that can estimate the value of the tender, unremitting attentions of their family. As to you & Charles I will say nothing. His precarious health in infancy, & your infirmity, God knows, regulated all our plans & motions for years. But, dear child, you then repaid us by your affection & agrémens ; & so it may be in future, I trust.

George [2] is Steward at Doncaster Races. He made an admirable speech on Canning's business, the unprepared part was the best part, which is a good sign. On the Catholic Question, Ld Francis Leveson made a better speech than usual ; but Brougham says it was in the exploded, vicious taste of, " coiled serpents, surges, scene, mountain tops, gilded hemisphere, foamy billows," & such high flown trifles.

Tuesday, May 19, 20 [Holland House].

I went to a ball at Mrs Baring's,[3] as they, you know, are great favorites of mine. The house was very handsome, & is adorned with splendid pictures, spoils from Talleyrand & many of the collections made under the Empire. The heat was intense, & I never penetrated

---

[1] Anthony Morris Storer (1746–99), collector of books and prints, and man of fashion. In ill health, 1787–8.

[2] Morpeth. The subject of his speech was a grant to one of Canning's sons of a pension of £3,000 a year, to get over the difficult question of law as to provision for his family. It was passed, not without strenuous opposition.

[4] Mrs. Alexander Baring.

beyond the room I first took my station in.   Lady Morley has written
a clever jeu d'esprit, a Petition on behalf of the Hens to Parliament
against the importation of foreign Eggs.   It is too bulky for a letter.
It is printed like a petition to Parliament.   It is too long, otherwise
very clever nonsense.   An answer has been written, which is even
better, but anonymously as yet.   W. Scott dined & slept here Saturday.
He was remarkably entertaining, full of legendary lore ; some of his
anecdotes he told admirably & briefly.   He told us he never had
known but two persons who were really persuaded they had seen
ghosts, & both fell by their own hands.   One was Lord Londonderry ;
the other he did not name.   His notion palpably is that it requires a
spice of lunacy to entertain the belief.   He enquired with great interest
about you.   I never saw any person admire more this lovely place.
The day was bright & fine ; the nightingales in full song, & the rich
blossoms & foliage quite magnificent.

The " Canningites " in the Government, Palmerston, Dudley, etc.,
followed Huskisson into retirement during the spring.

27th May.

Your dear father's foot is better ; the wound is quite healed, &
not made worse by the fatigue & exertion of going last night to the
King's Ball.   He only staid 20 minutes, just to be spoken to, & give
a short coup d'oeil to the brilliant scene.   Mary remained ; & I have
not seen her since, as she slept in town.   She looked *beautiful*, a new
dress, arrived 3 days before from Paris, à la Sévigné, became her :
shoulder knots, full plaits, & all that has been exploded this half century.
She is very lovely, very amiable, & will make some man very happy,
whenever there is one wise & lucky enough to try to win her.   Mary
is returned, mighty pleased with the splendor of the Ball.   I hope
next year la belle Natalie will be at a similar fête, & be one of its
brightest ornaments.[1]   Huskisson & Palmerson are certainly out.
Our Govt is becoming quite military, as Sir G. Murray is made Secy
of State for Colonies.   He is a distinguished General Officer.   Young
Stanley carries all before him in the H. of Commons.

3d June.

The strange political embarras is detailed at full length in the debate
of last night.   You will there see the eager avidity with which the
Duke of W. grasped at the possibility of getting rid of Mr H.

[1] The engagement between Henry Fox and Mademoiselle Potocka took new
life in March ; but at the end of a few months, it was finally broken off.

Whether this Peninsular Ministry will last or not can only be resolved by time. Ld Essex has bought a house in that swamp called Belgrave Square. He is very busy in planning & furnishing it.

Our dinner with Leopold went off very well.[1] He has more sense than appears from his cautious, cold manner. I have promised to dine with him some day this month. I had rather not, but must. My acquaintance with him arises from *you*.

6th June, [1828]. Hd H.

The whole population of beau monde, & all that of the lower classes, has turned out to Ascot Races, which have been more brilliant than ever. The King wishes them to surpass Newmarket, & has even added another week by cribbing from Egham. People are rather angry at the scheme, & do not send their best horses.

London is very festive after a great stagnation, breakfasts without end. One upon the water in the Barges, given by the D. of Clarence ; Dss of St Albans at Holly Lodge ; another by D. of Somerset at Wimbledon ; and balls without end.

August 26th. Hd H.

The Kensington people have quite won my heart ; all ranks & classes have been so anxious during Papa's illness, coming up, & stopping the servants to know about him.[2] The D. of Wellington even rode here, wet to the skin, to enquire. More was reported of his danger than I believe ever existed.

3d October. Hd H.

We spent a few days at Petworth, much pleased at finding Ld Egremont [3] well. Tho' he complains of feeling 20 years older than before his last illness, yet it does not appear ; he is active, shrewd, witty & friendly as ever. His house is a strange medley, as you may remember, artists & their wives & large numbers of their children. Of his own family, he had only Mrs King, her husband & children, & Ly E. Marsham, & some Riddell nieces, & another son of his own, Mr Crowle, *full* brother to Mrs Fitzclarence : they are neither of them the children of Lady Egremont. He is in the church ; very good natured, but not clever.

---

[1] Prince Leopold dined at Holland House on June 1, a large party to meet him.
[2] His usual chalkstones, and other gouty symptoms in an aggravated form.
[3] George, 3rd Earl (1751–1837), married, in 1801, Elizabeth Ilive, by whom he had six illegitimate children before marriage. Mrs. Fitzclarence later became Countess of Munster.

Kerry [1] is returned with his brother from their parents, one to his college duties, the other to school. They are both charming boys, Kerry full of affectionate, amiable qualities, the other a sturdy, original sort of character, very loveable. They appear as yet to be very excellent children, & to love their family.

We are much confounded to find the house in a more deplorable state than ever. More walls opened, & the roof taken down; & the expense will be enormous. I hardly ever saw Papa look more serious & annoyed.

10th October [1828].

The Govt have taken a most ill situated place for the residence of the young Queen. [2] It is low, damp, & often inundated by the Thames. She will scarcely escape an ague. Poor Palmella, from great adversity, poverty, exile & all manner of calamities, is restored to honors & importance. He has his credentials as Ambassador from Pedro, & is besides named *tuteur* or guardian, invested with such powers that no subject ever had before; & indeed they are puzzled at the Foreign Office how to treat him. In the meantime, I hope that the marriage with Miguel may be avoided. Quiet people are rather alarmed at the establishment & progress of these Brunswick Clubs. [3] It is an Association formed much upon the intolerant & violent principles of the *League*; fortunately they have no *Guises*. The D. of Northumberland is a very weak, silly man; & Lord Chandos, living with inferiors & always accompanied by a led Captain, his *bully back* as Congreve describes, is not formidable, from the contempt into which he has fallen & makes him quite insignificant. But it is an opening for parsons & country squires, & unless well resisted may have pernicious effects upon the Catholic Question, when it comes to be again agitated. The parties at Castle Howard and Chatsworth are described as very pleasant. I should have enjoyed being at the former so much. Luttrell describes it as having been quite perfection. The George Lambs [4] live entirely at Melbourne, in Derbyshire. Ld

---

[1] William Thomas, Earl of Kerry (1811–36), Lord Lansdowne's eldest son. The second, Henry, succeeded in 1863 as 4th Marquis. He took the name of Lord Shelburne on his brother's death.

[2] Doña Maria da Gloria, the dispossessed Queen of Portugal.

[3] Formed to repel the increasing sympathy with the Catholics. The Duke of Northumberland (Hugh Percy, 3rd Duke) had succeeded Lord Anglesey in Ireland; and the appointment gave rise to some agitation, as the new Lord-Lieutenant was well known as a " Protestant."

[4] George Lamb was Lord Melbourne's youngest son (1784–1834), lawyer and politician. He married Caroline St. Jules.

Melbourne has confirmed it to them for their residence during their lives, which they delight in : & she has made the old place very beautiful, a garden & sundial like mine, a terrace & steps; so I am bound to approve.

Lord Howard's [1] marriage with Lady Lucy Bentinck is settled. He has been very constant, & will, I think, be happy ; & the Portland family will do with a good grace what they agree to. It is a great thing for him in all ways. Her fortune is great, & the connexion must be advantageous ; besides that she is a very pretty girl. I am quite happy at the event.

17th October.

We shall go next Tuesday to Brighton, unless we are prevented by something disagreable. That place is so full that houses are not to be had ; neither the Duke of Bedford nor Mr Baring have been able to secure one. We go to the same house on the Steyne you remember Mrs Hope had ; & my mother has taken lodgings at the shoe-maker's adjoining, where she hopes to be able to give a gîte to Charles & his wife. They will all dine with us ; so we shall be snug. When one grows old, it is a comfort to have near & dear connexions at hand ; & my mother, tho' not infirm, is yet very old, so that unless she is under my roof or immediately under my eye I do not feel happy, as at her age she really requires all the tenderness of her family.

Lady Hardy [2] & family are established already at Brighton. She is at home every evening. Her daughters are admired : the eldest very clever. Ld John Russell wished to marry the young one, but she declined. It is a pity he has the rage to marry upon him, as he is so frequently repulsed, & should, as Binda says, be, as he would in Italy, content to be Prelato or Monsignore of the family, as he is a delightful person in all relations but those of lover or husband ; at least so I should think, & so do the young ladies. The death of the Q. of Würtemburg [3] throws us all into odious mourning, & has affected the D. of Clarence, who was very much attached to her. They were the pair in the family most united.

[1] Lord Howard de Walden.

[2] Anne Louisa Emily, daughter of Admiral Sir G. Cranfield Berkeley and widow of Vice-Admiral Sir Thomas Masterman Hardy, Nelson's friend. She had three daughters. In 1840, she married Lord Seaford, father of the 6th Lord Howard de Walden.

[3] George III's eldest daughter, Charlotte Augusta Matilda, Princess Royal.

November 20th.   Brighton.

Nothing fresh here occurs except arrivals without end.   The latest importations are Ld Dudley, Ly Lyndhurst, Ld Bessboro' preparatory to the Wm Ponsonbys.   Dss of Bedford is also come, & merry & well.   The stories of the King are so various & contradictory, that I cannot guess which is true.   It is certain he has lost considerably in bulk, & his face is much diminished in size.   The Brunswick Clubs do not get on as much as the violent party expected.   They are not encouraged by Govt, altho' it is whispered his Majesty underhand gives them support.   Parlt will not meet before February ; but we shall establish in London next month, as it is always good for Lord Hd to be seasoned to London before the meeting : that is to have *over* his smoke & fog cough, the inevitable consequence of the London atmosphere.   Agar & his family are all safe & well, much to his own & Ld Clifden's felicity.   Mr Huskisson is returned in full vigor, astonished at the ignorance & mismanagement of the A[ustrian] Govt in their commercial measures in the Milanese.   The high duties almost amount to prohibition ; & smuggling of course is very constant & successful.   So they have no revenue to pay for the expense of collection from their customs.   What a narrow escape we have had at Covent Garden.   The gasometer was *under* my box.   The accidents of the escape of gas to overpower the atmosphere during the performance arose from the malice of a dismissed workman.   How wicked !

1st December, [Brighton].

We are about leaving this favored spot as to climate ; & certainly it agrees remarkably well with Ld Hd, indeed with us all ; but he must be *seasoned* before Parlt opens, where there will be much to interest the mind & pique curiosity.   *Here* the gaieties are about to begin.   A ball under the patronage of Mrs Fitzherbert on Wednesday.   As she is anxious for its success, Mary goes.   D. of D. is come for 6 weeks without his establishment : hitherto he has generally dined with us.   He is, as we all have long known, remarkable for sound, good sense : but when seen so intimately he shews a great fund of drollery & fun, like Lady Granville ; & both from their mother.   His two charming nieces, Susan Leveson & Blanche Howard, are to appear the first time at a ball after Easter.   *They* will captivate, I foresee, abundantly.   *He* hopes one may please his heir, the future

Duke,[1] who hitherto has been the admiration of Cambridge for his mathematics & classical acquirements, & also remarkable for his skill in all field sports. Besides he is handsome, but too taciturn & reserved. Your friends the *Dawsons* [2] have under Lady Caroline Damer's will assumed the name of *Damer*. The inheritance has been very comfortable, a charming house *ready*, with furniture, plate, books & linen, for immediate possession in Dorsetshire, a pleasant county, surrounded by an estate of better than two thousand a year. This with her fortune & his own pittance as a younger son, will make them enjoy a competence ; which with merry, good humoured people is all that can be wished for, as in their dispositions they find felicity. Mrs Fitz. is really in remarkable *beauty*, tho' her age is great.

8th December, [1828. Brighton].

We are on the point of quitting this healthy, gay place : mean to take Petworth on our way home. I do not like, at Ld E.'s great age, to miss any opportunity of enjoying his society. As one grows old, one clings to those who have been friendly in early life & who from intimacy with family connexions almost stand in the line of relations. Besides his head & heart are unique, & his witty conversation is not easily found in others. Papa he likes, not only for his own sake, but for Ld Ossory's & others. His regard to me is quite personal, as I have not the advantages of connexions for him to have loved & known.

We have enjoyed agreable society here, many of my own intimates, with the infusion of a few novelties, Lady Lyndhurst, for instance, sparkling & brilliant in beauty, & with odd sallies, not from any affectation of being original or flashy in conversation, but really from coming into the beau monde when her ways were formed for another class. She is good hearted & good natured. She enjoys that her Lord has contributed to make the D. of W. urge poor Denman's suit to the King [3] ; who has acceded, & acknowledges that his prejudice against him was unfounded. So he has his *silk gown*. The silk gown only gives rank & enables him to receive briefs, which

[1] William Cavendish (1808–91), son of Col. William Cavendish, grandson of 4th Duke. He became in due course 2nd Earl of Burlington, and 7th Duke of Devonshire. He did marry Lady Blanche Howard in 1829.

[2] George Lionel, son of John, 1st Earl of Portarlington. Came, near Dorchester, was the Dorset estate. Lady Caroline Damer was the sole surviving heiress of the Earl of Dorchester, and died unmarried.

[3] Thomas Denman, 1st Baron (1779–1854). He had been Solicitor-General to Queen Caroline, and was never forgiven by the King for certain incidents at that time. Even at the end of November the King refused to see him.

otherwise he could not. This income will now be greatly augmented. Before this he had only a very scanty receipt, and a very large family to maintain. Few things have occurred to give us more pleasure.

[Holland House] *21st December.*

Montrond [1] brought over the celebrated man Louis, Talleyrand's famous cook, who lived some months with us at Paris. He has a vacance till the jour de l'an, & came over to see this country, & learn some *ragouts Anglais*. Bless the poor man, what can he learn beyond melted butter & raw beef steak. There is, however, a very common & good dish Montrond taught us to enquire about, which is really good & delicious to those who can eat potatoes, I am not one, called *Irish Stew.* . . . It is really good. Mrs Clefane doubtless knows it, as in Scotland it is made of moor fowl & venison. Try it one day. Were you a German, you would out of *sentiment* for me. We were delighted with our séjour at Petworth. Dear Ld Egremont is in excellent health, & in better spirits than he has been for years. One of the days was when he completed 77 years, much hospitality, he fed & clothed the villages 3 miles round. The poor have extended the benefaction, by coming sometimes as far as 8 miles. He is all generosity & goodness to those who need his services ; his wit & agrémens, added to a remarkably strong, acute mind, render him a most agreable person. He goes to bed at $\frac{1}{2}$ past nine, observing that at his age he must only think of lengthening life, not enjoying it for pleasure only. His formation & constitution are fine enough to carry him on to a very great age, should nothing untoward occur.

Mrs Norton's poems are beautiful, the songs & short things. The Poem is too melancholy ; so I shall never be able to judge of its merits. The crimes are much encreased everywhere in the country. Burglaries, robberies & such offences, springing out of a bad system of Poor Laws & the criminal law which makes punishment so extreme as to be inadequate to the offence ; & many will not prosecute, as they do not wish to inflict death upon petty offences. The penalty for forgery is to be reconsidered.

Charles's returned from Brighton yesterday. They flatter us by saying the Pier & our haunts were in mourning at our departure. A man like your father, who is much at home seeing people, must by his absence make a gap in society where his conversation is so delightful & enlightened. I really think after all he is now without comparison the most agreable man in England.

[1] Count Montrond, the friend and confidential agent of Talleyrand. He died in 1843.

CHAPTER VI

1829

5th January, 1829, [11] Berkeley Square.[1]

There has been a great party at Windsor Castle, where Lord Dudley was conspicuous from his temper & eccentricities. He scolded Wyatville because he felt chilly, the servants loudly at table for waiting ill, complained of the bad chère, said he had lately dined with a friend, a lady, where the soup was hot, the wine cool, & a fat woodcock. "Look at this wretched snipe." Objected to the Castle, said a large house would be better, as he did not believe the Danes were coming. In short, he was absurd beyond measure. The King could talk of nothing but the little Queen,[2] with whom he was quite enchanted, her beauty, manner & sense. He could not mention a little trait of feeling without emotion. He said he conducted her down stairs to her carriage, & on taking leave assured her of his wishes for her welfare, & that he would do all in his power to *re-instate* her in her rights. The child burst out into a fit of crying, & threw her little arms round his neck. This, he observed, was a spontaneous feeling ; "she could not have *been taught*, as they could not know what my conversation would be." The Castle is reckoned very splendid ; but the finest rooms are not finished. It can never be a comfortable residence, as the difficulty of getting out must always be an inconvenience.

The Blessington family do not succeed well at Paris. D'Orsay is censored for his treatment of his poor wife,[3] & laughed at for his dress, which is composed of sky blue pantaloons of silk & other strange mixtures. He wears his shirt, without a neckcloth, fastened with diamonds & coloured stones—in short a costume that *men* disapprove as effeminate & nondescript.

January 19th, [1829].

Ld Anglesey [4] leaves Dublin this day. He seems to have been

---

[1] "A very good & very cheap house."
[2] Of Portugal.
[3] D'Orsay had married Lady Harriet Gardiner, Lady Blessington's step-daughter, in 1827.
[4] The circumstances of Lord Anglesey's recall from Ireland as Lord-Lieutenant are fully set out, from the Holland House MSS., in the *Chronicles of Holland House*, pp. 103-4.

abominably used by the Governt here, most basely. The Devonshire meeting went off better than might have been expected in that foyer of intolerance & bigotry, Exeter. All the *freeholders* & persons of education & substance were on the liberal side. Ld Seymour made a good speech, & Ld Boringdon [1] did well at the public dinner. It is very creditable to the young men to come forward on this occasion. Indeed, the young ones seem to feel strongly upon great questions. One likes them to shew interest, even if it should be on a different side ; but now England & France are full of life & stir, compared to what they both were 80 years ago.

January 26th.

. . . Next week will be the tug-of-war ; tho' till Ld Plunket comes the 15th, I do not suppose the great question of Ireland will be discussed à fond, tho' it is one of such magnitude & every hour is fraught with alarm & danger. Good old Lord Fitzwilliam says he knows the Dss of Northumberland to be a great anti-Catholic vixen as ever breathed, & she has much influence in the ménage. [2] The Duke is a poor creature, vain, ostentatious & null. Young Cavendish, Lord George's grandson, is 2d wrangler at Cambridge. The 1st is a man of the name of Philpotts, but they were nearly equal, & Cavendish shewed great mathematical genius. Perhaps it is as well he was not first, as it might make him too devoted to that branch ; tho' he has great talents besides & is a good scholar. The young man of 21, Mr Brodrick, who has distinguished himself so brilliantly at the Irish meeting after Ld Anglesey's departure, tho' perhaps too much in the Irish manner, was one of the best mathematicians of his time at Trinity College. He is said to be a nephew of Mr Grattan's.

Much pressure was put upon the King by his Ministers during the winter, to agree to some measure of relief for the Catholics ; but he only gave way after many struggles. The Speech definitely recommended Parliament to consider whether their civil disabilities might be removed, under careful safeguards for Church and State. Peel resigned his seat for Oxford University, in duty bound, as he had been elected on Protestant grounds. The Catholic Association dissolved itself, forestalling the passage of a Bill to do away with it.

6th February. 1829. Berkeley Square.

I went last night into the Ventilator, & heard Mr Peel's commentary on the King's Speech. The comment is much more satis-

---

[1] Edmund Parker (1810–64), who succeeded as 2nd Earl of Morley in 1840.
[2] The 3rd Duke (Hugh Percy) was the new Lord-Lieutenant.

factory than the Speech itself, in which there is much put as to securities, etc., to please the violent anti-Catholics, than will be enforced when it comes to be enacted. What has effected this great change is not announced ; but probably the power of the Association & the Clare election have had their weight. In short, come from what hand it may, [it] is a great blessing to the country, & is by all well-wishers hailed as such most heartily. It is to be hoped the Irish will follow the advice of Brougham & others who gave it in their speeches last night, & many today by letters to Ireland, to close the Association, & not let the Bill for putting it down operate at all.

It is a delightful concession, & so surprizing that one feels in a dream. Peel is the only *honest* one. The great Duke is what one always thought, devoid of principle, gratitude, generosity ; but he is the only man who could now carry the measure, & as such will be supported in it by all who are really attached to the welfare of the Country. The King has been circumvented, as he ought to be when great benefits are necessary for the country.

I do hope we shall not have any Protestant tumults. Fortunately there is no Lord George Gordon to head them ; but one must see that every effort will be made to rouse the bigoted, not dormant spirit of the Protestant devotees. Already there are placards about the streets, & endeavours to obtain, as they will do, petitions from all quarters against it. But the D. of W., being in earnest, will be brisk & not let the grass grow under his feet.

Remember your Papa was the *first* man who moved C. Emancipation in the House of Lords, when he was very young.[1] It is a proud thing for him. It is comical to see the change of language in the most violent. To have Ld Bathurst [2] speaking in favor of the measure : Ld Ashley ! too, who by the bye spoke so low that I did not hear a word of his speech. In short, it is quite a comedy ; but, as it is all for the good cause, nothing should be said to mortify them or stop them in their career of coat turning. Neither Lds Grey nor Lauderdale are come up. Ld Anglesey with great forbearance & generosity, forbore making his statement, not to mingle private concerns with the great measure : but what he did say was admirable. To *him*, we shall owe the measure very much by his reports of the state of Ireland ; & the quiet of it is chiefly owing to his good government,

---

[1] In 1800. *See* his *Whig Party*, i, 153.

[2] Lady Holland wrote on February 10 : " Your friend Lord Bathurst, the champion formerly of every opinion that was narrow, is now liberal. He was very manly in his turn and disdained every petty palliation, but firmly acknowledged a downright change of opinion."

by which he gained the confidence of the political & Catholic Church leaders. He is a fine, gallant, high-minded, disinterested man, with very *great* talents & sound understanding.

It is stated *distinctly*, that the measure is adopted without any compact or arrangement with any foreign powers, purely *domestic* ; so his Holiness has nothing to do with our internal arrangements. The Catholics will be admitted into Parliament & enjoy every civil right in common with their fellow subjects. Only exception is, I believe, the office of Ld Chancellor. One is so absorbed in this wonderful event, that there is not time to think even of other things. . . .

14th February [1829].

. . . This great question goes on briskly. The petition against Catholics was defeated at Cambridge by a majority in the Senate. It did not even come to the Juniors, who were numerous & would have had a much greater proportion against it. Oxford, the scoffers say, was not enough aware of the determination of Govt to carry it through, so pledged themselves too soon against, & accepted Mr Peel's resignation. The King is not suspected of any foul play or under hand intrigue to counteract his Ministers. Indeed, he could not form any Ministry, were he so disposed. The chief opposition to the measure lies among the Bishops & a few Lords ; but the Bishops are only dissentient, & will probably not act with any violence. Some of the Lords are really de bonne foi, such as Lord Winchelsea,[1] who is not a very able man, but who is honest, frank & truly zealous in what he thinks the duty of a true Protestant. I like him personally for his warmth & sincerity. Ld Eldon[2] is an old politician of the Machiavel school, acute & able, but always good humoured. He ascribes the whole of this business to Papa, whom he said last year, with Will. Smith, *trafficked* with the D. of W. upon the Test Act ; for the carrying of the Test Act was in truth breaking the barrier of the Coronation oath. It is not true that your Papa did so ; but it virtually was done by the passing the Act last sessions, which he was so active in doing. It is impossible to imagine any conduct more disinterested & honorable than that of the old Opposition & Ld Anglesey—such generous, strong support of the Govt, devoid of all petty feelings which vulgar minds might feel at seeing their own

[1] George William, 10th Earl (1791–1858). Charles Greville wrote (I, 55): " Lord Winchelsea made a ass of himself, and would like to be sent to the Tower ; but no one will mind anything such a blockhead says."

[2] The Lord Chancellor.

measure adopted & brought to bear, & the palm of glory taken by others.

Ld Anglesey suspends his own case from an apprehension of doing mischief to the question ; & Papa suspends what is almost as near his heart as the C. Question, the Foreign policy. He is afraid any attacks against the Ministers might have a bad effect ; as the old Tories would vote perhaps with him & shew a force against Ministers which might have a bad effect upon the King's mind, supposing *he* was not as steady for this measure. But people never quite feel trust & security about Royal persons. I should say at this moment few stand higher than Papa & Ld Anglesey in their respective stations. Indeed, there never was a person who more deserved universal esteem than dear Papa, God bless him.

George [1] spoke well the other night. He has gained in self posses-sion & manliness prodigiously by his journey last summer to Ireland, where he had rather an embarrassing card to play, but he extricated himself admirably & with credit to his judgment. Poor Emily, Mss of Londonderry [2] died suddenly yesterday morning. I did not know her much ; but she was always good natured, & filled a space in a salon brilliantly. I really am sorry, & so are the Town I hear. Ld Lothian will get some thousands a year ; but whether the jewels, furs, etc. will be given to him or Lord Londonderry is not known yet. Ld Grey came yesterday. He brought his son George, a handsome lad, shy & modest, who was distinguished at Navarino. Ly Grey follows soon from Howick. Lady Jersey, I have only seen twice, each time but for a moment. She bounced out as soon as Lady Lyndhurst came into the room ; another time Ld Anglesey put her to flight. She is not improved in temper & manners by politics. Her son Villiers is reckoned very amiable.

20th February.

I last night took your Aunt with me to the H. of Lords. We heard an excellent debate, of which she will, I dare say, report the particulars to you. Lds Plunket, Grey & Eldon spoke, & the Chan-cellor very well. I was quite surprized at hearing Ld Clanricarde acquit himself so well, with great feeling, modesty, judgment, & good, even graceful language. The D. of Cumberland made a very violent speech ; but my suspicion is that he was allowed by the Govt to

---

[1] Lord Morpeth. He spoke upon the Catholic Association.

[2] Emily Hobart, daughter of 2nd Earl of Buckinghamshire, and wife of the late Foreign Secretary. Lord Lothian (7th Marquis) was her nephew. His mother, her sister, died in 1805.

do so & go out in a blaze, & that he will be no longer troublesome. The question will be carried by a great majority ; & I think Mr Peel is also pretty sure of his election.[1] *Even Blanco* [White] has written to say that *he* will vote for him, altho' his opinions remain unchanged as to the danger of granting any further relief to Catholics. It is quite delightful to see the D. of Norfolk upon the verge of being in his proper station.

6th March.   Berkeley Square.

. . . Mr Peel last night opened the question of what the Bill is to be. He spoke four hours remarkably well, & was cordially cheered.[2] The freeholders' qualification is to be raised to £10 from 40s ; & the only exclusion is the office of Lord Chancellor. The debate is adjourned, & few of the powerful speakers spoke. Mr Brougham will tonight. He is obliged to go off, the day after, to his circuit, a provoking contretemps, as his talents would be invaluable when the details of the Bill come on. There are sceptics still, who believe *Windsor*, now the D. of Cumberland is in full activity, will still overset the Bill, but it seems difficult. One is pleased at the admirable, honest, generous conduct of all who have professed themselves advocates for the Emancipation. They unite so sincerely, making but one head & hand with Govt upon the subject. Every curiosity upon other subjects is forgotten, or rather suspended. It was said, & with some authority, & believed, that the King meant to make overtures for forming a neutral Governt that would agree to defer this question for a year. The effect was a more decided declaration on all sides of the necessity of *immediate* concessions to Catholics. Even Mr Huskisson, about whom there had been very great suspicion, I believe unfounded, that he might be moulded to any purpose by the King, declared himself very explicitly. So unless the King tries Ld Sidmouth, there is nowhere for him to look ; & *he* could not supply a Minister to lead the H. of Commons.

The D. of D. brought young Cavendish to see me. He is very well looking, like his poor father, only with more intelligence in his

[1] Peel was beaten by 146 votes. Greville suggests that the election was mismanaged. He found a new seat at Westbury. Lady Holland wrote on March 12 : "All almost of the respectable resident clergy at Oxford voted for Peel. Only the outlying, ignorant country parsons, who poured down in torrents, were against him. 'Peel for ever' ! say I. If he would be *just* & merciful to Portugal, & correct the Game Laws, he will be in my opinion as a good a Minister as I can imagine."

[2] Charles Greville remarked that Peel's speech was the best he ever made. Brooks's were "full of satisfaction" at "the liberality of the measure."

countenance, *modest*, but not awkwardly shy. He is to stay in London & see the world. They say his pursuits are chiefly scientific & classical, & his pleasures shooting. He seems perfectly good humoured, & has, I doubt not, much of the sterling family sense.

9th March, [1829].

. . . The Bill is not quite so promising as we had expected. The K. is adverse in his heart : & making a great stir among his courtiers & household, the division in the Commons was great. But the minority was larger than is liked, & some names such as Lowthers, Manners & others give alarm. In the Lords, it is also nervous. Lord Shaftesbury is behaving abominably, & would not let his second son, William, who had promised, vote the other night. The D. of Wellington unluckily is not well or able to go to the King. The King's living at such a distance is a very serious evil to Ministry.

Ld Normanby will not come over for the Bill ; they say faute de moyens. He has £1100 a year to live upon, which can hardly do with theatre, balls, etc., and long frequent journeys. Ld Francis seems perfectly happy with his now *three* sons. He describes his life as very happy, "not in my usual amusements, but in an amusement quite new to me, *reading* ; & I have found the greatest pleasure in it . . . I have just finished *Herodotus*, in which I delighted. In short, my head is quite full of Greek wars & Roman quarrels, & my heart so full of my three sons."

19th, 20th March, [Berkeley Square].

The Duke of Richmond [1] has this session taken a great part, tho' on the wrong side ; & I have foreseen that will make him one of the most able & active members of H. of Lords. He is very fond of us both ; & I have seen him a good deal. He brought his five boys to see us the other morning. Sydney Smith has exchanged his living at Foston for an excellent one in Somersetshire : so with his Canonry at Bristol he will be enabled to live more in the warmer & better parts of the Island. At Foston he had literally no society. The few neighbours were remote, & he was not upon very good terms with them. Mrs Hibbert's [2] marriage has turned out well : a good sort

---

[1] Charles, 5th Duke (1791-1860).

[2] Lady Holland wrote : " She is a most distinguished-looking person, but so dark. Mrs Hibbert, her mother, has inherited from her brother near £10,000 pr am. Full half of this will come to her son, who is the husband of Emily Smith." She married Nathaniel Hibbert, whose father George sold his books on succeeding to Munden Hall, Herts., as it was too small—the sale here mentioned.

of young man, comfortable fortune, a family who like her, & a child coming immediately ; all good & happy. Saba, who is very amiable indeed, has not as yet been so lucky. W. De Ros's marriage has turned out happily.[1] He is become gardener, carpenter, mechanic, boatman, fisherman : in short, always occupied, & consequently always happy. Five children & much love ; in short, it is a beau ideal realised of happiness. A great sale of books is going on, the greatest since the Roxburghe. They sell well, a Mazarin Bible & other rarities. Prints also, at an extravagent price. Mr Wellesley, the clergyman of Flitton, near Ampthill, is the greatest collector now, a son of Ld W.

30th, 31st March, [1829].

The House of Lords did not do any mischief to Papa, tho' he stood upon his legs near half an hour ; but we are very careful of all fatigue or pleasure, to nurse & save him for the important Bill, which is expected to be ready for the Lords either tomorrow or Wednesday. There is a report the Brunswickers mean on the first report to oppose it, but this is so unusual & fatuous that it can hardly be done with any propriety. The D. of Gordon regrets having resigned the Great Seal [of Scotland]. Some say the office will be abolished ; others that it will be given to Lord Home. In short, there is no thought or conversation but upon this momentous question ; & it is is gratifying to find that the conduct of our friends is so admirable & well considered by all.

As soon as the Bill is disposed of, there are to be private theatricals at Hatfield, which will be gay ; & the troupe is good, Lady F. Leveson, Mr Ellice, George, Phipps & various others. You would be a great addition, if your acting powers are still in vigor. Stratford Canning[2] has resigned ; & Mr Gordon goes to Constantinople immediately. Some think Mr S. Canning disliked going among the Turks again ; others that he wishes to try his powers in Parlt. He is a clever, but not well tempered man. Lord Lothian is quite a convert to the C.Q., & votes steadily upon it. He was much affected by Lady London-derry's death. The accession to his fortune puts him quite at ease. He is a bit of a favorite with me, you know, & so is his cousin Valletort.

The Bill passed the Commons last night, & will be in the Lords today. I have an intention of going to the second reading by my

---

[1] William, later 23rd Baron de Ros (1797–1874), married 4th Duke of Richmond's daughter, Lady Georgina Lennox, in 1824.

[2] The diplomatist, created Lord Stratford de Redcliffe in 1852 (1786–1880). He was a member of Parliament.

curtain. They talk of making galleries, etc., as in the Queen's trial, for the accommodation, not only for the immense number of Peers, but for H. of Commons, who accommodate the Lords & ought to have some reciprocity. The ladies force their way, & are very troublesome upon the Throne, much to the annoyance of H. of C. & Peers' eldest sons, who have a right to the Throne.

The ball for the relief of the Portuguese in Paris yielded 30,000 frcs, a large sum for French Society; the Orleans family behaved nobly. There was the usual dose of squabbles among the ladies with each other, as upon such occasions is usual; but in such places as London & Paris the men have better pursuits than to be involved in such rubbish, & the pulling caps ended in due time. Lady Conyngham is ill. Halford's attendance at Windsor is for her.

3d April.

I am tired to death, having been shut in my old baize curtain at the H. of Lds; but am going again tonight, it being an adjourned debate, & is really most interesting. Ld Lansdowne's was the speech of the night, quite admirable. The Bishop of Oxford made an excellent speech, full of ability & learning: quite worth your while to read, if such matters at all interest you. What does the Court of Rome say? Not pleased, I dare say, at there being no Concordat. It is much better for this country; for, as your father states it, this is only the *repeal* of two obnoxious laws. These once repealed leave the Catholics as they were ever since the Reformation, when they were admitted into Council & Command exactly upon a footing with any other English subjects.

10th April.

The Catholic Bill is as good as done. Today is the third reading; & the Royal Assent will be given on Monday. The D. of Wellington has conducted the matter in a true workmanlike style. He alone could have awed the King & subdued the Tories, at least the bulk of them. The world are very just, & ascribe the merit entirely to Fox & Grattan & those worthies who first agitated the matter. Those at the eleventh hour, & Canning even, have not the glory. The old Whigs have acted admirably, & are much respected for their high, disinterested & zealous conduct. How matters will go on, when this is done, is more than anyone can say; but I conclude the foreign policy will still be a bone of contention.

17th April, [1829]. Hd H.

We came to sleep two nights in London, in order to dine in town at the Gowers's & Agar Ellis's, & meant to have done much this morning ; but the weather has been so tormenting from rain that it was impossible to think of museum or pictures or anything, either to see, or drip in & out of carriage. Lord Wm Russell arrived, & breakfasted yesterday with us. He is in good plight. He has the offer of a regiment at Xante, but has not decided. It would be a sad banishment to live there for a few years : & not on a service that speaks much to the imagination, which a command at Malta or Corfu might do more in these bustling times in the East. But his heart is among his family & friends ; & if they could manage a decent income, he would live at Brighton, where so much is combined that they both like, society, good medical advice & climate. Wrio., whom I have not yet seen, is much approved, they say, in every respect, excellent in all essential qualities, & a most agreable companion & inmate. Our dinner at the Gowers's from the intense heat of the rooms was insufferable. It gave us all headaches ; tho' the party was well composed, Belgraves, Granvilles, Clanwilliam, etc., etc. Yesterday was a delightful day at Agar's. The rooms cool ; & somehow we were all in high spirits, the Granvilles, the Mount Charles's, Lyndhursts, Plunket, Lord Anglesey & several others quite pleasant. Ly Mt Charles is very pleasing ; when one knows her well, that scowl from short-sight becomes a sweet smile.[1] Lady Granville was uncommonly entertaining. In short, we all agreed we had never spent a more agreable day. We all staid till 12, very unusual at a London dinner. The Dsse de Baden[2] is coming over, with a lovely, rich young daughter. She dislikes the notion of her marrying a German Prince, & prefers England to all countries, & Englishmen accordingly : & she hopes to win the D. of Buccleuch. *He* is amused & half flattered. The only objection the Dsse sees is that the Duke has only three Dukedoms, so the fourth son must go into the Church. How little they know of our customs & laws. Papa is anxious the Dukedom of Monmouth should be restored to D. of Buccleuch. The D. of Richmond has no objection, tho' it loses *a pas* in precedence.

[1] Lady Jane Paget, Lord Anglesey's daughter, married, in 1824, Lord Francis Nathaniel Conyngham (1797–1876), who succeeded as 2nd Marquis in 1832. The latter's elder brother died unmarried in 1824.

[2] Vicomtesse Stephanie Tascher de la Pagerie, cousin of Empress Josephine. She married Charles Louis Frederic, Grand-Duke of Baden. Although her quest was doomed to failure on this occasion, she married her youngest daughter to the 11th Duke of Hamilton in 1843.

We are just returned to this gay old mansion, having slept two nights at Granny's. We expect Ld Plunket & his son to dine & sleep ; also Seymour & his friend Ld Acheson & some others.

I never touch much upon politics, but hear the Ministers dislike the D. of Cumberland continuing on in this country, as he ear wigs the K., & makes him sullen & barely civil. I do not see him in such a formidable light. À propos of the Dsse of Baden, they say Leopold is an aspirant ; but he has no chance with the young lady. All London are gone to Newmarket. Papa is dying to go there once, but he has always been stopped by gout. Indeed that gout crosses us with many schemes ; as I am afraid, ever since the chalk stone of last summer, of venturing far from home or advice.

[April] 21st. Hd H.

Next week the King comes for fêtes, etc. for Ly Maria Conyngham, who is tired of Windsor so long together ; & as he cannot do without that family, very malgré himself he is to pass a month in London. People are scandalized at Mrs Grattan [1] not being more, or rather at all, elated at the carrying of this great question. She ought, for the sake of her illustrious husband's memory, with whom it was so nearly interwoven with his whole existence ; but she is a bit of an evangelical. Her brother had in Italy a sort of patito in some family connected with the Littas, a narrow minded, silly man, as I have heard—an Irishman of course . . .

18th, 19th May.

. . . Yesterday the D. of Norfolk [2] gave a great dinner to the Duke of Wellington & Peel & all the leading supporters of the C. Bill, & to the Catholic peers. Papa would not miss on any account, tho' he was obliged to go on his crutches. He enjoyed, almost as much as the Duke himself, seeing him in possession of all his rights as an Englishman ; indeed the Duke's felicity is not to be described. Ld Surrey sits for Horsham, & has taken his seat ; you may guess with what delight to *her* family. They are excellent people, & deserve the good that befalls them.

I have not yet seen Seymour Bathurst,[3] but am told he is so altered !

[1] Mrs. Grattan's maiden name was Fitzgerald.

[2] Bernard Edward, 12th Duke (1765–1842). His son, Earl of Surrey, later 13th Duke, had married, in 1814, Lady Charlotte Leveson-Gower, Marquis of Stafford's daughter.

[3] Lieut.-Col. Hon. Thomas Seymour Bathurst, son of 3rd Earl. He held a post in Malta, but died suddenly in 1834.

become what the French call a bel homme, which means portly, clumsy, pink & white, & heavy ; but this is only from hearsay. Lady Byron is in great affliction.[1] Her only child, Ida ! (sic), the poet's name, has suddenly been deprived of the use of her limbs, & is at Brighton quite deprived of the power of motion. Brodie went down ; but, from what I heard from Ld Melbourne, fear he has not made a very favorable report. Mrs Lamb with her usual good nature & kindness of heart is gone to see her.

1st June, [1829].

You will hear all the news from your Aunt. She is going tonight to the Ventilator. The debate will be upon Sir J. Mackintosh's motion upon Terceira, which will bring in all the question of Portugal. Some persons are in hopes that there is a more favorable [feeling] towards that unfortunate nation, but of *this*, nothing I notice has transpired. Lord Beresford,[2] in full Portuguese Marshal's uniform, visited the young Queen at Laleham, on his knees kissed her hand, & asked if there was anything for her service he could execute, a complete offer of duty & obedience to her commands. The King gave a Ball of young ones, where she met the future Queen Victoria. It was very pretty. Poor little soul, she fell down just as she was leaving & cut her lip. Upon seeing her own blood she was nearly fainting away. Were she in Don Miguel's power, he would accustom her to such sights, & perhaps more of her own. At the grand military inspection of Cavalry before the French Princes, the D. of W. appeared as Colonel at the head of his regiment. By some strange untoward chance his horse became restive & threw him off. The Tories exulted, & said it was a good omen, as he fell at the feet of the D. of Cumber-land. I was sorry, as it was a vexatious mortification ; & that is not what he ought to have in what one may call his *own* department. That he should flounder & blunder in a speech, I should not mind. Some ascribe the accident to the great fur cap he wore, which was high, & the wind caught it. At the Ball the King said to Ld Anglesey, " Why Paget, how came you to be so clumsy as to fall before the foreigners ? Was it the want of your leg ? " " I did not fall, Sir, nor should I, even if I had to wear a high cap." " Bravo, that's the best thing I ever heard ; " & his Majesty called people about him to laugh at Ld A.'s reply. The D. of W. was not far off, & tho' too

---

[1] Hon. Ada Augusta Byron, afterwards Countess of Lovelace.
[2] William, Viscount Beresford (1768–1854) reorganised and commanded the Portuguese army in the Peninsular war. Master-General of Ordance, 1828–30.

deaf to hear, it was of course immediately repeated to him.[1] We rejoice much at Scarlett being made Attorney General. It is a public benefit to have a man of his character & abilities so forward. Ld Rosslyn is Privy Seal. Many other changes are making, for now the C.Q. is carried, there is a complete dissolution of all party ties.

Ly Ellenborough has completely shocked the public, & worn out the patience even of her Lord. Poor wretched woman, she is to be pitied, as she is young & has the prospect of a long life of wretchedness before her.[2] He is to separate, & has sold all her carriages & little ponies.

Henry Fox was in Paris in August 1829, and came on to England. Consequently there are few letters of interest at this period. He left again for the Continent at the end of January.

[*October* 20, 1829. Brighton.]

. . . Mr Tierney declared, had he not beheld with his own eyes a scene in Lady Downshire's drawing room, he could not have believed the report. He saw a cradle, at the foot of which a very smart femme de chambre was sitting. Ly D. told him she was placed *there* to amuse the dog, who was lying covered up like a Royal infant. One of the bulletins reported the animal " had passed a restless night." However it is mending, & the doctors have saved its eye ; so her journey which was delayed on its account for a week is to take effect today ! ! What a woman. The Tierneys dined yesterday, & we had Kenney [3] to meet them, as his style of conversation is sure of diverting T. It succeeded ; he told some stories of his own adventures with different actors & actresses with considerable point, & yet simplicity & truth. He was to write an Opera for Braham & Stenau that was called *False Alarms.* Braham suggested, by way of novelty, that there should be a drawing room scene, where he might sit to a piano & accompany himself, for which Kenney should write suitable words. He did, once, twice, three times, the last ungraciously accepted, saying, " Send 2 or 3 more, & then I will decide." " No," said the author, " the third must be the last." The play was acted, & the song " a fatto fanatismo," " The Smile & the Tear." Braham then published, & got £500 for it, & called

[1] Lady Holland wrote next day : " Lord Anglesey came yesterday. He says all is true of the King's speech to him, but *not* his reply."

[2] Lady Holland elsewhere remarks that she was said to have been corrupted by Princesse Esterhazy.

[3] James Kenney (1780–1849), dramatist. John Braham (1776?–1856) was a celebrated tenor.

it Mr Braham's celebrated song, etc., without any acknowledgment
to poor Kenney, even of thanks or good will.

[*December 3rd*, 1829. Brighton.]

We have a sad corvée today. The Dss of St Albans dines here.
Nothing but Mrs B.[1] could have done this, not to please her, but to
counteract her mischief; as I have good reason to believe she amused
herself with telling the Dss, as I did not go to her breakfasts, that I
had resolved never to shew or accept civilities from her; & this is
by no means the case. I should be sorry on account of Lord Dudley
Stuart that she should believe this. Mary, who likes to write *long*
stories, will tell you how Mrs B. was put to the blush, if that were
possible, at a public disclosure of one of her calumnies, & properly
rebuked by Lady Aldboro' for it. D. of D. wanted me to dine
today, but his house is too distant for timid persons after sunset.
There is no back road to it; & I always fear the Cliff. . . .

<hr/>

[1] ? Baring.

CHAPTER VII

1830–1831

George Tierney had died early in 1830, creating a vacancy at Knaresborough, a seat in the gift of the Duke of Devonshire. The latter had been persuaded by Lord Holland to offer it to Brougham, who had been obliged to withdraw from Winchelsea.

Saturday, [*January* 30, 1830].

. . . D. of Devon. has most kindly offered his, alas, now vacant seat at Knaresboro' to Mr Brougham, who has been it is supposed very much hampered by the change of Ld Cleveland's politics. I do not know whether he accepts or not ; but if he does, it will make a great change in the state of the H. of Commons, as Mr Peel single handed cannot stand up against B. There is a report that the new Lord of the Treasury will be John Wortley, but this is only rumour ; yet there are certain little circumstances which make it probable. There has been a very serious rumpus among Ministers & King, which was made up by Lady C., the first time she has openly appeared in a political strife. People do not guess why she appears as a peace-maker, because she never seemed to like the D. of W. ; & her son has by his resignation shewn that *he* dislikes him. Some say she is jealous even of Mt Charles's favor with the King. Poor Vesey Fitzgerald is worse. Ld Ellenboro's correspondence with Sir John Malcolm, which has been published, not par parenthèse very handsomely to him, diverts people much, & will do Ld E. some harm in the world & with the King, whom he treats very flippantly in his language about knighthood, etc. ; & the stanch ones will be offended at the "Nice Bishop." [1] We hear that Schwarzenberg, who is at Paris with Ly E., has promised to marry her. This is not believed here.[2] Ld Sefton came last night; & described having gone with all

---

[1] Lord Ellenborough was a member of the Board of Control. His letter, written a year earlier, took Malcolm's part in a dispute between him as Governor of Bombay and the Judges of the Supreme Court.

[2] Lady Holland wrote on March 17 : " Ld Ellenboro's Bill has gone through the Lords, *much* helped by Papa's good nature & assistance, but an opposition is threatened in the Commons. It will be hard upon her ; as I know her whiskered lover is very honorable & right, & ready to make her every reparation in his power."

his family in one of the new steam machines on the rail road, which is to annihilate the canals, at the rate of 28 miles per hour. He only went 5 miles, but said the velocity was marvellous & not disagreable. This looks but ill for Ld Francis's [Leveson-Gower] prospects. Addio.

5th February, 1830.

Mr Brougham has accepted the handsome offer of D. of D. Ministers have offered, & it is I believe accepted, the office of Chief Baron of Scotland to Mr Abercromby. It is a place quite professional, for life, & worth £6,000 pr am. He could not for a moment hesitate ; but the reason of its being offered is very evident. They wish an unpopular man to be Speaker, Mr Goulburn, & were afraid of the *concurrence* ; as Abercromby is so universally liked & respected that he, who has always been looking to the Chair, would probably have beat him by a considerable majority.[1] Abercromby has sacrificed more than any man to strict adherence to his political opinions & friends ; & one is glad to see him late in life no longer pinched in his circumstances, which he has been most narrowly these last few years. Ld Lansdowne has the Borough of Calne open, which is never an agreable thing ; altho' the place is very secure.[2]

26th February, 1830.

I am extremely languid & peaking today, from having sat 7 hours & three quarters behind the red curtains in a very small space during the debate in H. of Lords. Imagine all the time hearing nothing but long-winded speeches upon currency, corn, silver standard, consumption, circulation & such topics ; only enlivened by a most shrewd, hard, biting, sarcastic speech from Ld Radnor, full of point & many painful truths, upon the state of the labourers, farmers, landlords, their relative situations & the sort of animosity sprung up among them against each other. I took Lady Stanhope with me. She heard as good a speech from her husband as the dull nature of the subject

---

[1] The sitting Speaker, Charles Manners-Sutton, was re-elected, Goulburn retaining the post of Chancellor of the Exchequer. Abercromby's post was abolished two years later ; upon which he returned to Parliamentary work and defeated Manners-Sutton for the Speakership in 1835. On his retirement, in 1839, as Viscount Dunfermline, Henry Goulburn was proposed as his successor, but was beaten by Shaw-Lefevre.

[2] Lady Holland wrote four days later : " Lord Lansdowne brings in young Macaulay for Calne. It is an experiment, as he is only known as a clever writer in E. Review. I never saw him, & hear he is not pleasant nor good to look at. His father is the great Saint, Zachariah, & the bitterest foe to all W. India concerns."

will admit. I met Henry Greville at the Chancellor's at dinner last Sunday, & was sorry to see him looking so emaciated, pale & worn. He thinks the Irish climate destructive to his health, as he never feels a moment of ease from rheumatism when there. . . . The party was very gay & agreable ; Ly Lyndhurst in splendid beauty & spirits. The house brilliant, & the best in London after the great hotels. I could not stay as late as I should have liked, to have gone through the party, but had people of my own waiting for me here.[1]

12th March.

. . . Lady Byron is getting into a silly controversy with Moore upon some passages in his book. She will be the loser ; as many suppressed passages will now be disclosed, & she will not like it. Your Papa is doing his utmost to quell her restlessness, but in vain. I am afraid she is a cold, obstinate woman ; but do not mention this opinion.

9th April, [1830].

Mary will herself apprise you of her own feelings & concerns. All I shall say is that yesterday she accepted Ld Lilford,[2] & her counte-nance today betrays her felicity. He has never swerved from the most devoted love for her : & certainly he has not been to her an object of indifference. The seeing her so happy, makes us so ; tho' we are not yet sufficiently acquainted with him or his family to appreciate all the good qualities people give him. What is well known is that he was an admirable son, & to a numerous set of brothers & sisters has acted like a parent. He is beloved & popular near his own residence. We are pleased at seeing her so, & feel no responsibility ; as the whole decision & choice has been her own doing. She says the only alloy is not having your sanction, nor can she think it ratified without your dear presence. I dread the loneliness of this great house, when we are left by all. When I was younger, my spirits were better, & I always had a nursery which I used in my mind's eye to build castles in the air of how when they grew up they might become. Strange visionary ideas ! We shall now be alone at the

----

[1] It was of that dinner party that Creevey wrote (I. 375) : " The first time I met her (Lady Holland) in company since our separation (for we have never quarrelled). She is mighty anxious to get me back, for no other reason but because I won't go."

[2] Thomas Atherton Powys, 3rd Lord Lilford (1801–61). The marriage took place by special licence in the library at Holland House on May 24.

period of life when every tender tie ought to be tightened. Alas !
Alas ! I can grow quite dismal in pitying myself.

Before the next letter which we print was written, George IV had
passed away. He died on June 26, so the reference which follows
denotes the Duke of Clarence, who had become William IV.

23d July, [1830].

. . . The King is making himself extremely popular. His manners
are unaffected, & he has a real desire of pleasing & making people
happy ; which when the source is from goodness of heart always
succeeds. He goes today in person to prorogue Parlt ; & all the ladies
to shew their zeal will fill the House, which will make it insufferably
hot. Persons are surprized at Mrs Hope being a *Woman* of the Bedchamber. The services are not dignified ; & at Court she cannot
be admitted into the Circle, or be spoken to as her own station entitles
her to otherwise. She gains the fan & gloves. There are many
jokes about the Maids of Honor. The Duke of Buckingham & Lord
Howe are contending which is to have control over them. The
other day the Queen was rather suddenly to appear in ceremony.
Her Ladies were summoned. The answer was that only three Maids
of Honor could be found, the other three having slept out. This
sounded oddly, & made a joke.

Great changes took place in France shortly after the last letter was
written. A revolution in Paris led to the proclamation of Louis
Phillippe, Duc D'Orléans, as Lieutenant of the Kingdom at the end
of the month, with the offer of the Crown a week later. King
Charles X left France, and came over to England in August. Wellington's Government were not long in recognizing the new King ; and
on September 25 Prince Talleyrand arrived in London as Ambassador,
much to some people's surprise, as he had reached the age of 76.
His niece by marriage, the Duchesse de Dino, came to keep house
for him. The British Ministry itself was on its last legs, and after
riding for a fall was defeated in the Commons. The King then sent
for Lord Grey on November 16. Had Lord Holland been in a reasonable state of health, it seems improbable that Grey would have looked
further for his Foreign Secretary. But he had been seriously ill
recently ; and we find his wife advising a less exacting post than the
Foreign Office, though as a matter of fact there is no real evidence
to show that any offer was made. Henry Fox, driven from Italy
by illness and grief at the death of his friend Lady Compton, was again
on his way home, and actually reached England on the very day on
which his father kissed hands for the Duchy of Lancaster, on
November 25.

Tuesday. (*November* 2, 1830. Hd. H.)

We have John [Russell] staying for a few days, but his Parliamentary duties will soon take him off. But en attendant, he is a comfort, in which I trust he may speedily have a successor in you, my dear Boy. Your Papa made a point of my going, tho' he could not, to a splendid dinner at D. House, given to Talleyrand & Dsse de Dino. John was my Cavalier, & Allen remained with Papa. It was very handsome, & had the desired effect of pleasing those who were the object of it. Nevertheless the want of intelligence from Paris, both as to the Govt & the instructions how he is to proceed in these Conferences, are embarrassing to Talleyrand. The negotiations with Ld Palmerston & his friends were going on still as late as the day before yesterday, I was told ; but there has been another complete refusal. Some say the Govt cannot go on, unless there are fresh accessions ; but of this I know nothing.

[*November* 19 ? 1830.]

Your father is in very tolerable health ; but till the sore heals, I cannot feel easy, tho' I am assured there is no cause whatever for alarm. This has influenced my feeling in urging him not to accept the Seals of the Foreign Office. He will, therefore, only have a very quiet office, where he will not be called upon for much exertion. We have moved to London.

As the outcome of the change of government in France, Belgium rose in revolt against the domination of Holland, to which it had been united for military reasons by the Powers in 1814. To avoid Prussian aggression, Louis Philippe announced that if that country took a hand, he should support the Belgians with an army. The question was then referred to a Conference sitting in London ; for Wellington realised that the situation was dangerous, and agreed to the separation of the two countries, if France would take no separate action. The Whigs came in ; and Palmerston replaced Wellington as Foreign Secretary. After the Duc de Nemours, Louis Philippe's son, had refused the Belgian crown, England and France proposed Prince Leopold, who was proclaimed King in July 1831. Holland, aggrieved, attacked Belgium, which suffered initial defeats, until the arrival of French troops.

As the Whigs were now firmly in office, Henry Fox had no difficulty in obtaining a diplomatic post where he could train for his new career. And so August 1831 found him an Attaché at Brussels, under that old friend of the family, Sir Robert Adair, who had been sent there on a special mission.

Reform had been initiated by a Bill, which only passed in the Commons by one vote. A dissolution soon followed in the summer of 1831 ; and a very similar Bill was introduced by Lord John Russell on June 24.

Tuesday, 16th August, [1831].

Your letters are highly satisfactory, &, even to those who see the dispatches, are interesting as they contain many details of value. You do not mention what makes a stir here, the rudeness of the D. of Saxe Weimar & his phrase of " honte de mon beau-frère." [1] Your reports please Papa much for their clearness & observation. Perhaps your hurry of writing renders your hand sometimes difficult to decypher, but I can always contrive to read even the most twisted word.

Lady Jersey & some Tories dined here on Sunday. They are elated & disposed to be saucy upon the Belgian discomfiture & the successes of the Dutch. They pant for war, & hope the French may drive all Europe to confusion. A violent diatribe against the French, Poles, & all Liberals or insurgents, which she treats as synonymous. The unpardonable behaviour of the Irish members a few nights ago, contributes to their spirits. Indeed the Irish, if they purpose the same line of conduct, will injure the Govt essentially ; but we must hope for their becoming more reasonable & trusting a little to their *only* friends. But they are impatient, & do not consider sufficiently how much the Govt are delayed in all matters & harassed by the Reform Bill, which is in *slow* progress. Lady Jersey had heard that Ly Harriet D'Orsay had quitted her worthless companion & joined her aunt, the wife of an Irish Bishop. I wish she may be able to annul her imperfect marriage & recover the enjoyment of her own property. Ly J. says Ld Burghursh [2] refused to allow the marriage they celebrated in his house in Florence, in consequence of a private message from Lady Harriet declaring her reluctance to the union. All this may or may not be true.

I am sorry the *burnings* are begun again in different parts of England. In Bedfordshire ricks have been burnt at Flitton. How lucky for Leopold to have Wm [Russell]. His head & knowledge are invaluable

[1] Bernard, Duke of Saxe-Weimar, married Queen Adelaide's sister. Lady Holland had written a few days before, " Windsor is overrun with Germans. The Dsse de Saxe Weimar, the King complains of, as being quite mad upon this Dutch business, abusing him, his Govt & country."

[2] John Fane (1784–1859), son of 10th Earl of Westmorland by his 1st wife, Lady Jersey's brother. He succeeded as 11th Earl in 1841. D'Orsay's marriage was celebrated in Naples. Henry Fox had been asked to attend as a witness, but declined to be present.

upon this occasion. Tell him Ly J. is not pleased at his being there.[1]
We have Sir Thos Neve's house again from Sept. 1st.[2] Lady
Stafford most gallantly set off alone per steam to Dunrobin on
Saturday.

Hd H. 23d [August], [1831].

. . . Your Papa, John [Russell] & Ld Lansdowne returned from
the magnificent dinner at Windsor at ½ past two to join me at Richmond. Poor John looks like death, & has not rallied as much as
I had expected. He will be at it again today. The Lords look very
grim, & their scheme is to defeat the Bill by pressing an adjournment.
Nobody seems prepared to say how it may be met. D. of Bedford
is enjoying himself in quiet at Woburn, & wants us to go there, if
but for a day. If I am able, it is not impossible ; but Lord Grey
likes to have Ld Hd near him, & did stop once our going on that
account.

Friday, 26th August.

. . . I dined at Ld Grey's at East Sheen, an excellent house built
by T. Hope & now belonging to Ld Aylesbury. The garden is flat
& pretty, but dull & dismal, with a dirty large piece of water for
ducks too near the house for health. He means to pass his Xmas
there. We had the Lyndhursts. She was in excellent humour &
looked herself again in beauty. He is always pleasant & sensible.[3]
Your Papa was very comical in his remarks upon Ld Londonderry
yesterday in H. of Lords.[4] It was a mere nothing, but produced a
great effect, & made Ld L. so angry that the D. of W. pulled him by
the skirt when he jumped up to reply to Papa. What provoked him
was the peals of laughter at Papa supposing him pleased. Don
Pedro[5] is to return for the Coronation at his *own* request, & will
be lodged & conducted about in Royal carriages, etc., all free of expense. This is very right. He is a trump card, & should not have
been allowed to go off in a huff about nothings. Henry Webster is
again appointed to attend him.

[1] He was attached to Sir R. Adair's mission to the Low Countries.
[2] 30 Old Burlington Street.
[3] Charles Greville suggests (II, 86) that Grey's partiality for Lyndhurst in
1830 was due to a penchant for Lady Lyndhurst. As the Chancellorship was
destined for Brougham, Lyndhurst was made Chief Baron.
[4] Lord Londonderry asked Lord Grey whether the French troops had been
withdrawn from Belgium.
[5] The Emperor of Brazil, father of Doña Maria.

Everybody seems dead sick of the Bill ; but already they begin to see a little daylight, & hope another 10 days may bring them through with successful termination.

Tuesday. Hd H. [*August 30th*, 1831.]

. . . Your Papa had destined this day to writing you a letter, but he was off early to be in the Cabinet at *eleven* ; & there is business in Lords. They are anxious & busy. The Coronation & Peers are coming on, & I am not sure the French news is quite satisfactory. There seems a reluctance about the armistice ; but of this I only speak imperfectly, as I cannot see Papa a minute alone. He did not reply to Ld Londonderry yesterday, as the Ministerial notion is not to discuss pending affairs ; but he was displeased at his treachery in coming over the House & asking privately some question, which fortunately Papa answered very guardedly. You have no notion of the low, mean tricks the Opposition resort to in both Houses. The fires are beginning again. An incendiary in Bedfordshire the night before last destroyed many ricks. This is the *second* within a fortnight in that county.

The H. of Lords affect to be confident that the Country does not care at all about the Reform Bill now. If they attempt throwing out the Bill, they will see a frightful stir in Manchester, Bristol & Birmingham, & other unions in Middlesex, which are not pleasant to quiet people.

2d September. Hd H.

I am afraid you will be again disappointed, as Papa is obliged to go over to Sheen to see Ld Grey, who tho' *better* is still confined there by lumbago or sciatica, a *courbature*. However, he is decidedly better ; and the Tories need not cry out with any savage yell of triumph, as they *have* done about John. Ld Althorp is also better, & hopes to get on in the H. of Commons more rapidly ; indeed there are well founded expectations of the Bill being through next week. The King comes to town today or tomorrow to stay over the Coronation. I rather hope he may visit Sheen. It would have a very good effect ; but do not say this, as perhaps he may be too busy to stir. The question of Peerages must soon be settled. I hope our Ministerial friends will not be squeamish as to numbers. They ought not ; for those who cry out against numbers will only laugh, if they do not make enough to compass the job. Ld Wellesley says Queen Anne made 12 at a step. Had it been necessary she would have made 24, & 12 to that ; & she was but a woman. The numbers of the H. of Lords was then comparatively small, so such a batch was prodigious ; & there had been no Mr Pitt to familiarize the public to such an act of the Prerogative. If the Ministers halt, their Govt is up. I do not know who are to be the Peers. The only one, I believe, is certain is Mr Maule.[1]

I have been quite ill & hors de combat ; & we have been *literally* alone, so that I cannot give you any insight into the beau monde.

September 6.   Hd H. [1831].

. . . The Tories talk very big & are certainly in prodigious force, physical & moral. They have brought up many to take their seats who were considered dormant & done for, Ld Scarsdale & some of that trempe. It will be very unfortunate should the Bill be checked, such as moving for adjournment or any such obstacle. The people are getting impatient, & are organized in case of the Peers being refractory, which is anything but pleasant for quiet people.

The Coronation took place on September 8th. Lord John Russell was Paymaster of the Forces, and had an official residence in Whitehall.

September 9th.   Burlington St.

I spent the best part of the day at the Pay Office to see the procession pass, & then dined at Ld Essex's. The gorgeous sight was very gratifying. The King was most cordially greeted by his affectionate, attached people, looked well & happy. The D. of Sussex was cheered, & the Chancellor. Where we were, the D. of Cumberland escaped hissing, but at the Athenaeum and in Pall Mall he had a dose. I was sorry my *dérangement* prevented me from enjoying the comfortable seats kindly allotted to me by the D. of Norfolk, as the show in the Abbey was beautiful. The Peeresses looked beautiful, the first & foremost Dss of Richmond & Ly Gower. Afterwards the King underwent a dinner of 120 covers, but not at all the worse.

The ensuing fortnight will be one of considerable anxiety. The Tory Peers talk big ; & the Ministry stand or fall by the Bill. If they defeat it in the H. of Lds, the country will be dissatisfied ; & God knows what mischiefs may arise. I suppose with King, Country & H. of C. on side of Ministers, they are pretty safe ; as one would hardly think, with public opinion all over Europe upon such institutions, that they would hazard a collision with the two other powers of the State. But there is no knowing how far passion & intemperate party feeling may carry men. I shall be unfeignedly sorry, & feel

---

[1] William Ramsay Maule (1771–1852), created Baron Panmure.

that the King is entitled to everything from his Ministers, whom he likes & is so honourably disposed to sustain. Papa is at the Cabinet, & then goes to see the King after his yesterday's fatigues.

Tuesday. Hd H. 13 *September,* 1831.

A most melancholy catastrophe occurred last night. Poor Johnny Calcraft cut his throat.[1] He had long been in a very despondent state of mind, brought on by over-excitement. I am very sorry indeed. He was a quick, clever, agreable man, one of the sharpest & readiest in debate in the House of Commons, & would have been of great use to his friends. The opening the county of Dorsetshire is full of anxiety, as it is one of the least favourable to Reform in England ; & if old Banks should stand, he would have a great chance against any other candidate. The getting in an anti-reformer just now would have a bad effect on the House of Lords. People talk of Mr Sturt, Wm Ponsonby ; but as yet nothing is settled. Perhaps in the Cabinet today, they may manage for a good one ; but I tremble for the expense. Already the General Election swept from us some hundreds ; so that with subscriptions, *dresses*, robes, etc. the income of the Duchy has nearly been absorbed. I cannot give you any tolerable surmise as to the probable issue of the great struggle coming on among the Peers. You know I never see things on the bright side.

Yesterday Papa dined at St James's, a dinner of 100, foreigners, ex-diplomats & persons of all colors. The King made a speech in French for Talleyrand, which had some jokes perhaps not in the purest taste,[2] but he was full of good humour & universal kindness, & seemed well & happy. Some of the Princesses are gone ; when the others go it will be better. The Dss of Cambridge went off in a huff, at the steam boat being given to the Landgravine in preference to her. She is reckoned very hostile to the King personally & all his present Ministers. The ladies did not behave prettily or at all like grandes dames to the Dss of St Albans. They really *shouldered* her on their bench. How can women behave so to one another ! The Queen's maintien, grace & dignity was prodigiously admired. Her dress too was exquisite ; but your Aunt who was an eye witness can tell you all this better than from second hand.

[1] John Calcraft, the younger (1765–1831), M.P. He voted for Reform, although he had taken office under Wellington in 1828. Huskisson's death at the opening of the Liverpool Railway may quite possibly have had an adverse effect on his mind.

[2] " Talleyrand, when asked by Lord Sefton, ' Eh bien, que pensez-vous de celà,' replied, ' C'est bien remarquable.' "

The Greys left us yesterday. He is worn & harassed by the multiplicity of business and the want of sleep. He never gets a refreshing night's rest. We sleep in town tonight for a debate on Game Bill,[1] but shall return, & then proceed for a few nights to Ld Lansdowne's delicious villa at Richmond. It is nearly, if not more than 18 months, since I have had any change of air, except a fortnight in winter at Brighton & a night or two at Richmond & St Ann's, & this does not suit my health or former habits.

I daresay Ly William will have written the incident which occurred at St James's, of Lady Jersey turning out the Dss of Gloster, to force herself by the King at the Concert last night.

16 *September*, 1831. Hd House. *Friday.*

. . . Poor Leopold,[2] he must be perplexed ; but even annoyance is better than the tedium of the life he led here, so that he is a gainer by the exchange. For here, except in the tracasseries of his sister's little Court, he had nothing to do ; & his loss is felt *there*, for he was friendly & judicious in his advice & kept down all mischievous meddlers, who seem to be getting a head now & may do her personally harm in public opinion.

A most incomparable debate or rather conversation in the House of Lords on Wednesday.[3] Ld Londonderry, who is invaluable to the Ministers, enabled Ld Grey & Chancellor to make known their opinions upon our relations with France, which Ld Grey did with great effect & will produce considerable advantage ; & the Chancellor, they say, was admirable, so full of wit & sarcasm & excellent reasoning, not a word too much nor any sort of longeur or indiscretion. If Ld L. had been hired to help the Ministers, he could not have done them better service. The Tory Lords are still very clamorous, reckoning to defeat the Bill by hook or by crook. Nous verrons.

The rebel Poles had been defeated by the Russians at Praga in February, and finally submitted to them in September after the fall of Warsaw.

Tuesday, 20th September. Hd H.

. . . We spent two nights at Richmond,[4] where the Lievens unluckily were not. Perhaps she might have given us pain by her

---

[1] A Bill moved by the Duke of Richmond on September 19, to alter the Game laws.

[2] Prince Leopold had refused the Crown of Greece in 1830 before accepting that of Belgium. The Duchess of Kent was his sister.

[3] On the subject of Portugal.   [4] Lord Lansdowne's villa.

exaltation about the Poles ; so it was well not to see her just now.
The Lyndhursts came to us. She has quite recovered her looks, &
seemed very merry. She said she was going to give a dinner to the
Malignants, the Barings, Lds Aberdeen & Dudley. I hope Ld L. is
not so very hostile ; but his position in H. of Lords is portentous.
Ld Northampton came up for the Game Bill, about which he is more
eager than for other questions ; but he is very zealous in favour of
the Govt.

Friday. Old Burlington Street. 23 *September*, [1831].

. . . Talleyrand was very low on Wednesday. He dined with us,
as did Ld Grey & the Lyndhursts. He had evil forebodings about
Paris, tho' confidence in the civil courage displayed by C. Périer [1]
to the mobs ; even Sebastiani seems to have done his part well.
However, yesterday's accounts describe them as being afloat again,
& likely to weather this burst.

Is it not strange that the D. of W. has boarded with very thick
planks *all* his windows upstairs to Piccadilly & the Park ? The North
back front is not closed. The work of *darkness* began on the day
of the Coronation, & is now completed. He says, I hear, that it is
to protect his plate glass windows against the mob, who will assail
him on the Reform Bill ! As it cannot really be for thrift, it looks
like defiance ; & the mob will be irritated when they discover his
intentions. Monday se'ennight is the panicking day ; and I protest it
is not in my power to form a conjecture on the subject. Much will
depend upon Ld Lyndhurst, who is now the great card ; but I am
not without hopes of him. He is displeased at the Tories for having
deserted him on the Chancery Reform Bill, to which par parenthèse
they had pledged him to oppose when he was on the circuit, & without
any authority from him. He therefore says he is *not* a party man, &
is *absolved* by this proceeding ; but you know well that he is slippery.
They dine again with us on Sunday ; but there is a long week of
interval for him to be worked upon by others.

I am going to dine with Talleyrand alone, I am afraid ; as Allen
is at Dulwich, & Papa will be in Lords ; & I am very unequal to anything of the sort. But we have no establishment in town, & live
upon our friends. [2]

B. St. *Monday,* 26 *September.*

I understand that Lady Jersey gives out that she has *captivated* the
King ; but his language is certainly not very flattering to her in *any*

---

[1] Casimir Pierre Périer (1777–1832).   [2] Lord Holland also dined.

way.   The Greys are in great affliction at the loss of Lambton's lovely
boy.[1]   He had, as you know, long been lingering under the pressure
of an organic disease, which terminated fatally last week at Brighton.

2d Oct., 1831.

. . . The Town is full of anxiety as to the result of this great
question, which is to try its fate in H. of Lords today.   Ld Grey's
absence from *all* affairs for 8 days has been unlucky.   The results of
the lists vary so much that it is impossible to form any just estimate ;
& really many votes will depend upon the turn the debate may take,
as I really believe there are some who may be actuated by conscience,
tho' only a few, for the doubtful Sydney classes under the head of
the " *honest faibles.*"

4th October.   B. St.

I have already written today.   Ld Carlisle told me had a division
come on, the Opposition last night, by those in the House & proxies,
would have beat the Bill by 4.   Imagine !   That such a man as Ld
Harrowby should influence the destinies of Europe.[2]   For war, war
must ensue, with an ultra Ministry, and with such hostile feelings as
are entertained by most of the late Govt against the order of things
in France.   It will be bad for Leopold's stability.

[*October 7th.*]

My dear Child,

This tedious Bill is still working its boisterous course ; & some say
it may train on to Monday next.   The fatigues & heat quite overcome
Papa.   I never saw him so thoroughly knocked up when he comes
home.   The temperature is described as dreadful.[3]   We have had some
defections ; yet still there are those who think it may do.   That is
to say, there is a favorable majority of *living* bodies ; the proxies are
17 against perhaps nine.   This occasion ought to make Ld Wharncliffe bring forward his favorite scheme of a motion for depriving the
Lords of that privilege, which he had determined upon doing ; but
the abuse of such an advantage will at present be of service.

[1] " Master Lambton," whose name is well known from Lawrence's celebrated
picture.
[2] Lady Holland had written on September 30 : " Ld Harrowby declared
himself against the 2nd reading, which has produced a great sensation.   He is
quite an Apostle, writing circular letters in all directions, & is very busy among
the Bishops . . .   His decision has certainly produced a most mischievous
effect in Lords."
[3] " The oven," Lady Holland called the House of Lords a day or two earlier.

5 o'clock.

The division will take place certainly tonight; & the majority against very great. What will ensue remains to be seen. If King & Country continue as they have been, the Ministry may remain : else bon voyage to all your friends.

The division took place at 6 a.m. on October 8, a majority of 41 against the Bill. Although the King refused a large creation of peers, Grey undertook to remain in office on condition that he was allowed to introduce a third Bill on similar lines. To this the King agreed and withdrew his suggestion of a prorogation of Parliament.

Sunday, 9 October, 1831.

The fate of the Reform Bill is decided. That of the Ministry, depends upon their bringing in its twin brother. They are not at all out of heart. The King wishes them to remain ; & the Country has given them their confidence. But of course much must depend upon the extent of all these points. There is much excitement everywhere ; but a great hope that peace will be kept in all parts of the country. The Home Office for England & Ld Advocate for Scotland are busy uniting, & urging this necessity. Scotland is silently determined that Reform *shall* be ; & the accounts of the Birmingham Union, its organization & extent, are rather frightful. But as it is among a better class, they will be reasonable & remain quiet till they are convinced their cause is desperate ; & then Lds Kenyon, Worcester, Stormont, Valletort & such others may be gratified by seeing the blood of their countrymen. Those gentlemen, I understand, have expressed a wish to have a *fight* with the people, adding, " and the sooner the better."

Ld Hd felt very warm upon Ld Lyndhurst's sneers & sarcasms, & replied, as you see, very well & tartly. All intercourse in future must cease between *Ld* L. & me. I am an insignificant person, but he has lost my warm & cordial friendship ; & I think a friend & a good word is not entirely without value, let the individual be ever so unimportant. It is suggested the Queen, who is very ill surrounded, has given too much color to the stories of the Tories that she is extremely averse to Reform. She only sees Ld Howe, Ly Brownlow, Miss D'Este & a few of that trempe, reads the Mg Post for English intelligence, & the letters of the Dukes of Saxe-Meiningen & Weimar for foreign facts & opinions. It is said she boasts of never having called Leopold *King*, & in her letter of thanks to his congratulations upon her Coronation, skilfully avoided signing herself *Sister*, which is the common formula between crowned heads. Also when his Minister at Court was presented, all she said was, " I hope we shall soon see your *Sovereign here*," avoiding the use of the title *King*. These are nothings perhaps ; but they show the animus. You may mention this to Adair, but to nobody else ; as it would not be right from *this* house that there should be any critique upon that great Lady—who au reste they say has good qualities.

Tuesday, [October 11th].

Ld G.'s interview yesterday at Windsor [was] most highly satisfactory. The King, as he has always been, open, frank, good humoured, & friendly. The Country firm & cordial to the Govt. In short, as matters now stand, it is impossible they should be better. In all probability Parlt will be either prorogued or adjourned ; & next week we shall be released for Brighton. I long most ardently for change of air. Many a weary month has passed without my inhaling a breeze beyond what is tainted through the valley of the Thames. Your Aunt [1] has been indefatigable in her labors both in Lords & Commons. She will give you a curious report of the *ladies*. There are many anecdotes that would make you laugh, some disgusting of their violence. One, during Ld Grey's beautiful & touching reply, was furious, using most opprobrious epithets, *Scoundrel*, *Villain*, & some too strong for utterance for female lips. Ly Mansfield was the offender.

B. Street. *Friday*, 14 *Oct.*, 1831.

All apprehensions about the quiet of the Country or the change of Ministry must be allayed by this time ; & there is every appearance of tranquillity & perfect confidence. The King has been, as he is always, frank, & firm & cordially attached to his Ministers. You would have been amused at Ld Howe's [2] silly, intemperate letter. He is sore, angry & foolish beyond belief. The Queen in a pet declares she will not have another Chamberlain, but she will come round. Those on the tapis are Lds Cawdor & Clinton. Mulgrave would be too immoral, & play the deuce with the Maids of Honor, teaching them to enact Ophelias & Monimias. So I imagine there is no serious intention of proposing him.

Sir Walter is arrived in town. He is much decayed in faculties.

---

[1] Miss Caroline Fox.
[2] Richard William Penn Curzon, 1st Earl (1796–1870), Lord Chamberlain to the Queen, and her devoted adherent.

His friends are wavering whether he had better go to the Mediter-
ranean, where the sight of new objects may amuse & induce him to
form fresh habits ; or remain for the benefit of better medical advice
in case of a *third* seizure. His memory is greatly impaired ; tho' he
continues to write mechanically for 7 or 8 hours as formerly. But
his production is a repetition of what he had already composed, so
entirely has he become forgetful. It is melancholy. We dined
yesterday at the Pay Office, the Wms [Russells], & John upon a pair
from House, & Moore. The latter is not very friendly to the Govt,
nor indeed to mankind, being very much nettled that half the Irish
counties & towns did not ask him to be their representative, & that
Ld Lansdowne did not bring him for Calne.

I cannot give you a word of gossip. Dsse Dino goes to France
for a month in a few days. Talleyrand has Ld Grey's old house in
Hanover Square, lately Lieven's, who, to her delight, is again in one
of the pleasantest houses in London, Ashburnham House. The poor
Durhams are breaking their hearts at Sudbrooke. The day of the
funeral was one of anguish. Young Copley, Sir Joseph's son, is to
marry Miss Pelham, Ld Yarborough's daughter. She is very pretty,
& a great heiress. The fires are frequent in the country in farm yards ;
another within a mile of Woburn, very destructive to the D. of B.'s
property. I fear Dorsetshire will go against Wm Ponsonby [1] ; & Ld
F. Osborne has rashly given up Cambridgeshire & left it to an enemy
probably. The Lords seemed scared at their own proceedings. Lds
Wharncliffe, Haddington & Harrowby you see have put water into
their wine. I have seen the former here very much depressed ; he
is advised not to go to Wortley for a fortnight. He was burnt seven
times in effigy at Sheffield, which annoys him. If the Prorogation is
long enough to enjoy oneself and to let the Peers cool, I daresay the
new Bill will meet with a very different reception.

Lord Lilford behaved well in taking the Bedchamber at a *crise*, as
it was just possible he might have held it for a day or two only. Both
he & Mary lose money daily, & will be glad of the £1000 pr am &
the contact with the Court.

18 *October*, 1831.

Everything is going on well. Ld Howe's dismissal has been followed by that of Sir Byam Martin from the Admiralty, where he was
a bitter foe, & held language unbecoming a man acting with Govt.
Indeed he rarely voted. His removal is the strongest proof that could

---

[1] He resigned his seat at Poole, and was beaten by Lord Ashley, his cousin by
marriage.

be adduced of the cordiality of the King ; as Sir Byam is an old naval friend, with whom he is in daily habits of intercourse. I hope other changes may follow, & those in diplomacy. In *that* quarter, however, the retiring pensions are a difficulty, as the H. of Commons is stubborn upon money. The Opposition, out of sheer malignity, have kept on the Bankruptcy Bill in H. of Commons to delay the Prorogation : quite childish spite. I hope, however, it will take place on Thursday or Friday, & that we may be at Brighton early in the ensuing week.

Charles was requested by the King to attend on the Gd Duchess.[1] We all say he is smitten, as she is very pretty & winning ; & he became very anxious she should not encounter the dangers of the Baltic & cholera at this season, & even had a squabble with Mde Nesselrode, whom he calls a He-woman, quite a fierce dragon. However he will tell you all this with his gay humour. The Princess remains for a short time, but is to proceed to her sister, a *regnante* on the Rhine. Ly Wm has not seen the Queen except on great occasions of Coronation, etc.[2] Perhaps Ld Wm's brush with the brutal Saxe-Weimar may have influenced this conduct, as Her Majesty is very warm upon the subject of Holland.

21st October. [1831].

Poor Charles is half demolished by his attendance on the Gd Duchess. How indefatigable Royal persons are. He could only escort her to H. of Lords to see the Prorogation, & instead of accompanying her to the dinner at St James's, he went to bed. Papa, for the first time since his bad cold, went & dined there. The Queen was very gracious to him, Ld Lansdowne & Goderich, but never uttered to Chancellor or Ld Grey. She made it up in civility to Lady Grey & Georgina. She is silly in acting so ; but her mind has been poisoned by the bad entourage, who are doing their utmost to convince her the removal of Ld Howe is a *personal insult.* She will however soon get over this folly ; for such it is in truth. All her ladies to *a man* are furious, & encourage her perverseness. The worst of them is Lady Wellesley, the Republican !

An account of the interview between the opposing lords and Lord Grey is given by *Greville* (II, 228). The third Reform Bill was introduced in the Commons on December 12 by Lord John Russell. The second reading was carried on the 16th, 324–162. It passed from the Commons without a division on March 23, 1832.

[1] The Grand-Duchess Hélène, daughter of Prince Paul, brother of the King of Würtemberg, and wife of the Grand-Duke Michael, the Czar's brother.

[2] Apparently Lady William had some Court appointment.

[*December* 13, 1831.]

. . . The town was inundated with reports on Sunday in consequence of the interview between Ld Harrowby, Chandos & Wharncliffe, with Ld Grey, Chancellor, Althorp. It was *solicited* by the
first Lords, & granted by Ld G. ; but the Tories set about that they
had been *sent* for to negotiate & upon the failure Chancellor had gone
off to Brighton. Not one word of truth in it. Entre-nous, I do not
think the Lords acted quite fairly to give an air of negotiation, which
could only have a mischievous tendency to the Ministry. However,
the debate last night will set all matters to rights. Peel lost his temper,
exposed himself, & was deserted by his former adherents. Ld Clive's
speech was conciliatory ; but Mr Portman rather unluckily tried to
clench his vote, which naturally enough offended, & inclined him to
retract perhaps more than he intended. Ld Althorp was made very
indignant by Peel, spoke with warmth & vigor, all the better for his
anger ; in that the whole went off most advantageously to the Govt.

The Greys dined with us. They were both very *cheerful* & in good
health. Not very common, you will say.

The Czar Nicholas procrastinated as to signing the ratification of
the separation of Holland and Belgium ; and England and France
finally signed without Russia for the other Powers.

Tuesday, [*December* 27, 1831].

Your long letter delighted me. How pleasantly you write. It is
the only compensation for your absence, which would bear heavily
upon me anywhere but in London. We spent three days most
agreably at Sheen. Nothing could exceed the tenderness of Ly G.
I felt quite sorry at leaving them, & am confident they saw us go with
equal regret.

Russia is blowing as cold politically as the winds she sends us do
physically.[1] They have taken a *contemplative attitude*, an affected
phrase of M. Bressan's, & will do nothing to ratify until they obtain
the *consent* of the K. of Holland. This puts Zuylen his representative,
his *real* representative, into tip-top spirits. My dear Falck is very
seriously ill, confined for many days to his bed by suppressed gout.
. . . He is not able to move hand or foot. He is so frank & loyal,

---

[1] Lady Holland wrote on 19th : " Bülow came in evening from Richmond.
He described the Lievens as in a state of great anxiety, from knowing the
Moscow courier has arrived at Gravesend, detained by quarantine, but hourly
expecting the dispatches." Heinrich von Bülow (1792–1841), Prussian Minister
1827–41.

that the conduct of his King distresses him : & when he expresses his own views has made him liable to rebukes which have pained him greatly.   We dined on Xmas day at Ld Sefton's, an immense party, but nevertheless very cheerful.   Talleyrand has again lost a large sum of money owing to the roguery of an agent-de-change, & also the Dsse Dino.

Mde Apponyi [1] makes herself too much a chef de parti, & will from what I hear perhaps get a little hint from high quarters that she ought not to do so.   As to Lady G[ranville], nothing can ever make her political, & if she is so intimate, depend upon it, it is only the suite of former habits & probably renewed from ball arrangements with her daughters & some such trifling matters ; as Lady G. is as superior in understanding to the other as a hawk to a buzzard.

[1] Austrian Ambassadress in Paris.

CHAPTER VIII

1832–1833

Jour des Rois. Friday, [1832, *January*].

The King was very much pleased at Lord Grey's visit, & everything was as satisfactory as possible. The Queen was much more gracious than formerly ; & the King in excellent health. In short, nothing could be better. The Chancellor [Brougham] has been very ill : paid dearly for his frolic to the North into a house half pulled down & open to the weather, with all the damp of new walls. He was seized in the night with an attack of cholera, very severe. He had no bell, nor could he obtain assistance for two hours. In short, he was in danger for a few hours, and is safe, tho' recovering very slowly, & not yet able to be en route ; & then he will come up very leisurely. This is unlucky, as there are Cabinets which from his station he ought to attend & direct many of the legal points.

Much as we have all admired Ld Grey, I should say his colleagues if possible admire him more than ever, for his temper, moderation & judgment. The Chancellor is quite eloquent in his eulogium. Talleyrand, rather contre-cœur for a country excursion at this season, was to go to Panshanger to bring back Pauline [1] today, who has been making herself merry during the holidays.

[*Jan.* 12, 1832.] East Sheen.

We came here yesterday. The house is warm & comfortable ; & both my hosts are in excellent health. Yesterday we had *only* the family, which really suited me better & was very agreable. Mde de Lieven came for a morning visit at 5. Entre-nous I suspect the whooping cough in her family is no calamity of the ladies of *this*, as it is a pretext for diminished intercourse. [2] Russia is a very reluctant ratifier, if she will do so at all. But we are in a fuss at the affair of the Fortresses, in which T. has not acted with either his usual temper or

---

[1] Daughter of Madame de Dino, who later married Henri de Castellane.

[2] Lady Holland wrote a week later : " Psse Lieven perceives she has greatly lost her influence with Ld G. : & has by her address made her friend rekindle an almost extinguished flame, which strange to say now burns with fresh ardor. Thus she obtains knowledge of all that is going on, and with her skill & talents you may judge whether she is idle in taking the full benefit of such an advantage."

definition on the subject. It will be too provoking, if such an insignificant thing should be the cause of serious misunderstanding between the Govts. I hope he will dine here today, so that he may be made to see the danger ; as both Ld G. & Papa think him wrong, but also Ld P[almerston] who is hot, & that is not a condition in which grave matters ought to be discussed. Nothing can be more unfeignedly cordial than the King to Ld G., treating him quite as a equal & almost with tenderness, hoping he does not vex himself at the opposition to the Bill, which he adds *must* be read a second time ; & then expressing a warm wish to see him in the holidays. Yesterday Ld G. folded up a letter, which he said was the 102 application for peerages. I think you will see a few soon, & more if necessary.

Friday, [January 20, 1832].

. . . Were you not diverted at the Lievens complaining at Ld G. seeing Czartorisky.[1] Ld G. was nettled. She called him a " criminel d'état." She must be greatly provoked at its being followed up by *all* the Ministers making a point of shewing him civility. Lord Palmerston dined two days running with us on *purpose* to be sure of meeting him on one. Esterhazy made a point of calling & sitting an hour with him. In short, everything that can prove sympathy & deep interest to him personally he has found here.

[January 23 or 24.]

Papa is vexed at not being either able to attend the Cabinet, or keep an appointment with Ld Palmerston to go over the papers for this odious motion on Belgium.[2] The Reform goes on smoothly & rapidly in Commons, so that the tussle will come speedily to the Lords. Be assured there is no truth in any of the stories you were told of the King's giving only a certain number of peers. He is all that an honest Minister could wish ; & he is full of confidence in that Minister. Attendance in Lords is much wanted for daily matters.

Friday, [February 3, 1832].

. . . I went to the English version of *Henri III* by Ld F. Leveson. The two first acts are rather heavy, the last full of powerful interest &

---

[1] Prince Adam Czartoryski (1770–1861) was elected President of Poland on December 30, 1830, but resigned in the following August. He was proscribed by the Czar, and lived in Paris for the rest of his life.

[2] Lord Aberdeen moved on January 26 an Address to the Crown censuring the political policy pursued towards Holland and Belgium.

lively action ; but a more thoroughly disagreable composition I
never witnessed, painful in the extreme.   The acting excellent ; even
Warde,[1] generally so harsh & offensive, in the stern part of Guise
did well.   Fanny Kemble remarkably good ; & poor Charles, her
father,[2] well as he is always, but evidently labouring under the effects
of recent illness.   Ld F. did his share well ; only his choice of a subject
is surprising, it being so very, very disagreable.

The weather is so damp that I am compelled to take my exercise,
such as it is, under cover.   Yesterday at the British Museum ; today
is Westminster Hall, a peep into the Court of Chancery to see
Brougham in his wig, & then to H. of Commons library, Lords, etc.
Being anxious to hear of the case of cholera reported to have occurred
in a London hospital, I went to the Bd of Health, saw & questioned
Dr Russell.   He says it certainly is not cholera, nor anything re-
sembling that malady.[3]

Lord Harrowby wrote a circular letter to various Peers, as to their
vote on Reform.   This he refused to show to Lord Grey, but gave
Lord Ebrington a copy.   A garbled version got into the *Times*,
perhaps through Lord Durham.   (See *Greville*, II, 264–5.)

Tuesday, 27 February, 1832.   Old B. Street.

. . . Ld G. Bentinck [4] is doing all the harm he can to Govt, by
saying they wish to be beat tonight on the Metropolitan members.
That letter in the *Times* is *not* a fair transcript, tho' the spirit of it is
nearly so ; but still the wording is so different that it does not bear
an exact interpretation.   I think matters are in a very ticklish state
from the great reluctance to make peers ; so that the second reading
will be trusted to the chance support of the frightened.   Many declare,
even among our own supporters, that they will vote against it if there
are any creations.   What strange folly !   But so it is ; even supposing
the *very* doubtful vote, there will then only be a majority of *two*.
And then in Committee the Bill will be so worked & altered, that it
will no longer be that which Ld Grey is to stand or fall by.   In short,
the tenure is most precarious.   The Tories are in prodigious spirits,
& look forward to office immediately.   It is said the D. of W. has

---

[1] James Prescott Warde (1792–1840).

[2] Charles Kemble (1775–1854), and his daughter Frances Anne (Fanny)
(1809–93), acted together with great success, especially on a tour in America
1832–4.

[3] Ly Holland wrote : " People are not much afraid of cholera.   Should it
extend to Lambeth, Parliament may move to Oxford.   So is the talk."

[4] (1802–48), son of 4th Duke of Portland, politician and racing magnate.

sent emissaries to the French Court to assure them, in case of a change here, that the present policy towards France & other foreign countries will be preserved, as it now is.

There was an extraordinary damp fog on the night of Drawing Room & D. of Devon.'s ball. Accidents of various sorts occurred, loss of diamonds, etc. The ladies *walked*; & one was set on fire by the link boys, Miss Mitchell, I think, & hurt a good deal. Many never reached the house, from the coachmen not knowing their way, Dsse Dino, Ly Belhaven & others. Great difficulties in Downing Street, where Lds Grey, Althorp & Palmerston gave official dinners. D. of Bedford was coming to me, but after half an hour & upwards spent in Belgrave Square, his coachman said he could not find his way; so he got out, & with some difficulty found his own door by the help of many servants & link boys. . . .

March 9, 1832.

. . . I believe they are quite sure of passing the second reading; so peers will only be required for the Committee. For the Ministers are inflexible, & will not yield one particle of the principle of the Bill, however they may be ready to accept them in adapting some of the details to use. Be assured of this; & let no saucy Tory or Conservative pretend to the contrary.

Lord Mulgrave [1] has just been here to say he has made up his mind to accept the Govt of Jamaica. He has been sometime wavering; but she has come to town, & is willing to go with him there. It is a most advantageous appointment for the Govt; &, if the " Saints " would allow, may be the means of settling that distracted country into some peaceable state. But *that* is very doubtful.

Lord Eldon did Govt much service last night by attacking the bench of Bishops. The Archbishops were disposed to be shabby & silent; but, worm-like, the Primate even turned at the insult, spoke for & supported the Govt upon subject of tithes. [2] The Tories are furious at the defection of some of their own squad & of the Bishops; & Lord Eldon, injudiciously for his cause, goaded them. D. of W. has never recovered his temper since his illness; so that even his warmest private friends are less at their ease with him than formerly. You know that he never goes near Ly Jersey, a complete alienation. Papa is busy out, so may not perhaps have time to write. He is pretty well,

[1] Lord Normanby had succeeded his father as Earl of Mulgrave in the previous year. He later was created Marquis of Normanby.
[2] On the report stage of the Tithe Bill for Ireland.

but worried at the malignant attacks in the *Times* against Ld G., who
feels the personality much.   But they are so violent & unjust, that the
effect produced is rather contrary to the mischief intended.

Tuesday, March 20.

. . . We went on Saturday to Hd. H.   The air was delicious, so fresh
& clear after this horrid thick atmosphere.   Papa got upon his pony
& enjoyed himself among his sheep & trees, as if he had been 18.
Poor I could see nothing but through the windows of my rolling
chair.[1]

Friday, March 30, [1832].

. . . I send some beautiful verses by Mrs Norton upon the death
of Lady Gower's child.   They are fully equal to any she has written.
It is a pity, with so much talent & real genius even, her taste is so
indifferent.   The choice of subjects is often disgusting : imagine a
coffin maker being the hero of one of her stories, the one she considers
her chef d'œuvre.   I would not read it, from the disagreable details
which I was told would be quite offensive to me.   She is writing a
novel, which will have, in my opinion, the unpardonable offence of
ending very ill.   This will also be the case with Ld Mulgrave's, from
what is said of his new publication.[2]

The intelligence of the ratification from Vienna was signified by
telegraph from Paris at ¼ after four p.m. Wednesday, & reached
London at a few minutes after 12 o'clock on Thursday morning.
What a wonderful power man has obtained over space & time, to
convey in so short a period information from such distant points.   As
it happened, it was of no very particular use ; but had Peel or Ld Aberdeen been asking any of their taunting questions upon foreign matters,
it might have been agreable to have had such a ready answer.   Nevertheless I should like to have the ratification here bodily.   The fact is,
all hang back till the Reform Bill is settled ; and some enemies choose
to suppose Ministers will go out if they should meet with another
repulse.   But that may be an erroneous speculation.   However, en
attendant, I hope they may not be *beat*, whatever may ensue.   The
King is very sanguine & talks of *we* & *us*, says he is sure we shall have
a majority of at *least* 18.   Kings can *do* no wrong, but Kings may be
misled into believing wrong.   The Bishop of Lincoln & Ld Braybroke

---

[1] Lady Holland had met with an accident a month before, and had damaged
some of the muscles of her back.
[2] *The Contrast.*

have written long handsome letters announcing their intention of voting second reading.

Yet I hardly know what to say for the upshot ; but be careful not to whisper even to Adair that I have a shadow of doubt, as somehow or other things come round ; & the intercourse is very brisk between London & Bruxelles. Two, that held out promises, but were never trusted, are off : Lds Coventry & Glengall, a pretty pair. The day of struggle will be Monday se'ennight. Ld Grey is inclined to sen'night ; tho' it now stands for Thursday, but is to be altered for the convenience of some lords who have sessions, etc. in country. It is far from decided the bringing up Ld Althorp ; the Commons are so reluctant to spare him. He is desirous of coming up, but like a real friend & honorable man leaves entirely the decision to the judgment of those who want his services. I do like, & almost love Ld A. very much.

Holland House. *Monday, 2d April,* [1832].

Just arrived under your natal roof. Bright day, birds singing, & all looking brilliant and agreable in every way. Poor dear Papa shut up in D. Street in a Committee to study the clauses of the Bill ! with Lds Goderich, Lansdowne, Melbourne, D. of Richmond. They have very wisely invited Ld Radnor, who has very kindly yielded his services. He will be invaluable to assist in fighting the Bill, should no roguery occur to defeat its second reading on Monday next. Papa then goes to Lords, & the Chancellor & he *come out*, as the Scotch say, to dine & sleep tonight. Tomorrow Papa has the same duties to perform beginning at one o'clock, & so on till Monday. His health is good, & he is glad to be employed, for he says his nervousness prevents his being as useful as he thinks he ought to be about speaking in the House.

At Dsse Dino's ball for le petit peuple, I staid to see Orloff.[1] He is a fine Hercules built man, with rather an agreable countenance. He is not the *chef* de famille, but an illegitimate son of the great Prince Orloff's 3rd brother, Theodore. He is however very rich, & a great favorite at present with the Emperor. He sided in his favor on the death of Alexander, & had great influence with the soldiers in their decision ; whereas another brother took part against the Emperor, & has been ever since in disgrace. The Lievens are not mortified at his coming, as they rejoice at anything that diminishes the influence

[1] Count Alexis Orloff (1786–1861), who had just arrived from Russia on a special mission.

of Matuscevitz, who is nettled at his superior importance.[1] Austrian ratification as you know is come, but contingent on Prussia's first, a strange thing for Austrian morgue, that anything issuing from the Aulic Chamber should not take the lead before a mushroom power like Prussia.

Monday, 9 *April,* [1832].

. . . The King is so anxious for the fate of the Bill, that he has anticipated by two days his coming to town, & will be here tomorrow. His presence with a friendly interest may counteract the mischief (*Private, Private, Private*) of the indiscreet visit of Lord Howe for the whole of last week at Windsor, under very peculiar circumstances. He succeeded Lds Grey & Palmerston. The Tory papers boasted that altho' he was not Ld Chamberlain de jure, he was de facto, as he handed her Majesty daily to dinner. Add to this he left his wife in the country, where his children were dangerously ill of the measles & his wife wanting him at home, & the clamour in the neighbourhood at his absence. To say the *least* it is very indiscreet in the Great Lady for her own, as well as the sake of others.

I am going to dine at Pay Office, & pass my time between it & Chancellor's room [2] : for I never will go up to the hen coop with the ladies, & prefer not hearing the debate ! There was a tussle, it was said, last night between Ly Jersey & Sir Thos Tyrwhitt.[3] As you may be curious about lists, I send you the last, which has been of course kept secret. Lord Stanhope very handsomely has taken his seat, & votes for second reading. Shew the list to Adair. We always when we meet have a great exchange of civilities with the Lyndhursts. She has called upon me ; & he & I chat freely. She is in great beauty. The on dit is that she is very sullen at the sudden restraint upon Ld D.[4] as there was a draft for £5000 on his table which was destined to her ; but the banker had been ordered not to make payments. Poor Ld D. is becoming more calm & reconciled to his condition. He reads & writes Latin orations, all good & correct. I do hope he may soon be returned to his former state, for there is something taking about him.

The second reading division in the House of Lords took place at 7 a.m. on April 14. The Bill was carried by a majority of 9.

[1] Count Matuscevitz was First Secretary in the Russian Foreign Office, sent over to England by Nesselrode to assist Prince Lieven.

[2] The second Reading debate began on April 9.

[3] Usher of the Black Rod.

[4] Lord Dudley had shown signs of madness, and had recently been placed under restraint.

13th April.

I am *very* nervous about the division tonight. *Some* relied upon are tripping, & have decided against. De Ros ! ! !, pledged doubly, is again wavering : Hastings, Waldegrave, Ravensworth, Grantham. Hélas ! it is very bad—bad for Europe. The power & ratification are already in London, *known* to be, but kept contingent upon the success of Bill there. Never was a Govt so cruelly hampered & ill-used as this has been, but if they weather it, the more the glory. Ld Grey rises with the peril, both in energy of speaking & promptitude of decision ; & even his bitterest foes are struck with his discretion, courtesy & ability, to say nothing of the fairness of his whole conduct, which has been through out most remarkable. His health is sustained marvellously without air or exercise, mind always harassed, & living in a most noisome, foul atmosphere ; as Downing Street is the sink of London, *really* not metaphorically.

Monday, 16th April, [1832].

The news got to Paris of the success of the second reading on the same day ; a very speedy communication, as the messenger only started from Talleyrand's door $\frac{1}{4}$ before 8. The weather must have been very bright & clear for telegraph. Papa is not the worse. On his return at $\frac{1}{2}$ past 7, he eat a roast chicken & drank a bottle of claret, slept well, & has kept so. Allen & I sat up for him, greeting him as cordially as we felt. I think all is very promising. Some who croak say difficulties are only just beginning. Perhaps so, but I do not feel intimidated by the bullying language of the Tories, who call the victory the death blow to Lord Grey's Govt. Some of the doubtful peers & some of the pledged voted against. Hastings behaved admirably ; Lord Ravensworth also. In that the thing is well done, if not entirely. I hear Ld Harrowby means to be pugnacious in Committee ; but Ld Wharncliffe is rather more reasonable. The Queen had a sad headache the day of the news ; but the King had a light heart, & went off to Windsor in spirits. I send you a Penny Magazine which is said to be superintended by the Chancellor. It has a great sale, forming part of the Education system, of which he is the head & promoted. His health is greatly improved.

P. Lieven has been ill some days, I *believe* really ill ; but some fancy he is vexed. He is an excellent man & thorough gentleman, galant homme au possible, unlike the rest of his Embassy. There is no Court in Europe of more importance at this moment than that of Berlin ; where our Govt *ought* to be put on a right & respectable footing. The D. of C[umberland] is full of machinations there. Our Minister at Petersburg [1] aids & abets, & Ancillon [2] is the greatest anti-Liberal in Europe. We cut a sad figure there ; & it is most important. At Vienna, Esterhazy was received as if he had been the rankest Jacobin of '93. It is said Neumann [3] is very crestfallen at the division, having expected it quite the reverse. He is a bitter foe.

Some think the ratifications will be signed today ; tho' the Russians make a push to wait for the answer to Orloff's courier who went on 14th from the Hague.

I am going to be very gay. On Thursday we go to Stoke, Ld Sefton's, for 2 nights. He has invited those he thought agreable to me, Chancellor, Melbourne, Luttrell. We return to Hd H. on Saturday ; & then Papa, like a schoolboy for holidays, looks forward to Ampthill on Monday.

Good Friday, 20th April, [1832].   Stoke Farm.

We have now quitted B. St : came here yesterday. A beautiful ferme ornée, most comfortable house tho' small ; every room abounds with all that is wanted, luxe more than in Palaces. A recherche in all things imaginable for use or agrémens ; the best cuisine in Europe, delicious German baker, Italian office, gardens to vie with Holland for vegetables, & flowers as good as Haarlem : in short, all that man or woman can wish for. A shrewd, sensible, lively, good hearted host with gay, lively conversation ; & the best natured wife that ever lived, & cheerful daughters. We have Chancellor, Wm Lamb, Luttrell whom we brought down, many of the family. Today guests are expected ; tomorrow we return. Chancellor not quite himself in spirits, but his health is good. He never recovered his sharp attack of cholera in the winter, has remained too low ever since. But he does all his duties perfectly ; so it is only his private friends who have reason to complain from his want of his former gaiety, tho' today he is however full of stories & fun. À propos Charles has made his first speech, on behalf of the Poles, but has not had the honor & glory of a specification, as he is described as an unknown member.[4]

---

[1] Lord Heytesbury was British Ambassador in Russia from 1828 until the summer of this year, when he retired.

[2] Minister for Foreign Affairs in Berlin.

[3] Philipp von Neumann, Austrian Secretary of Legation in England.

[4] Charles Fox had been elected M.P. for Calne in 1831. Allen also wrote to Henry Fox : " It was short. The reporters, not knowing who he was, have designated him, ' a member, name unknown.' Some one should tell them it was a name not quite unknown to their predecessors."

Easter Sunday, 22 April, [1832].

. . . Your opinion & pleasure at the Russians lagging behind the other powers is universal. It will mortify & shew them they are not of the importance they affect to be ; & this spirit rising against them upon Polish injustice & cruelty may bring them to reason. *Here* the hostility of party was never stronger, nor more activity shewn. It is apprehended there is a close alliance formed between Lds Lyndhurst, Ellenboro', Wharncliffe & Harrowby, which through the former is in direct communication with D. of W. upon the clauses in the Bill, how they are to be treated. Our only hope is their not agreeing ; else it will be a desperate case for Govt, as those that made the majority will almost all follow the above Lords, & perhaps many of our *own*. So that without creations, or what is the same, callings up, I cannot imagine the *Bill* being otherwise than so mutilated that those who brought it in cannot submit to, nor the Country be satisfied with. There are meetings 2 or 3 times a day in Charles St under the vigilant control of Messrs Holmes, Croker, Ld Rosslyn, etc., from whence they write to & see peers, to ascertain about attendance, etc. Poor Lauderdale, who has been *very* seriously, dangerously ill, is to be dragged up. He comes with Tweedale & Maitland, each become as furious as wild bulls. From Scotland, the General in Command writes that he requires more troops, as he has only a few, & the spirit is very turbulent among the people. The clauses in the Bill the most disliked by its opponents, are the £10 freeholders & the additional numbers for the Metropolitan district. *Some* slight modifications of objectionable parts may be yielded ; but nothing that touches the principle of the Bill can be admitted. It is really very disagreable to see people look so angry, quite to outrageous wrath, & some that one has known formerly in softer moods. The Greys are at East Sheen. The quiet & repose of that excellent house is most essentially necessary to his health, which has stood miraculously but will be all the better for calmness & domestic pleasures. He is so happy surrounded by all his children & grand-children, & now he has that nice person, Ly Elizabeth ; & I suppose they do not much mind her husband, who is very good natured at least.[1] Dreadful sudden case of cholera ; Lady Ann Wyndham expired shortly after her seizure. Sir M. Tierney attended, & acknowledged it was the *first* case he had ever seen ; tho' hitherto he had very obstinately asserted that he cured Lady Clanricarde & others with castor oil.

[1] Lady Elizabeth Grey married John Bulteel in 1826.

Ampthill. 26 *April.*

. . . We return on Monday ; & I hope the King will settle in town.
For he is surrounded by a very bad entourage at the Castle : & cannot,
I suspect, venture to invite his Ministers even to dinner, altho' they
have been in the neighbourhood for some days.   Never was so fierce
a foe as the Greatest Lady in the Land ; & this she keeps up by stories
from Germany of the too great alliance between England & France.
She cannot digest Belgium, & would have a crusade for K. of Holland
to recover it, in order that her sister might live again at Ghent.   In
short, nothing can be worse than the whole Court is towards the
present Ministry & their policy, domestic & foreign.

On May 7, Lord Lyndhurst moved in Committee to postpone the
disenfranchising clauses until after the enfranchising ones had been
passed, and carried it by 35.   Ministers would not agree, as they feared
that the Bill would be emasculated and reappear in an entirely new
form.   Lord Grey's Government resigned on May 8, upon the King's
refusal to make 50 peers to carry the Bill.   Henry Fox was one of
the eldest sons selected to be sent to the House of Lords, in the event
of the creation of peers.

May 8th, Tuesday, [1832].

In a very few hours much will be known, tho' not perhaps before
the departure of the mail.   The defeat of the Bill was complete :
& unless rectified by creations the Ministry must yield.   There has
been much going on to work upon the King's mind these last two
months, so that there would be no surprize in that quarter.   I shall
lament it for public & private reasons, not unmingled with apprehension too ; as the people are warm & determined, & one can never
quite feel secure when there is agitation.

Since writing the above, the Cabinet is up ; Ld Grey & Chancellor
gone to the King, who is at Windsor.   Upon the issue of that interview depends the Govt ; but my belief upon the whole is that it will
end so well as to make it imperative that you should be here ; & that,
you know, I never thought before.   So, darling, do as your Papa
wishes, & come off.

It is impossible to use language sufficiently strong to reprobate the
disingenuous misbehaviour of Lds Harrowby & Wharncliffe.   What
a contrast to Ld Manners !   Even Ld Hastings, torn as he is at home,
behaved consistently with his former vote.   Tankerville deserted ; as
did the sneaking Archbishop of York.   But you will hear all this,
I hope, within 72 hours or thereabouts.

Papa spoke extremely well last night, which delights me so much that it is quite a set off against the defeat ; for he had become nervous & fancied he had lost the faculty of speaking. He is very brisk & well.

Friday. South Street. [*May* 18, 1832.]

. . . I have never till within these 48 hours been seriously alarmed at the state of the country, always ascribing much to exaggeration & vapouring. But now it really appears there is, bona fide, an organization of the people amounting to a national guard, all ready equipped, disciplined, & as *yet* obedient to their leaders. These Unions have such immense influence upon the financial part of the country that they can regulate the Savings Banks, &, if they so direct these, millions of money can be drawn *out.* The day before Ld Grey had the communication from the King, there was a run to the amount of one million upon the Bank, & to a great extent upon private Banks. Rothschild had an interview with D. of W. ; & it is conjectured *his* report of the state of the money market had great influence in his abandonment of the Ministry. Last night Ld Grey & his friends entered the H. of Lords convinced & satisfied, from the assurances they had received from the highest quarter, that W. & Co. would make a declaration to say they should withdraw their opposition from the Bill. Instead of that you see they only *abused* the late Ministry, & expressed a stronger than ever abhorrence of the Bill of Reform. Never were men placed in a more embarrassing position, a cleft stick, a cul de sac, & in short in all the impossible situations to go on or get out. How it will end, God knows : not well for general peace & quiet. Peel, it is said, is coming sneaking again on the scene, to rescue the King & rally round the throne. Much will depend upon the conduct in H. of Commons tonight.

Poor Talleyrand is cruelly cut up by the death of Périer, & also at the uncertainty of things here. I am afraid the Queen has been very active. She says sooner than the King should yield, she would prefer seeing him by the side of Charles X at Holyrood House.

Henry Fox came over to England, as his father desired, towards the end of May, and remained for two months. The Duke of Wellington, however, failed to form a Government ; and the King having informed the Opposition Lords that he was prepared to create more peers, the Bill passed in June. After supplementary Bills for Scotland and Ireland had been passed, Parliament was dissolved early in December.

Saturday. H. Hd. *August 4, 1832.*

. . . We had the most appalling thunderstorm I almost ever recollect in any country, accompanied by a deluge. The water burst into 7 or 8 rooms. In my dressing room, a cataract that only missed Papa's head by a few inches. It would have knocked him down, had it caught his head, so large was the column of water, also my wardrobe. The Library was not habitable in the evening, & many other rooms were inundated. Your Aunt gives a very comical account of the flood that burst into her house. The lightning burnt a house in Sloane Street. The newspapers will also tell how mischievous the storm was on the river. The roads are as deep as winter.

19th October, 1832. Hd H.

. . . The Chancellor is in a very excellent plight, cheerful, *even* spirits, & doing all unanimously with his colleagues. I should not observe upon this ; but previous to his return from the country there were all sorts of rumours, which those who knew him best did not credit ; but it threw a sort of curiosity over his proceedings. Ly Wm [Russell] was to leave town yesterday to join Ld Wm at Lisbon.[1] She is to sail in the *Britannia*. The worst part of her expedition is the necessity of quitting the great ship of war to be lowered into a steam vessel in the open sea, as the *Viper* is the only vessel, a sort of Cartel, which Miguel's Govt allow to enter the Tagus. Like you, she hates England so much, that she would go anywhere. She has neither kin nor home, or anything to bestow affections upon, or very much receive them from others, from her selfishness of character. Her children are charming. Perhaps it is unlucky for Hastings to become such a wanderer, but he is a delightful boy, full of good dispositions & kindness of heart. The Lambs [2] come over to us from Richmond often. She is not in very good health, which all must regret, as she is one of the most amiable, agreable persons I know.

Talleyrand is thinner, but in all other respects perfectly as before. He shudders when he mentions how ill he had been. Lady Keith, who is in England, disturbs him by her language as to the new French Ministry.[3] He considers it injurious, & very wrong considering how she is connected by favor with the Palais Royale. The Greys are

---

[1] Lord William was sent on a special mission to Portugal in 1832, and became Minister when England recognized Doña Maria as Queen.

[2] The George Lambs.

[3] Louis Philippe had much difficulty in forming a Government after Casimir Périer's death.

at Sheen from whence they cannot stir, as D. St is painting & under-going thorough repairs.

December 12th, 1832. B. St.

The Metropolitan elections are going on well in all ways, both as to the choice of representatives in better mode of voting, which is remarkably quiet & easy. No mobs, no obstacles to those who go up to vote ; two days finish the whole, & the candidates do not appear until they do so to return thanks from the hustings. . . .

Henry Fox had returned to the Continent in August, and joined the staff of Sir Augustus Foster at Turin, an an Attaché, in September. Early in January a letter arrived from him asking for his parents' consent to his marriage to Lady Mary Augusta Coventry, a young lady of 20, daughter of George William, 7th Earl of Coventry (who succeeded in 1831), and Mary, daughter of Aubrey, 6th Duke of St Albans. Her mother was separated from her father. Fox, being a friend of Lady Coventry, or Lady Mary Deerhurst as she was then known, had had opportunities of getting to know his future wife during his previous stay in Italy, so his attraction to her was no sudden passion. The wedding took place in Florence, at the house of the British Minister in Florence, George Hamilton Seymour. None of the family were able to make the journey to be present.

22d January, 1833.

All that we hear makes our feelings much more comfortable upon the subject of your projected alliance. The education of the young lady, & her mother's remarkable attention & prudence towards her, are very satisfactory topics. Incidentally, I have heard that nothing can be more in good taste than Lady Augusta's whole deportment ; and she does great honor to the judicious attentions of her mother. Lady Coventry is said to be very good natured, which is a great point. Indeed, the prospect of seeing you happily married, an event I have so long wished, makes me quite happy ; as I am sure you are formed for the quiet & soothing pleasures of domestic life, & will yourself be a different person. I am much mistaken in you, if Ly Augusta will not have great cause to rejoice in her choice of you ; but the whole is a lottery, unless grounded upon strong affection & mutual esteem, which is I trust the case in your instance.

22d February, 1833.

. . . All I hear of Lady Augusta is charming : not a dissentient voice, both as to beauty, manners & agrémens of every sort. I think

Lady Coventry has done herself great honor in her mode of bringing her up, & wish much I was en relation with her to express it ; but on no occasion have, or will I ever put myself forward, & Papa is awkward, for only this moment I asked him to write, but he declares he felt it so strange & liable to misinterpretation that he will not. When Ld Coventry is congratulated, I hear he speaks handsomely & kindly upon the subject. This he did in the H. of Lords.

Mde Vestris, for the first time in her life is with child, & she is in despair. Ld Castlereagh,[1] for the honor of Ireland, is enchanted at his feat.

1st March, 1833.

. . . The dénoument of the roman of the Dsse de Berri is ludicrous.[2] The Carlists must be confounded. These devoted ladies at Paris, who had worn des bourres à la prisonnière, renounced dress & dancing for her sake, must console themselves with the benevolent reflection that their little Princess has not been altogether so dreary & desolate in her wanderings, as their loyalty might make them fear. It is puzzling for Louis Philippe to decide what is best & ought to be done with her.

M. de Talleyrand is a good deal better : was able to go out yesterday. The injury was done to the *well* foot, so it probably got better sooner than the other would have done. I heard yesterday poor Ld Dudley was not likely to survive many hours. Life is no blessing to him with all his sufferings, so it is hardly kind to regret its termination. His understanding has long been so clouded that he is not conscious of what is going on around him, or with whom he was speaking.

Mr Stanley's speech[3] has produced an extraordinary sensation.

[1] Frederick William Robert Stewart, afterwards 4th Marquis of Londonderry. He married the widow of 6th Viscount Powerscourt and daughter of Earl of Roden in 1846, and had no children, dying in 1872.

[2] Caroline (1798–1870), daughter of Francis I, King of Naples, and widow of the Duc de Berri, murdered in Paris in 1820, son of Charles X. Creevey wrote : " What say you to the Duchesse de Berri's approaching accouchement, young Bourmont is said to be the lucky lover. What a termination to all her heroism to save the Crown of France for her son." She was imprisoned after the ineffective legitimist rising of her son, the Duc de Bordeaux, and had a son during her incarceration. Count Hector Palli was the father. She was released in June 1833.

[3] On the Irish Coercion Bill. He attacked and pulverised O'Connell. Greville (II, 363) wrote : " Stanley seems to have set the whole thing right like a great man."

Old George Byng, who has been 43 years in the H. of Commons, says neither Pitt nor Fox ever produced such an effect. To be sure the circumstances were very peculiar under which it was delivered. But politics are not topics to amuse you at present.

24th May, 1833.

. . . It was such a relief to hear the ceremony was over ; as till it was, I had terrors & apprehensions of an interruption, either from your health or some of the unforeseen casualties of life. The only notification was your own letter from Lucca, & one from Lord Palmerston to tell us. Mr Seymour had announced it to him.

Tuesday, June 10 or 11, 1833.

My dear Henry & Augusta,

We had the pleasure of a visit from Lady Coventry yesterday, who in the most obliging manner passed over etiquette & came to visit us. She also has accepted an invitation to dine here on Sunday ; & Lady Grey has offered herself & Ld G. with her. She is a cousin of Lady Grey. Lady C. seems brisk, lively & agreable. She is pretty but small. She told us Augusta was a size less than herself. Her eyes are very brilliant, quite magnificent. Lauderdale cannot leave his home on account of health ; and as she is very anxious to see him, must go to Dunbar for that purpose, which she seems inclined to do. She spoke of you with great regard, & expressed having felt much anxiety about your health when you were at Albano. She gives an excellent account of Lady Augusta's constitution & health, which I am happy to say those who saw her in Italy confirm. Let her cherish it ; for be assured without health there is no felicity in life.

There is a sad instance of that in this house, poor Agar,[1] who has every earthly blessing, but he is in so precarious a state that it gives too great a feeling of insecurity to render it availing. However, he bears up very manfully, from his great natural spirits. They have been here some days : leave us tomorrow. He is ordered perpetual change of air, so hovers about London for a few nights together, not to be far from medical aid. They have 6 fine children, another coming in August.

Last night we saw the fireworks from Syon, where the Duke of Northumberland gave a splendid fête to their Majesties & some of

[1] Lord Dover, as he had been created in 1831, died a month later. Lady Holland wrote : " It has been a most afflicting event, & to none more out of his more immediate connexions than to me."

the élite of Society, none under Ambassadors. We were sitting in the large bow-window of the Library, which is now my salon since the hot weather; a great many persons came both from Syon & London. Poor Mde de Lieven made me quite unhappy at taking leave. She is so affected at going, which she is to do on Saturday. She is a very great coward; & the voyage in the steam vessel frightens her a great deal. She is to spend 3 weeks with the Imperial family at Peterhof, & be here again by 12th August. I conclude, however, that the return, tho' apparently certain, is never quite sure with such despotic masters as Russian despots.

16th July, 1833.

. . . We are again in this vast town, on account of what had till yesterday all the appearance of complete defeat. But the Tories flinch when it comes to the point; & nous voilà perhaps even through the Committee.[1] Some, when they thought there was real peril, behaved well; for instance Ld Chichester lost no time in tendering his proxy. A Bishop or two disposed to slink away; but on the whole no great cause for complaint. Ld Grey is better; but the old complaint of gall stones hangs over him, & produces at times much pain & occasional inconvenience.

The good news from Portugal is a pill to the Tories,[2] & possibly may have had the effect of making them think twice before they rashly tried to overthrow this Govt. My own pleasure is great; but very much founded upon poor Palmella's safety & prospect of well doing; as, poor fellow, these last two years my heart has ached at the sight of his deep grief & despair. Find out about his property in Piedmont, whether it is tolerably good & unencumbered. But I much fear he has embarked his all in the cause of Doña Maria. If there ever was such a thing as a Saint, it is his angelic wife. With all the qualities belonging to a wife & mother, she has such noble courage & heroism, and is without intolerance so sincerely religious. I hardly know the character that calls for more respect & admiration.

People are bored to death with breakfasts; that at Syon was a complete failure. The weather & bad local made the Dss of Buccleuch's very disagreable & catch cold. Today Ld Westminster gives one at Moor Park to their Majesties & the Town, a distance of nearly 20 miles! What a thirst for pleasure. The Lansdownes, etc., are to sleep at Cassiobury, a very good distribution of distance.

---

[1] On the Irish Church Bill.

[2] Dom Miguel's fleet had been defeated off Cape St Vincent on July 5 by Dom Pedro's, under the command of Sir Charles Napier.

CHAPTER IX

1834–1835

The Foxes arrived in England at the end of August, and remained until the early days of the New Year, when they returned to Turin.

14th January, [1834. To Lady Augusta Fox].

I cannot tell you what an excellent impression you have left upon the minds of all who saw you, & what regret, alas ! at your departure. " Bonne renommée vaut mieux que l'écriture dorée " ; & that you have, dearest little one, in all quarters. I conclude you will see Mrs Pellew.¹ Tell me *frankly* what you think of her. Is she pretty, clever, pleasing ? In short, what is she ? I have had a very obliging note, expressing much kindness & good affection. I hope her daughter is a nice girl & will be satisfactory to her. Mde de Lieven has continued her passion for whist, & has her regular party every evening. Dr Holland ² has been accepted by Miss Smith, Sydney Smith's daughter. It is a very suitable & promising marriage. Her father jokes with her upon the certainty of the Doctor's being knighted, & her becoming *Lady Holland* : & bids her provide in time her coterie of Luttrells & Rogers's, etc.

4th February, 1834.

. . . I assure dear little Augusta there are many enquiries made with real feeling & kindness about her. She is a little meteor that has blazed amongst us, & alas ! vanished. Our carriage was asked for on Saturday to attend the funeral of Lady Lyndhurst.³ I have a

¹ This was Lady Holland's daughter, Harriet Webster, born in 1794. She had married, in 1816, Fleetwood Pellew, later K.C.B. and an Admiral, son of Lord Exmouth. Mother and daughter had not met for many years, as all intercourse was forbidden after Sir Godfrey Webster's death by his executors. The Pellews dined at Holland House later in the year. Their daughter, Harriet, married Lord Walpole, later 4th Earl of Orford, in 1841. His sister was Lady Dorothy Nevill, so well known in London society.

² Henry Holland, M.D. (1787–1873), created a Baronet in 1853. Saba Smith was his second wife.

³ She died after a short illness, premature labour. Lady Holland wrote on January 28 : " Poor Lady L., a melancholy finale indeed ! It was always my apprehension that she was a condemned person, how I could not say ; but her temper and character denoted a fatal catastrophe, as she was always a wretched woman in her most brilliant days."

letter from him brim full of feeling about her, & assurances that however appearances might be for the last two years, she always considered with gratitude Ld Hd & me among her best friends. He will come & see me soon.

Today is the King's opening Speech. It is not known whether the Opposition will move an amendment in either house ; tho' O'Connell must in ye Commons, to keep up his *agitation*. The Tories are likely to support the Ministers against the Radicals, in the hope of its being the most mischievous thing to their Govt.

Talleyrand was 80 on 2d February. Your Papa sent him a beautiful pair of reading glasses for his fête. He is well. The Dsse has never quite recovered the effects of the sea, & is really unwell. There are nightly *whist* parties at Mde de Lieven's, Talleyrand's, & sometimes here.

Charles Greville spoke of a violent declaration against O'Connell in the King's Speech, " that is, against Irish agitation." And as he might have, and did take a strong line in reply, the position had its dangers.

Friday, February 21, [1834].

. . . The King told Ld G. that he never left town with so much ease of mind & content as he did now. In short, all is going on perfectly well, if our *own* people do not spoil their game ; but this business is ugly in H. of C., & your brother is half afraid of a second Wilkes's business if expulsion is attempted. Otherwise from all I see & hear, *never* was Govt so respected & looked to with confidence. The Queen saw Ly G. yesterday, & was very gracious, & expressed herself in a friendly way towards Ld G. If anything goes wrong it will be from their own blunders.

March 4th. B. St.

The Kerry marriage is fixed for 18th.[1] By that they will get Holy week & Easter for their honey at Bowood. Ld L. has behaved very handsomely about settlements & allowance. I am glad the world praise him now, as they did, perhaps with reason, censure the delay about the marriage unmercifully. Lady Duncannon is very ill, so enfeebled by fever & cough, that one cannot but fear that the worst

---

[1] Lord Kerry, the Lansdownes' eldest son, married Lady Augusta Lavinia, daughter of John, Viscount Duncannon, later 4th Earl of Bessborough. Lady Duncannon, who died later in the month, was a daughter of 10th Earl of Westmorland by his 1st wife.

is fast approaching. It will be a dreadful blow to D., who is not well prepared for such a loss, being naturally of a sanguine temper.

I have not been well enough to go even *once* to Psse Lieven's Wednesdays, Ly Grey's Thursdays, Dsse Dino's Fridays, or Mrs Baring's Saturdays : yet I want to make an effort for one if I can. London is reckoned very agreable, & some young beauties are approved, Miss Harcourt, Ly E. Vernon's daughter, and a dozen more—Tant bien que mal, but what pleases in a great town, Novelty. I am sorry there has been a fracas between Ly Keith & Mrs Dawson.[1] It was about Sunday parties. One will not go out on that day ; the other receives all the town. But Mrs D., instead of being in a *sober minded* state of religious abstraction, which are the phrases used upon those occasions by persons who withdraw from society, she opened her doors & attracted Ly Keith's guests, & to a degree spoilt her soirées. I daresay, like most squabbles, they are both in the wrong ; one in doing the thing, the other in her mode of discussing it ; but I am sorry, as I like both very much, and abominate hearing of tracasseries. Ld Westmorland has quite got over the bad effects of swallowing laudanum instead of a cough draught. The stomach pump saved him, & a vigorous constitution.

11th March, [1834].

. . . Ly Lansdowne is much troubled & alarmed at a distressing double vision in one of her eyes, which prevents her from seeing distinctly. She is not a nervous person, or one like me giving in too readily to a dismal state of things. Therefore, she is of course more readily listened to than another. I am very sincerely sorry, as she is full of estimable, useful qualities, & very necessary in her family. Ld L. gives Kerry £3,000 pr am.[2] Unluckily they have taken a house this year to be near Ly Duncannon in Cavendish Square ; but probably next year a portion of L.H. may be fitted up separately for them, which would be comfortable for all parties, as they have hitherto been a family of love.

What an unlucky country is Spain from the libertinage of its Queens. The present is conducting herself so madly, from a violent passion she has conceived for a very mauvais sujet, that it brings the

[1] Mrs. Dawson-Damer (*see ante,* p. 91).

[2] Lady Holland wrote on March 18 : " Today is Kerry's wedding. I hope Ly D. will go through it well. She is in a sad weak state, totally unfit for any exertion. So the ceremony was to be in her own apartment : consequently limited to the very immediates of the family."

cause of her daughter into jeopardy.[1] The sober part of the community are disgusted at the effrontery of the Regent, tho', if she conducted herself decently in public, would wink at private frailties. Here we are going wild about the better observance of the Sabbath. It is proposed to shut up the Parks, & put barriers across the streets to prevent the passage of carriages. You would be astonished at the numbers who are inclined to give ear to this proposition. It is strange that people should meddle with the opinions & conduct of others upon religious matters ; but so it has been & ever will be.

10th, 11th April. 1834. Hd H.

... We go to town tomorrow. Parlt begins on Monday, & there will be important, if not anxious questions discussed. This cold weather also makes it agreable ; for altho' the house is very warm, & indeed the drawing room too much so, yet people cannot drop in so readily of evenings as in London ; or can I, if I have a fancy, go out for an hour. M. de Talleyrand grows thin, & looks wretched since the news of Broglie's resignation : tho' he is now more satisfied, as there is every assurance & probability that the same line of policy that directed the conseils of the French Cabinet for these last 18 months will be persevered in. Pozzo [2] is horridly mortified that his friend Molé was not appointed. Much as I like Molé personally, it would have been the worst nomination possible ; as he is so decidedly *Russian*, & we should not long have been on good terms with France. Confidence is a plant of very slow growth ; & it will require great steadiness & straight forward conduct in the French Cabinet to inspire the necessary conviction of bonne foi. The probity, truth & character of Broglie altogether made everybody sure that all was *fair*, as long as he remained in power. He is so much regretted, that I do not think it unlikely both Chambers & King may get him back in the fulness of time, which would be a great blessing to Europe. The Russians are baffled in hoping to sow discord between the two countries, & now have recourse to fifty little stories & tracasseries de société. One is that Ld P. is jealous of Talleyrand, which has produced a coolness. This is false : at least they are on such terms of intimacy

---

[1] Marie Christina of Naples, 4th wife of Ferdinand VII, who, as the result of persuading her late husband to repeal the Salic Law, was ruling as Regent for her infant daughter Isabella II, to the detriment of the claims of Ferdinand's brother, Don Carlos.

[2] Count Carlo Andrea Pozzo di Borgo (1764-1842), a native of Corsica, who entered diplomacy in Russia in 1804, and was Russian Ambassador in Paris 1814-35, and London 1835-9. Thiers had succeeded the Duc de Broglie.

that T. wanted to go to Broadlands ; & the other frankly told him he went solely for visiting his constituents, & should be en garçon not sleeping regularly at home. This sort of franchise is very unlike coolness.

May 6.

The debate last night went off in favor of Govt ; so they have fresh breathing time till the next pinch. I do not foresee any immediately yet.[1] Lady Mulgrave, who is in charming health & looks, was much diverted by the manners of the Jamaica magnates at dinner one day at the Govt House. A great man asked if he should have the pleasure of *wining* with her. She knowing they liked rum or brandy, desired him to drink what he preferred, but she drank port. He gallantly replied, " I will take your liquor, Madam."

13th May. 1834.

. . . We are to dine today, a family congregation, at my Mother's to meet Mrs Pellew. Papa cannot join us till $\frac{1}{2}$ past 8 ; but that is perhaps better, as the space is small & the guests numerous. I am but poorly for all these matters, as it rather puts me out. However, it is *right*, so must be done ; & Mrs Pellew seems very clever & disposed to like us, which is a good thing. The *beauty* at the Queen's Ball was Miss Louisa Paget, Sir Arthur's daughter. Miss Byron is reckoned a very ordinary young lady ; none of the paternal sparkle.

23d May. B. St.

We came here for 2 nights, partly for H. of Lds, & besides to see a play, & dine at Ld Grey's. The play was admirably acted, the last part of *Henry IVth*. Little as I like Macready, it must be admitted that his acting in the scene where the Prince of Wales takes the Crown is excellent. Farren's Shallow & Dowton's Falstaff were also very good. The Coronation show was tedious, too much so for endurance. Papa came from Lords in time to accompany me. The event of the day is the recall of the Lievens, which seems to afflict most people. The Emperor had long determined in his own mind to have Lieven as Governor to his son.[2] But it was hoped the fancy had gone by ;

---

[1] Lady Holland wrote on May 2 : " On Monday comes on the question upon Pensions, the result of which is very doubtful, & may cause the dissolution of this Govt. It is hardly an equal bet, as people are inflamed & wrongheaded."

[2] Later Alexander II (1818–81).

& Mde de Lieven returned in great spirits from Russia fancying all was safe. But those barbarian Princes have a volonté futé ; & it is now come upon them like a clap of thunder. She is more wretched than can well be imagined. M. de Medem [1] is reckoned an able man. He belongs to Pozzo's Embassy, and is a Courlandais related to Mde de Dino. He left Paris on the 9th May for instructions, so may be here in a month. It will be a sad loss to Society. Esterhazy is also very much missed, but he will return for another year in October.

But what is more important than these foreign concerns are those *here*, which look very gloomy ; & we are in the moment of the crisis. It is a long story, but all arises out of Ld John's unlucky declaration on the Irish Appropriation of Tithe, which Lambton underhand has worked up with some members of Parlt, in order to force Govt prematurely to do *that* which perhaps a little time might otherwise accomplish. In short, I believe the whole fabric is crumbling, which is most annoying, especially as it is so thoroughly absurd & unnecessary. Lambton & a parti du mouvement will be uppermost. The Tories are utterly out of the question, as all this is levelled against the possibility of their winning, happen what may. The less you talk of these matters the better. The question will be settled by tomorrow ; but my hopes are slender of a good termination. It is all a H. of C. affair ; nothing to do with Lords, King, or even Ld Grey.

Charles Greville thus describes the position of the Ministry as mentioned above (III, 33) May 11 : " A little breeze was stirred up by Johnny Russell, making a declaration without any necessity, that he was unable to agree to the *appropriation* of Irish Church Property, and that he might feel obliged to separate from his friends upon it. This disgusted his colleagues, and a Cabinet sat to decide whether he should go out or not, and they very unwisely settled that he should not stir." But by May 27, the breeze had become a gale (p. 38), " There is the devil to pay with the Government, which is on the very brink of dissolution : Stanley and Graham standing up against the majority of the Cabinet with regard to the Appropriation Clause."

10th June, [1834]. [Holland House.]

I have been very negligent in not writing, but really not having been very well : & also being extremely annoyed at passing events,

[1] Comte de Medem, 1st Secretary of the Russian Legation in Paris, 1835–44. Lady Holland wrote in September : " Cte Medem dined here on Sunday. He is bright & quick, & pleases Ld Palmerston by his mode of doing business. His health is but indifferent, & his personal charms very limited, but he will be high in his career, as he takes pains, has means, & is full of ambition."

I had not spirits. Well, it is over & done, & the wisest thing now is to make the best of a sorry affair ; but our four defaulters [1] carry off the polish & splendor of the Cabinet, and to me personally are an irreparable loss, as I was in great habits of intimacy with three of them & always in admiration of Stanley. As nothing is *sure* till done, do not mention that Abercromby most probably will tomorrow kiss hands for the Mint & a seat in the Cabinet ; it is quite a profound secret. The unpopularity of Ld A.'s appointment to the Admiralty beggars description from foes & friends, perhaps even more among the latter, tho' the cry is universal ; & no one exactly knows why it was done, as he was so well before, & this change may expose the Govt to defend his pension in H. of C. In short, there is no common sense in it. Crusty [2] will be particularly popular, especially in H. of C., where he carries great weight from the influence of his private character, & has considerable following. There have been some unlucky mal-entendus about Ld Mulgrave, who perhaps put too high an estimate upon himself ; yet he was entitled to much, for having done so well in his Govt. We are almost constantly here, only sleeping occasionally in town for dinners, which however are but rare.

20th June, [1834]. Hd H.

. . . The political horizon is murky ; the Tories, excessively elated by their success at Oxford,[3] ready to plunge all into confusion to expel this Govt. The high flyers, such as D. Newcastle, Lds Winchelsea, Londonderry, Wynford, etc., are for a motion to remove Ministers. The D. of W., with his accustomed craft & discretion by pretending to acquiesce, has taken the business *out* of their hands, pretending he will do it in a manner more consistent with the forms of the House, but in fact to prevent any such headlong mischief. In the Commons all goes on à vau l'eau. *There* as yet Ministers have nothing to apprehend. The admission of Abercromby into Govt has given them strength, as he has *opinion* & following in his favor in the House. I cannot say how much Ld Mulgrave's conduct vexes me, greatly for his own sake. He is really too high for his pretensions, nothing

[1] Stanley, Graham, Richmond and Ripon. Lansdowne and Spring-Rice shared their views. The Government was reconstituted, Lord Auckland taking the Admiralty ; Rice the Colonial office ; Lord Carlisle, Lord Privy Seal. Lord Grey was with difficulty restrained from resignation.

[2] Abercromby's nickname.

[3] The Duke of Wellington was installed as Chancellor of Oxford University on June 10.

under a Cabinet place, no mission under an Embassy ! He is a quick, dexterous speaker, & would be useful in Lords : besides for himself he is so poor, that any office would be of value. I fear we shall lose a very valuable, useful man in Ld Clanricarde, who is mortified at not having been promoted at these openings, especially for the Post Office. The wags say Ld Grey sent to Crauford's for a brace of Dandies, & got Lds Conyngham & Byng ; but they are there for their *uncles'* merits.

The King has notified his intention of dining here immediately after the Queen's departure, which now stands for the 4th July.[1] All the King's sisters are annoyed at the Queen's going ; but he is determined not to deprive her of so much pleasure. He is always considerate & good natured for others. He is remarkably well in health & spirits, I hear. Kiss Augusta for me.

27th June. 1834. [Old Burlington Street.]

. . . We slept here last night, as we had to dine in town ; & this morning Ld Hd is going to the King. Our dinner was very agreable yesterday at the Ladies Fitzpatricks'. Papa's foot has cured itself, in the marvellous way you used to describe of chalkstones. The Govt are going on very well. *A crisis* was expected last Monday in Commons, but nothing came of it. Peel has now decidedly accepted the office of Leader of the Tories. He had always hung back ; but some say his acquiescence was quickened by an apprehension of Stanley getting influence among them to his disadvantage. But I believe better of Stanley, & hope he will soon again be in our ranks. You are wrong about Ld Durham ; nobody of weight wants him. He has just Paul Methuen & Mr Stanley,[2] the husband of Miss Dillon, & some of the Radical press, which he pays highly & writes in.

Old Jekyll has not, with all his infirmities, lost the knacks of punning. At the dinner the other day, he asked for some *Cabinet pudding,* saying, " I have not tasted any since they put *Rice* into it." I believe in my last I mentioned the marriage of young Ellice [3] with Miss Balfour. It sprung out of the Highland parties last year. She is a near relation of the Dss of Bedford ; her mother was a Fordyce. She is a buxom, nice young Scotchwoman. They are all good natured, & are to live in town with Ellice senior.

[1] The Queen went to Germany on a visit.
[2] Edward John, created Baron Eddisbury in 1848, later 2nd Lord Stanley of Alderley (1802–69).
[3] (1810–80), son of Edward (" Bear ") Ellice.

Edward John Littleton (later Baron Hatherton) was Irish Secretary at this time. His negotiations with O'Connell were much called in questions at the time, as with the Lord-Lieutenant, Lord Wellesley, he seems to have given assurances, which he could not carry out. This was the direct reason for the fall of the Government, for Lord Althorp resigned the Chancellorship of the Exchequer and Leadership of the Commons : and Lord Grey at once followed suit. The King asked Lord Melbourne (W. Lamb.) to form a Coalition Government, but this was impossible, so a patched up Whig Government resulted.

4th July, 1834.

Did I mention that the Dss Countess [1] has put forward among the ladies a subscription for a bracelet to present to Psse Lieven as a token of their regard & regret at her absence ? This by bad management has been made so extensive, to secure money, that several ladies have had the gratification not only of saving their money, but of being impertinent in refusing. It is rather hard upon Mde L. to expose her to have a pert thing said by Mrs Baring !

11th July.

Your father's letter must have prepared your mind for the *crash*, which is over. The Ministry is dissolved, & all are out. It is a great blow, public & private. So are we all constituted, that the latter makes one feel more immediately the event. To us, who could hardly keep afloat, the loss of *upwards* of £3000 a year is calamitous indeed. Besides, I grieve at the privation of occupation & much amusement to your father, who enjoyed it much, & who, poor fellow, from his infirmities is deprived of many pleasures. The notion of a Coalition Govt is utterly rejected ; & indeed, the truth is a communication is already made to D. of W., Peel & Stanley— how far the latter may accept is doubtful. But *all* the present are *out*.

July 25th. [Old Burlington St.]

. . . All these political changes have made me very unhappy. Nothing could have induced yr Father to have remained in this mutilated Govt, but that it is a legacy of Ld Grey's made & urged by him. The King when he saw Ld Melbourne told him that it was by the advice & at the suggestion of Ld G. that he applied to *him* ; & you will read with painful interest Ld G.'s speech upon its formation in H. of Lords how much he approved. The Tories are endeavouring

---

[1] Elizabeth, Countess of Sutherland in her own right, married George, 2nd Marquis of Stafford, created Duke of Sutherland in 1833, the year of his death.

to sow discontent in the Grey family, by extolling him & abusing his former colleagues ; but this is such a gross trick that it must defeat itself. However a Whig Govt without Ld G. at its head seems impossible to last long or be reputable ; nor can I or will I, believe the curtain is dropped over him. When he complained of the arduous duties last year & wanted to throw it up, Ld Hd & others proposed that he should make over the laborious part to Ld Althorp, & reserve the *power & communication* with the King himself, & only hold some office of dignity without labor. This would have been the best, & given his friends the advantage of his talents & great powers. It was what Lord Chatham did when he was overcome by the gout.

29th *July*, [1834. Holland House.]

. . . You see all matters are adjusted, & this Govt is entirely Ld Grey's. *All* that has been done is in compliance with his wishes. The P. Seal was first offered to Ld Dacre, who from health declined it ; & now it is given to Ld Mulgrave, & the blue ribband to the D. of Grafton. In short, this Govt is Ld Grey's legacy. There is a threat from O'Connell which rather alarms, it being no less than his intention of fighting every clause in the Poor Law Bill, which would extend the session 8 weeks longer. What will become of people, nobody knows ; as half seem already completely knocked up by the fatigue. Poor Ld Hd was from 12 to 1 in H. of Lords, 13 hours ! His foot, which he exerted too much, is already much the worse for the exertion.

Ld Palmerston laughs at being the confidant of so many diplomats. His last confidence is from Sir A. Malet,[1] who wants promotion to enable him to marry a nice young woman, a friend of ours, & who has the support of the most active of men in the universe. The Chancellor has fallen desperately in love with Mrs Petre ; there are perpetual junkets & dinners. She seems flattered.

August 1st.

. . . Our Royal dinner went off admirably.[2] King well & cheerful. Ld & Ly Grey very much sought by the King, & warmly invited with all their family to Windsor next Monday. Yesterday we had a very dismal dinner, the last of the Lievens. She was so overcome, that it was painful, & he is also as low. They embark at daybreak today, or rather tomorrow. The dinner was at Ld Palmerston's.

[1] Sir Alexander Malet, 2nd Bart. (1800-86). He married Lord Brougham's step-daughter, Mary Anne Spalding, in 1834.
[2] On July 30.

It is not pleasant either the approaching departure of Talleyrand, tho'
he calls it but a congé for 3 months ; yet his age & the chance of
events makes it always disagreable to see him go, & I never feel quite
sure how she [1] may fancy things.

Saturday, August 2, 1834.

Your remark is very just & obvious, that it would have been better
for Govt to have had the grace of doing themselves what O'Connell
has compelled ; but I am told it is for better, but neither believing
nor understanding the *why*, I cannot explain.   The majority yesterday
was tremendous against Dissenters. [2]   We all regret Ld G.'s absence,
as it was a measure he had brought in.   Alas ! things are bad in that
quarter, & tho' very painful do not surprize me.   Indeed, I always
said it, the want of occupation works ; & living in D. St with all the
outline of office, yet not the substance, is not bearable.   I know my
man, & a little of human nature.   Ld G. is not a reading man, &
what tastes he had for sporting he has outlived.   He is so constituted
that he ought to have lived & died in harness, or, as he was formerly,
hourly expecting the trammels ; but now from his *hasty* decision &
previous morbid language he has dropped the curtain, & the last
comfort in Pandora's box is withdrawn.   I protest to you I love him
so much that it pains me to contemplate the barren, dry prospect
for him of the future.   For even if *hope* lurked in any quarter, it would
impair the hitherto pure dignity of his reputation, as it could only be
realized by changing his friends.   I can assure you, without any
exaggeration, I feel quite grieved & wounded at the present state
of things for his sake, as it will lower him in public estimation
very greatly ; & when I used to teaze him so much not to hold
the silly language of being *tired & worn out*, it was chiefly for his
sake, foreseeing what was probable.   Ly G. is very, very miserable,
but really does not betray so much anger & soreness.   His health is
perfect, & his faculties as bright & powerful as ever.

11th August.

Some of the Dandies such as Lds Chesterfield, Worcester, Wilton,
Mr Smith (Carrington), & some penniless ones, yesterday gave a
fête at Craven Cottage to the fine ladies.   The local is very small
& bad : the access so difficult, that those foolish men *bought* a field

[1] Duchesse de Dino.
[2] The Dissenters Bill was thrown out on August 1, by 187 to 85.

for space to turn the carriages in. There was a dinner, a concert, Grisi, Lablache & all the great singers, bands of Bohemian & Hungarian minstrels, a ball, &, splendid fireworks on the river. It will cost *immensely*, & from the specimen I had of those who had been there, gave little or no pleasure.

3d October.

Dsse Dino writes from Valençay that the London fogs even agree better with her health than the brilliant suns of Touraine & Valençay. From all I hear, it seems she is desirous of inhaling this climate again ; but the Duc d'Orléans has proposed a visit to Valençay, which will retard their quitting it till November. Talleyrand complains much of the feebleness of his legs, which have encreased upon him this last year. He writes in a letter to Ld Hd today, that he is trying baths of hot water with Spirits of Wine, but that as yet they have not done him good nor harm. Some advise the use of baths made of strong bouillon of meat. I shall suggest this to him.

Lord Althorp's elevation to the Upper House gave the King a chance for a change of Government, for which he had been waiting. The Ministry was summarily dismissed, but not without consultation with Melbourne, who advised Lord John Russell for the Leadership of the Commons. This was refused ; and Wellington was summoned, who recommended that Peel should form a Government. The latter, however, was on holiday in Italy. He hurried home, formed a weak Ministry, and dissolved Parliament ; whereby the Tory majority was increased, but in insufficient numbers to stave off small defeats. The task became more and more hopeless as the spring went on ; and a new series of sets-back on Irish Church matters made resignation necessary early in April.

14th November, [1834].

. . . Your father will tell you all about the present dilemma occasioned by the death of Lord Spencer, & the consequent removal of Lord Althorp from the lead in the H. of Commons. Never was there a more severe blow inflicted on a Govt than his loss. His truth, probity, & the universal conviction in every man's mind that he was sincere & dealing fairly, gave him weight & power quite unexampled in political annals. He was the best son, husband, master that ever existed, without ostentation, but remarkable for his simplicity of manners.

21st November, 1834. " Papa's Birthday."

I cannot but feel in all this sad overthrow that we are in luck in
not having a great house at Brighton at a high rent, & amidst a nest
of violent high flying Tories. But hélas ! we are encumbered by
one in town for a *long session* ; & the shabby man will not let me
return to our former mode of only having it till Easter.

The dismissal of the Ministers has been most offensive in the mode,
so abrupt, so unlike anything gentlemanlike. To those who had
very active affairs, it was really most inconvenient. Ld Palmerston
sat up the whole of Sunday night to arrange in the office his public
& private papers, to be ready to obey the peremptory order of sur-
rendering his Seal at two o'clock on Monday. As soon as Lady
Jersey heard the news, she drank the King's health, " *Now* he has
behaved like a gentleman." However, at present she is said to be
very indignant at not going to Ireland, or if at home in the Cabinet,
angry at only the offer of Ld Steward.

4th December, 1834.

. . . Rogers has been staying with us some time. He is returned
from his Northern tour in excellent health, temper & spirits. However it is evident he rejoices at the absence of the red boxes. The
sight of them always produced a fit of grievous spleen.[1]

23rd January, 1835.

. . . The world are full of the report which gains ground in belief
of the grossesse of the Queen. Alvanley has made a coarse joke but
very expressive of the general opinion, " Oh ! Lord ! *Howe* wonderful are thy ways." It is an unlucky event should it be realised, as it
would have been a happy one had it occurred 10 years ago. But
the prospect of a long minority with such a Regent is not promising
for the Country.

Young Canning [2] is just returned from Petersburgh. He travelled
rapidly, but unfortunately not in time to stand for the boro' that had
solicited him. He is a fine young man, with considerable abilities
& quickness, & probably will distinguish himself in public life when
he has an opportunity of so doing.

[1] Elsewhere Lady Holland spoke of, " Rogers, who is talking most pleasantly
& dislikes one writing."

[2] Charles John Canning (1812–62), son of George Canning, and later Viscount
and Earl Canning. He was elected M.P. in 1836.

March 24th. B. St.

. . . There has been a buzz this month of Ld John's [Russell] marriage ; but it now seems to assume a serious aspect since the arrival of the Morleys. It is to Lady Ribblesdale,[1] a very pretty widow of 27 years old with *four* children. She is reckoned good natured, & her size is more suitable than Emily Hardy's to the stature of her prétendu. She is the sister of Mr Lister, & is living with them under the same roof with Lady Morley at Kent House ; so you may suppose there has been no slackness in reopening the business. John's friends regret his marrying at all ; his habits of a batchelor being so confirmed that they think he will be unhappy. However the lady, with the exception of the four children, is very well, only she is extremely poor.

Ld Sefton has had a very severe struggle for life. He is now safe & able to move : but he had for eight days & nights a dreadful hiccup. He was much pleased with Dr Chambers. He & Halford seem to have done most skilfully.

Friday, 24th April, [1835]. Holland House.

Your Papa is very busy indeed. He is at one office or the other every day, there being a Committee of the Cabinet upon Corporations, Tithes, etc. He is very well, & now fairly installed, having kissed hands yesterday for the Seals ; [2] for as long as it lasts, it is very good ; but I am anything but sanguine, as the first opportunity a dog's trick will be played. The example of last November takes away all confidence.

It is most satisfactory to Lord Palmerston to find that all the dispatches to foreign Powers by the D. of W. are entirely founded upon his policy, & that there are frequent & specific references made to his opinion for a basis. I have hardly seen him since he was fairly installed, & beyond his giving your Papa the précis writership for a son of Ld Suffolk's, do not know anything of his arrangements. Ld Hd fancies from his silence about you that he has written, but I have no guess upon the subject, or even if your wish is to be promoted or employed.

---

[1] Adelaide Lister (1806–38), daughter of Thomas Lister, of Armitage Park, married, in 1826, Thomas, 2nd Lord Ribblesdale, who died 6 years later.
[2] Lord Holland had returned to his former post at the Duchy of Lancaster. Palmerston again took the Foreign Office.

Hd H. *May 8th ?*

You probably have not heard of a severe act of authority in the Emperor, who, on account of Psse Lieven's illness & grief upon the death of her sons, quitted Petersburgh for Berlin. He allowed Lieven to accompany her to the *gates* of Berlin, but forbad his entering the town & ordered him to return straight without delay to Petersburgh ! What tyranny & real cruelty.

With the Whigs again in the saddle, Henry Fox's position in diplomacy again became stabilized, and at the end of June he was directed to Vienna by Lord Palmerston. Sir Frederick Lamb, the Ambassador there, was absent in England, ill, so Fox on arrival found himself Chargé d'Affaires.

28th July, [1835].

. . . Mde de Lieven's friends are all dissuading her from executing her present project of coming to England, & leading a life des *châteaux* among her friends, Howick the first. I like her, therefore hope for her own sake she will not come, as it would only vex & mortify her. She cannot bear the original scheme of Italy ; so it will probably end in her establishing herself at Paris, with trips to Berlin ; for I hear she will not be a welcome visitor where *you* are. With all my partiality for her, one must admit she did the greatest mischief here. You would be astonished to find the great difference of language held by the C. Diplomatique, to what it was when she was prompting & urging them to really *misbehave*, Esterhazy & his Secy excepted. They both acted thoroughly well & like gentlemen. The latter, *Hummilauer*, we see often. He is a very sensible, upright man ; & pleasant conversation, well informed upon history, etc. Esterhazy, since his sister's departure, has been rambling over the country.

The steam carriage will, I am afraid, succeed. It goes down this road to Reading & Marlborough in an incredibly short time, & back again. The rate is 16, 17 miles an hour !

14th August.

I am still full of curiosity & expectation of hearing Augusta is arrived. I shall begin to tremble if she delays, as the Cholera seems gaining fast. Many persons have their doubts upon going abroad. Even Ld Hertford is full of apprehension ; & the Sutherlands also waver. Ly Carlisle is so very nervous & averse to taking any step, that it would not surprize me if she did not even attempt Paris. Pozzo has taken a house at Tonbridge for his niece, & will hover

between it & London. He is almost a suppléant for Talleyrand, as
he often comes at night & stays sociably long. He is delightful when
il s'y donne, which is often ; & he has no sort of restraint upon his
conversation. He has seen & knows so much. He is not of your
opinion about society at Vienna, which he calls quite a family. The
women are charming ; but the men go too early into the army to
know much that is not military. But there are exceptions ; & I have
known them in Merveldt, Cluny, Clairfayt & de Ligne.

Hd H. *Michaelmas Day, 29th September*, [1835].

Ld Melbourne is staying here a few days : very happy, cheerful &
agreable. His conversation is pleasant, rich in matter & full of genius
& originality. Frederick [Lamb] is much better. A letter today
from Panshanger, where he is, reports him so greatly improved that
he contemplates setting off to Vienna the middle of October ; but
he is liable to gouty relapses, so that till he is off, it must be doubtful.

Last night the Duc de Nemours,[1] most graciously, accompanied
by Sebastiani, came here. He is a pleasing stripling, talks well &
shews that he is well educated ; his smile is very agreable. He goes
tomorrow to Ramsgate to meet his sister & Leopold, who are to
make a visit to the Dss of Kent, but *they* do not proceed further.
The tour of the Princesses [2] in England has been successful, & must
have been flattering. Of all the places they visited, their reception
at Bishopsthorpe was said to be the most agreable. Harewood was
dull & ill-managed. The singing of Mother & Daughter was execrably
inharmonious, but of course was highly lauded. Their progress
through the country gave umbrage to a higher power. Nothing
can be worse than the terms on which their Courts are together.
Yet I believe the rising sun is more to blame in the contest than the
elders. But I know little, indeed nothing, of their tracasseries, but
what appears before the public.

Hd H. *1st December*, [1835].

This dreadful catastrophe at Hatfield drives everything out of one's
mind. The poor old lady fell a victim to her wilfulness.[3] She never

---

[1] Louis Philippe's 2nd son (1814–96). After his father's abdication in 1848,
he lived in England until 1870. His sister, Princesse Louise Marie (1812–50)
married King Leopold in 1832.

[2] Princess Victoria and her Mother.

[3] Emily Mary, Dowager-Marchioness of Salisbury, widow of James, 1st
Marquis, and daughter of Wills, 1st Marquis of Downshire.

allowed any of her attendants to be with her. She had the habit of perpetually dropping asleep, & had been on fire frequently. No vestige of her, nor her diamonds have been found. Ld S. was always an excellent son, & as careful as she would allow him. Fortunately the magnificent old structure is not destroyed. MSS., Library & State rooms are all safe ; offices & bedrooms are burnt. But the injury is not so great as we dreaded, except in the loss of the poor old lady, which is very horrible.

" Nutshell." [1] *8th December,* [1835. To Lady Augusta Fox].

I am not sure whether the daughter of Lady Glengall, who is going to be married to the great rich Mr Talbot, of Wales, is Henry's favorite.[2] At all events she is a very captivating person ; as her prétendu says, but for the interference of Lady Glengall, he should have proposed four years ago, but he abominates *her*. So it is a triumph of the little God over what seemed an insuperable obstacle, the mother.

My poor old friend, Mr Whishaw, is declining fast. His sight fails, & he is so scrupulous about his duties that he will not remain eight months longer in his office, as *that* period would qualify him for the full pension of retreat. He is a high minded, excellent man ; but this scruple is beyond the mark. Lady Jersey is said to have tired the whole party at the Pavilion. She never quitted the King's side,[3] & talked him into snoring : besides boring him, by preventing his talking—which he likes to do himself—a good deal.

Sir Chas Greville has a good legacy & house from Mr Churchill.[4] All the Ladies Greville have £3,000 à faire, & poor Lady Warwick, who nursed & tended him for years, not a token, merely because she had no Greville blood in her veins. Poodle Byng has £500. He died very rich, & was a good natured miser : but has left nothing to any who have not Churchill or Greville blood.

[1] Lady Holland's mother, Lady Affleck, had died in February, leaving to her daughter the tiny house in South Street where she lived.

[2] Charlotte Butler, daughter of 1st Earl of Glengall and his wife Emily Jefferys, of Castle Blarney, married Christopher Rice-Mansel Talbot, of Margam.

[3] Yet she is reported once to have said, " Why should we have Germans to reign over us ! "

[4] William Churchill, of Henbury, and Hill Street, Berkeley Square, a friend of George IV.

CHAPTER X

1836, 1837, 1838

January 15th, 1836. South St.

. . . The law arrangements are now terminated, and the most important secured by Campbell [1] not being lost to the Govt as Attorney-General; & he is very well satisfied to have his honor saved & a pledge that he is to have the first high judicial post that may become vacant. One cannot but feel pain at Ld Brougham being so completely put on the shelf; but it was impossible to do otherwise. The King would not have acquiesced; & the whole country would have supported His Majesty in his refusal, for it is but too true that every man's hand is up against him. There are few to whom he has not broken his promise, & then quarrelled with them. In short, the total want of *truth* has been his ruin. Sir Samuel Romilly above 20 years ago foretold, in spite of all his personal affection & high opinion of his great powers, that he would fail from that defect. He inspires no man with confidence. He is at present with his venerable, remarkable mother in Westmorland, his health greatly improving. [2] The Malets are in town with Ly B. They dine here today, & embark tomorrow for Rotterdam. She is, as you may remember, somewhat of a favorite of mine; & she fancies, perhaps not without truth, that I am the means of their being better off in their destination, as they neither of them had any fancy for Italy.

Ld Melbourne is laid up with the gout. Halford has given him colchicum to patch him up to go to the Council at Brighton tomorrow. He is now in bed, & I think it will be rather hazardous; but he must finish all the legal appointments directly, as the business in the Courts, for want of a Lord Chancellor, has accumulated prodigiously, much to the detriment of the suitors.

---

[1] John Campbell (1779–1861), later Lord Chief Justice, Lord Chancellor and Baron Campbell. His wife was created Baroness Stratheden in 1836. Lord Melbourne did not offer Lord Brougham the Great Seal, which was placed in Commission.

[2] Lady Holland wrote at the end of December, 1828: " He is so fond of his mother that he never lets an opportunity of seeing her pass . . . Merely to see the good old lady, he renounces Althorp, Bowood and various other festive scenes."

Prince Adam Czartoryski brought with him to England a collection of copies of Russian official papers, letters sent by Russian agents abroad from time to time to Warsaw for the Viceroy of Poland, the Grand-Duke Constantine. They had fallen into the hands of the Poles there during the insurrection of 1830. They were published by David Urquhart (1805–77), Secretary of Embassy at Constantinople, in the *Portfolio*, a periodical devoted to diplomatic affairs which only lasted for a few years.

2d February, 1836.

. . . You will find the *Portfolios* a curious & valuable possession. Of the authenticity of the documents nobody entertains a doubt ; even Pozzo feebly says there may be interpolations. His last despatch will nettle Metternich, but all his despatches shew great ability & cleverness. The universal opinion is that Mr U. is the Editor, altho' he has quite publicly denied it in a newspaper. It is a mysterious affair, in which many minds of different nations are concerned. Poor Pozzo ! He is so wretched, vexed, mortified & bored. He says he has *dégringolé* five years since he has been at this Embassy. It is generally thought his Court do not write to him ; or is he by any of his colleagues put au courant of the projects or proceedings of the Cabinet he nominally represents. His loss of favor is ascribed to two causes : partly the hatred & envy of the real Russian party, but mainly to his continuing in Paris when Charles X left it for St Cloud. Certain it is, the effect of all the Corps Diplomatique remaining Paris was most propitious to the success of Louis Philippe during les trois jours. Pozzo's enemies ascribe his conduct more to the device of keeping the French funds *firm*, in which he has a prodigious interest, than to any desire for the mere peace & welfare of Europe. He frets himself quite ill ; & I, who so much enjoy his society, feel quite unhappy about him. Besides, his *foyer domestique* is not comfortable to him. Sa nièce [1] is a *Crillon*, as proud as Lucifer. When he gives a dinner, it is of 35 covers ! quite odious to the giver & receivers. I do not think he can remain, altho' he is fond of the emoluments of office : indeed, nothing but *that* could have induced him to remain an hour after the slights cast upon him by his Emperor. Sebastiani is in very indifferent health, but better, & very friendly to this country. His wife [2] is the most imbecile person I ever beheld. What do you

[1] From a letter to Lady Holland in 1832, Pozzo's nephew, Charles, had married Mademoiselle de Crillon.

[2] Lady Holland wrote in 1833 : " Sebastiani is to marry Mde Davidoff, Lady Tankerville's sister. She will demolish him."

all say to the Duc of Orléans marrying an Austrian, the daughter of A.-Duke Charles ?   It is a project of Mde de Lieven's & Talleyrand. The French nation have had enough of Archduchesses, so it could not be made palatable to them.   It gives me sincere pleasure to hear of peace & amity between Talleyrand & Flahault ; & even the ladies are reconciled.   Probably this has arisen from the deep affliction of the Flahaults, in which everybody sympathizes.   Poor people ! who more than I can feel the extent of their grief ?   She was her father's darling, tho' he is fond of all his children.   Lady Keith lived at Ampthill during her grossesse, and ascribed to the air & quiet of that place the healthiness of the child, who was never ill till this last fatal fever.

15th July, 1836.

. . . Henry Greville is diverting himself in London, making skilful selections of the music for concerts.   That he made for the enchanting, splendid sight at S[tafford ?] House did great credit to his taste.   The Granvilles are here for a short time.   They spend the best part of their holidays on the Rhine with their two daughters. Our French Ambassador is gone to Paris, not useless, for my old friend from Valençay is coming there ; & Sebastiani may, from his influence with the K., counteract his extremely high Tory principles, at least the principles with him à l'ordre du jour.   Dsse Dino has again been baffled in another matrimonial scheme, one not a little mortifying to her, when she lowered herself to propose for a cadet of the Noailles's ; but the young man would not listen for a moment, on the score of the nice girl being ugly, which however she is not. He is the handsomest man in Paris, Antonin de Noailles.   The marriage would have been very advantageous in point of money to him ; but all T.'s family loathe Me de D. so much that probably that feeling had its weight in the rejection of the proposal.

Owing to the Ambassador's continued absence from Vienna, the Foxes had, with his permission, moved into the Embassy, where they were able to entertain Viennese society with great success.

1st November, [1836].

Your ears ought to have *tingled* last night.   Esterhazy spoke of you in a way most gratifying to parental ears, of your talents, *tacte* & success.   He backed his opinion very strongly by what Metternich thought & said ; who says he never met a person of your age so formed to be distinguished in diplomatic career.[1] So much sense & skill in your intercourse with him. As to Augusta, Esterhazy is full of praise, in which he adds that all Vienna join ; her popularity was universal, that you did quite right to go to the Embassy, where your parties just at the Carnival have been most acceptable & unique for agrémens. In short, the whole account he gave was very pleasing to hear. He is himself looking quite well, but will not, I fear, remain beyond a few months. Indeed he has an almost royal domain to govern in his own property. It is a pity the family, by being Catholics, cannot marry *our Vic.*, as Nicholas [2] is handsome & very pleasing ; & they surely have quarterings enough for any marriage, however royal & high.

2d December. South St.

We had on Tuesday one of the most violent hurricanes I ever saw ; indeed the mischief & accidents are numerous. Ld Lansdowne had a narrow escape, for had the gale been in the night he might have been sorely hurt. An immense stack of chimneys fell upon the roof over his bedchamber & broke through, & shattered one side of the great wall. We had little or no damage at Hd H. ; but some of the fine old trees at Ampthill were uprooted. If you ever read our English newspapers you will find a string of disasters enumerated.

Your friend Lady Blessington has taken Wilberforce's house ! at Knightsbridge, adjoining Ly E. Whitbread's. D'Orsay lives nominally in a small Bijou, for such it is described, adjoining. The house is fitted up with the greatest splendor & good taste. She gives large dinners to literary men, & directs some periodical journals which are being productive. She writes very poor novels, but obtains from them near £1000 pr am. A name will sell any trash.

Hd H. 27th December, 1836.

We came here, where in former times we should have been frozen, but thanks to the skill of the great architect, Mr Barry,[3] the house is really as warm as the most chilly could desire. In the dining room, the staircase you may remember I made from Gréfulhe at Paris, is

---

[1] Lady Holland wrote in July : " Lord Palmerston told me much of what he had heard, adding that Metternich is not a man to make endless flowery compliments."

[2] Prince Nicholas Esterhazy, Prince Paul's eldest son. He married Lady Sarah Villiers, Lady Jersey's daughter, in 1842, and died in 1894.

[3] Sir Charles Barry, R.A. (1795–1860), the architect of the Houses of Parliament.

become quite warm, not from *hot air* but a beautiful method of warming too long to detail, but it is done without vapor or smell of any kind. We have Rogers & his sister, & Russell,[1] who par parenthèse is no longer the inanimate being he was, quite gay & agreable, laughing & merry. He is extremely fond of me ; indeed I deserve it from him, nor is he ever happier than under my wing. We have had large parties, to get over some *proper* dinners, quite a season of *bombance* & good cheer for family & dependants ; but the most valuable, alas ! are absent. Now we grow old & think of you, mingled with sad feelings of how little we have for years & years enjoyed happiness from your presence ; yet still cling to one's own blood, & cannot be indifferent to the future for you.

We had the American Minister & his wife to dinner.[2] She is rather pleasing, but diverted Mr Hallam whom she sat next to at dinner, by lamenting that the people in this country did not speak English, only a bad jargon. In the meantime she is often herself unintelligible from her accent & very strange *locutions*. Ld Palmerston has invited a whole bevy of diplomats to Broadlands, where he means to indulge in 10 days of holidays.

Very few letters in the year 1837 seem to have survived. Owing to Lady Augusta Fox's, and indeed his own, health, they had left Vienna, and were living mostly at Florence : but Fox made two trips to England during that period, once accompanied by his wife. At the time of the following letter, he was on his return to Italy.

16th June, 1837.

Your entertaining account of Versailles is just come, with a pretty portrait of the Dsse of Orléans.[3] It has amused your dear Father very much. He says she looks very much like Gertrude, Dss of Bedford,[4] on her marriage, when George Selwyn called her an *olive branch*. She is so yellow : but she seems shrewd, keen & penetrating ; & your conjecture is not improbable that our friend may find her

---

[1] William, Lord Russell (1809–72), eldest son of Francis, 7th Duke, who succeeded in 1839; and he himself became 8th Duke in 1861. He never married. M.P. for Tavistock 1832–41.

[2] Andrew Stevenson, who remained in England till 1841. He had been Speaker of United States Congress for seven years.

[3] Princess Hélène of Mecklenburg-Schwerin had married Louis Philippe's eldest son, Ferdinand Philippe, Duc d'Orléans (1810–42) in 1836. He was killed in a carriage accident.

[4] Second wife of John, 4th Duke, whom she married in 1737. She had for some years taken charge of Caroline Fox, Lord Holland's sister, after their mother's death in 1778.

too much so, if there should be a struggle for influence over the Duke. I shall be sorry were anything to occur to annoy, or render the séjour of Paris less agreable than it has been hitherto. I should have enjoyed seeing Versailles ! perhaps more in solitude & daylight than in the vast crowds & turmoil of the fête.

We have in an equally illustrious spot, scenes of a very different character. Windsor Castle presents most afflicting views. Nothing can be more painful, so feelingly expressed, than Charles's description of the *genuine* sorrow there. Indeed, the whole public sympathize with the sufferings of the King, and eagerly catch at any glimpse or hope of his amendment. He is much beloved for his bonhomie ; & equally certain that there never was a King who, not *liking* particularly his Ministers, behaved with more honor & fairness than he has invariably done towards them. People can form no expectation of the future ; because nothing is known of the character and dispositions of the young one, nothing wrong, which is always something ; but from the extreme seclusion in which she has been kept, nothing can be known, as she has no friends nor intimate associates, even of her own sex. Charles is very frequently at Windsor, where Ly Mary is attending with the most affectionate tenderness, & her services in the sick chamber very important. The Queen is indefatigable in her attentions, shewing herself very good hearted & affectionate to all around her. Poor woman, her own health is a good deal tried, as she is but a frail subject herself.

28th June, 1837. Hd H.

The poor King expired last night. No doubt you will have had from Charles or your Aunt more particulars than I can give. He is a great loss to *All*, even to the young Queen, who would have derived benefit from a few years more experience. In the meantime, She appeared at her Council this morning, conducted by her Uncles, spoke her Speech, & signed the Declaration. She did it *admirably*, a little nervous at first, but recovered her self-possession. Her voice is described as distinct & pleasing : she marked evidently that she thoroughly understood all she uttered. Your Papa was not able to attend, but will, I trust, in a few days : & will then take the oaths as a Peer & for the Duchy, but of course, as *She* is potential, all the future must be uncertain.

18th July. Hd H.

The dissolution of Parlt, as you may suppose, breaks up London. This is the only busy week, Levée & *first* Drawing Room. Yesterday the Queen won all hearts by her deportment & beautifully delivered Speech. *All* agree in admiring the harmony, sweetness of her voice, & her pleasing manner of reading. The only occasions she had of shewing pretty attentions to yr Father, she did so with consideration for his lameness. He is really much struck by her good sense and conduct upon all important matters.

Monday, [February 5, 1838].

. . . I am much shocked at the sudden death this morning of poor Creevey. His life was useful & valuable to many ; & his wit & agrémens made him a most agreable member of society. To me & mine he has always been friendly. We used to compare notes on our *hearts.* He had an affection very like mine ; & his remedies were the same. It was of *that* he died. This has shocked & frightened me a good deal.

[February 6, 1838.]

. . . Bülow [1] made his first appearance here last night. He amused us by the account of the state of agitation in which he describes the young Princes in Germany to be all in at the prospect of our Coronation. Myriads mean to come to take their chance of winning the favor of the Queen. By his account the Wm Russells [2] lead a singular & recluse life at *Potsdam* ; from whence *she* never stirs, & he only on post days for a few hours to Berlin, always returning at night. The fine son, Hastings, is withdrawn from attending the lectures of a celebrated professor, as the association with the young students might lead him into mischief. Altogether it is very strange. Ld L. & your Papa proposed S. Smith to the Literary Club. He was chosen.

Yesterday previous to the Council, they all waited in an ante-chamber, which was extremely cold with an expiring fire. Your Papa got a chill, which has brought on tenderness in his feet. He is not quite well, so nurses himself to-day. A melancholy catastrophe at Petworth House. Five servants, very chilly, took a large brazier of charcoal into their sleeping room. They were all suffocated. The story rests on the authority of Ld Munster. Our magnanimous, good natured Queen has notified to the Fitzclarences that she will not alter the pensions on the Privy Purse given to them by the late King : that she does not know them, but wishes them well : but takes this

---

[1] Baron Heinrich von Bülow (1792–1846), Prussian Minister in London, 1827–41.

[2] Lord William had become Minister in Berlin.

line out of respect to her Uncle, whom she always loved & respected. This is a large sum for her to pay, £1200 pr am to the sons, £500 to the daughters, nine of them or more I believe. It is very noble & dignified in the little Lady, quite en grande dame.

[17th February, 1838.]

Sydney Smith is going to publish another attack upon the Church Commission.[1] To be sure the *mischief is done* by his former publication ; but he is shutting the door closer to a Bishopric, as the Archbishop would strongly resist any disposition in his favor from the Ministry. But with all his wit & talents, he is woefully deficient in tacte, or as dear Lauderdale calls it *tack*. By the bye, L. complains of his health chiefly from the state of the weather. He & Ld Brougham are the only persons who object to Ld Durham's appointment [2] ; for, strange to say, it is popular even among Whigs & Tories.

Monday. S. St. [19th February, 1838.]

With some peril & much discomfort on account of snow, sleet & hail, we made our way on Saturday to C. Square [Lord Duncannon's]. I was rewarded by the pleasure of seeing O'Connell. He struck me much : his conversation is rich & sensible, his manners perfectly well bred & easy, his deportment, countenance & expression quite admirable. In short, I liked him much, & hope to have him at our own table as soon as a fitting day can be found. Lord Lansdowne will meet him.

Yesterday we had the great Irish *Star*, Sheil,[3] a cheerful, witty little man, enchanted at his office. He goes tonight to Ireland for his re-election, of which he is perfectly secure. We had also the American Stevensons & the Lansdownes. Poor Ly L., is still suffering from the fatigue of standing so long at the Levée, but is not otherwise ill.

In May, Fox was offered the post of Minister at Frankfort, and somewhat unwillingly accepted. He left for the Continent forthwith without his wife, who was to join him later.

26th June, [1838]. Hd H.

The state of the town is curious to behold. It really does not seem large enough to contain the vast congregation of human beings.

---

[1] His attack on the newly appointed Ecclesiastical Commission in *Letters to Archdeacon Singleton.*

[2] As Governor-General of the British Provinces in Canada.

[3] Richard Lalor Sheil (1791–1851), the politician. He had just been appointed Vice-President of Board of Trade.

The streets unquestionably are much too narrow for the enormous mass of carriages ; daily several important points are closed for hours. For instance today when we go to South Street, we can neither get in via Knightsbridge or Piccadilly. Ld Willoughby kindly gave Mr A. & me tickets for his Great Chamberlain's box ; but upon due consideration after some days I returned the tickets. The length of time to sit, & the confinement so complete & hopeless, made me weak with nervous alarm. As at present advised, we shall content ourselves with the show outside & go to the Bd of Trade ; to attain which, however, we must be in the carriage by 8 o'clock, an early hour. There will be a very pretty fair of 3 days in Hyde Park, which delights the people ; & at night in both Parks fireworks, and the whole town illuminated. It is very pleasant to see the general excitement & good humour which prevails everywhere. As yet I have seen few only of the foreigners, as I was not able to go either to Ld Hertford's or Esterhazy's. On Sunday we shall have the Palmellas & Brignollés.[1] The latter I conclude either you or Augusta are acquainted with. Papa well : & is to dine at all the great dinners, such as Strogonoffs' and Soults'. All that one feels anxious about now is the *weather* ; if that should fail, it would be distressing to thousands. Ld Palmerston in the midst of all these arrivals fell sick unluckily, the gout in *both* feet ; most provoking. He was obliged to get Lord Glenelg to present for him : nor has he been able to do much even in seeing them yet.

30th July, [1838].

My dear Augusta,

Henry writes that you wish for letters from England. This is sufficient to induce me to comply, tho' I feel rather inadequate to the task of contributing in the smallest degree to your amusement ; as my health & spirits disqualify me totally from gleaning anything interesting. In all this turmoil of pleasure during the Coronation gaieties, I partook of few. The crowds of carriages at balls terrified & kept me away. That which was most worthy to be seen was Strogonoffs' ; & that night I was more ailing than usual. They were by far the most magnificent in all they did ; indeed the Russians are always splendid. Pozzo told me last night the Strogonoffs had spent £17,000 during their Grand Embassy. I went to the Psse Schwarzen-

---

[1] The Sardinian Envoy-Extraordinary. Prince Strogonoff and Marshal Soult were those from Russia and France respectively.

berg's [1] breakfast at Richmond. It was very perfect, gay & pretty. She is a most captivating woman, clever & pretty. She was much liked here. They are to see the interior : are already off to Ld Cowper's, Woburn, & to end in Scotland at the Duke of Buccleuch's. The town is quite empty ; people are sick of Parlt & pleasure.

In the autumn the Hollands decided upon a trip to Paris, and set off on September 5, accompanied by their physician, Sir Stephen Hammick, and John Allen. Lady Holland, according to her own account, was so shaken by the French pavé that she was forced to take to her couch on arrival. Lady Granville wrote to Lady Carlisle (*Letters*, ii. 270) : " She says it is the fatigue of the journey. I say it is such a dinner as I never saw anybody eat before." The party returned to Holland House on November 5.

[*25th September*, 1838. Paris. *Tuesday*.]

. . . Yesterday I was carried up the stairs to the Louvre. It was a private day, so we could be rolled about & see all at our leisure. The Queen's platform with two chairs opposite were for Papa ; I went in my own, as the motion is easier. The new Galleries are grand & immense. Papa was rather disappointed from all he had heard with the Spanish Collection ; but they delighted me, especially the portraits of the Infantes, male & female, such exact Spanish faces, & the strange baroque attire. The bed chamber of Henry IV, & Anne of Austria's Cabinet, are very interesting & magnificent. What a palace ! I am afraid the honor of being shewn Versailles by its Master is impending. It will very greatly disconcert me if so, as I am become dreadfully nervous again in the mornings, which I was much less during the journey than I am now again. Ld Granville is a close prisoner to his sofa from a fierce boil. This is most vexatious when we are here and he would enjoy so much being with Papa. However we have daily intercourse, & with Mr Aston,[2] who is a very sensible as well as agreable man. Walewski [3] is become editor of a Journal called *Le Messager*, the wags say, La Mensongière. He takes it up as an *industrie* to qualify himself for becoming a French citizen. I hear from England Flahault is still in hopes of bringing about the Shelburne marriage. This I *hear*, but do not know. Certainly, however, he always appeared most eager, perhaps too much so for success.

[1] Count Gregory Schwarzenberg (1770–1857), German Ambassador-Extraordinary.

[2] Arthur Aston, First Secretary in Paris under Lord Granville.

[3] Count Alexandre Florian Walewski (1810–68), illegitimate son of Napoleon and Comtesse Marie Walewska. French Ambassador in London, 1851–5.

[*15th November*, 1838.]

. . . The Lansdownes spent a few days with us, fewer than they intended ; but Ld Melbourne wished to see Ld L. & Papa together, so all my schemes were overset, of his going later & my combining it with St Ann's. So they three set off yesterday to the Castle, & I came to the Nutshell for a little dissipation in the shape of theatres, & a few to dine. I am startled at the thinness of Lord Melbourne. It is too much ; but it may be partly ascribed to the hard riding of those who are the attendants of the Queen. It is also too much for her. She has a small, active, safe, but very fleet horse, nor does she undervalue the last quality or allow it to rust for want of using : the pace at which she returns is tremendous. Ld Palmerston is looking deadly, so pale, thin & haggard : he kills himself by work. He has, however, gained just credit by his Treaties ; even the Tories & the *Times* praise him for his success. He has great abilities & great excellencies of character.

November 21st.

Poor Ld Sefton expired yesterday. He is one of the few cases where release is not to be deplored. . . . But his poor wife I sincerely pity ; her existence was bound up with his. She was but his shadow, leaning upon him for everything. She was an admirable wife & mother.

Ld John [1] is with the 6 children at Cassiobury, still dejected, following to a limited degree his official labors, both as duty & occupation. His strong sense of the first makes him devote many hours to *her* children, as he says they have him only for instruction and principles. I very much fear he will hardly be equal to all the tasks his situation imposes upon him, especially with this view he takes.

The Ministers are all with one exception in town : assemble today at the Cabinet. They have much to discuss. The last accounts from Canada are alarming. Ld Durham [2] has renounced his plan of visiting the U. States, & intended coming home on 1st November in the *Inconstant*. For the joke, it ought to have been the *Pique*. He has made a silly, & for himself, discreditable affair of the whole business, leaving the country in a worse state than he found it.

[1] Lord John Russell's wife died in November. She left two Russell daughters, besides a family by her first husband.

[2] Lord Durham had resigned his post in Canada at the end of 5 months, as the Home Government had refused to ratify his Ordinance for the transportation of rebels.

CHAPTER XI

1839–1840

1st January, 1839.

. . . As the scene of strife approaches people get keen, some dismayed. Certainly the Ministerial prospects are not bright ; but you hate politics, so shall spare you the conjectures. But you must not entirely trust *Galignani* ; for truth it is a very pleasant Journal to handle, but is all on one side of the question. Lady Breadalbane has accepted the office of Lady of the Bedchamber.[1] The Queen is in luck to have such a lovely, graceful, pure person. Her health is not strong ; she cannot stand, but that must be mitigated for her.

I know you think me blindly partial to all that belongs to my oldest, dearest friend Lord Carlisle ; but I think a Court so honored by his two daughters must command respect anywhere. Indeed it does very much from the entourage in general ; and this last appointment adds great lustre.[2] The Normanbys[3] are sorry not to prolong their stay, as this is a very sociable season. They dined again yesterday, & we are to meet them for the last time at Chas Greville's today.

January 8th, 1839. Hd H.

. . . I am surprized that Lord Normanby's brothers are to become Ld Charles & Ld Edmund, etc. ; as that is a perfect disqualification for any profession except army, etc. We have spent five very agreable days here, with society such as is suited to our taste. Last night we had a posse of foreigners, & some very sensible that I like mightily. Sampft & Bülow, both however from the detested country of Germany, and a Werter & a Thün. What you might have liked

---

[1] Eliza, Marchioness of Breadalbane, sister of 10th Earl of Haddington, married the 2nd Marquis in 1821.

[2] The Duchess of Sutherland was Mistress of the Robes, her sister Lady Burlington having just become a Lady of the Bedchamber.

[3] Lord Mulgrave had been created Marquis of Normanby in 1838. He was Lord-Lieutenant of Ireland at this time, but was shortly afterwards transferred to Secretaryship of the Colonies. Lady Holland wrote at the end of February : " Lord Normanby is installed in his new office, rejoicing very naturally at being quit of his Viceregal duties. People laugh good humouredly at his grand manner, which retains a little of the condescending airs of a Royal Deputy. But this will rub off when he is fairly *aux prises* with Ld Brougham & some rough opponents in Parlt."

better was Van de Weyer,[1] who is to be married on 31st. He begged me to negociate that Lord Melbourne & Papa should assist at the ceremony on 31st. He is to live with the rich parents of the lady. The house in Portland Place, which belongs to Lady Barbara,[2] & has often been Ambassadorial residences, is taken for that purpose by Mr Bates, the immensely rich father. Poor little man, his health is not sufficiently established to make one feel quite easy about him. He is very clever, good & popular.

The Queen comes today to town. She is resolved to amuse herself & go often to the theatres. Unluckily the early Italian Opera of last season does not perform ; & she cannot from etiquette go to the only amusing one, the Olympic. Her range is confined to the Old Drury Lane & Covent Garden, but she will go to the Haymarket, which contrary to usage is still open. At D.L. she will see Van Amberg & the wild beasts.

12th *February*.

Macaulay has just been here, looking remarkably after his journey.[3] He was enchanted with Rome & struck with Genoa. Florence, with the exception of the Gallery, was a disappointment.

People are much surprized at the Italian report of P. Albert being the intended King Consort ; probably none more than the Queen, if she hears it. It does not seem that the Coburg connexion would be popular, however winning the young man may be. I hope you like Stockmar ?[4] He is a very sensible, upright man. There was a story of his being less well with Leopold than formerly.

South St. 12th *March*, 1839.

The Court stories must have reached you with their various versions.[5] The truth still lies at the bottom of a well ; as far as my reading of the case, there was originally more folly than malice, some prudery but no malignity. Upon this the Tories have grounded

---

[1] Sylvain Van de Weyer (1802–74), Belgian Minister in England 1831–67. Mr Bates was a member of the firm of Baring.

[2] Ponsonby.

[3] Macaulay had been a member of the Supreme Council of India since 1834.

[4] Baron Stockmar (1787–1863) was King Leopold's secret agent. Originally an army doctor.

[5] Lady Holland here refers to the unfortunate case of Lady Flora Hastings, the Duchess of Kent's Lady of the Bedchamber, which was magnified by lying report into a major scandal. She was daughter of the 1st Marquis of Hastings, and died a few months later. Sir James Clark was the doctor.

very cruel stories disparaging of the Queen's good nature ; whereas on the contrary she has shewn sympathy & tenderness upon the case forced upon her notice. She made a point of Lady Flora appearing with her at chapel & dining constantly at her table. Poor Ly F. is in a dreadful state of health, evidently in an alarming condition. The Doctor seems to be chiefly to blame. He is a vain, presumptuous, meddling man, like most modern medicos, much inclined to meddle with the private concerns of patients, from the days of poor Farquhar down to this day. Ed. Lytton Bulwer has written a long, admirable play called *Richelieu.*[1] It has all the advantages which can be given by the accessories of scenery & costume. It is full of striking passages, many of which are as effective in reading as in the acting. I shall send you the play, *if it is to be had,* for already two editions have been purchased. He has a great power of writing.

Macaulay is plunged deep into his historical work. He takes up the period where Mackintosh left off, with the intention of continuing it down to our own days. He has great abilities & excellent power of selecting his points & arguing them well. A volume will soon appear of Lord Durham's correspondence with the Bishop of Exeter. If the public approve, more will follow. It is doubtful how it may succeed ; tho' there can be no doubt of Ld D.'s wit, eloquence of language, & learning, but perhaps it may be *Caviar to the Multitude.*

March 26th.

Matters here are in a very disjointed condition. Indeed, they are so complicated that the probability of their *righting* again is greatly diminished. The *movement* party are doing all possible mischief ; & tho' there is not the remotest chance of their winning to benefit themselves, yet their malice & activity may overset the Govt, should they withdraw their support on the day of appeal to H. of C., as the loss of their 8 or 10 votes will be felt in the division. I shall extremely regret the overthrow, as the occupation of public affairs has been most advantageous to the health of your Father ; it amuses & occupies his mind & time, the latter especially, as he is from infirmity very much disabled from the common resources of exercise & out of doors amusements—to say nothing of the benefit to our shattered finances. These are not my own gloomy presages ; but unfortunately many of the most sanguine & clear sighted are of the same opinion.

Ld John is a good deal annoyed at the behaviour of some of his

---

[1] Edward George Lytton Bulwer-Lytton (1803-73), created Baron Lytton in 1866. Charles Greville was in a box with Lady Blessington and D'Orsay on the first night, and gives an account of it in his *Memoirs* (IV, 133).

friends in H. of C., besides being in great alarm as to the health of Lady John's eldest daughter, whom it is apprehended has mischief forming in the head. She is a very clever child, remarkably précoce in understanding. Really the old women's maxim, that clever children never live, is too fearfully true. Many examples within my own knowledge justify the belief.

Bülow is really in a very wretched state. He will not see anyone, only waits for the signature of the Treaty. His wife has not, that I hear, stirred a peg to come to England. They say she is a selfish, stubborn person ; being a great heiress she likes to mark her independance.

Good Friday, [*March 29,* 1839. South Street].

. . . The frequent Cabinets have deranged our plans of going one step beyond home, to which we move today. The Lansdownes are also coming, for him to recruit from his long confinement. They have lent their villa at Richmond to Ld John, who will remain there with la petite famille. He is much recovered in spirits. I believe I told you all Mivart's hotels were engaged for the Gd Duke of Russia,[1] so that he may be surrounded by his Governors, Generals, Preceptors, Aides-de-camp, Physicians, etc. It would seem that Ld Durham will not be outdone by the young autocrat, as he has secured the *whole* of the Star and Garter at Richmond, to the exclusion of sundry visitors, and expelled Bülow from his apartment.

The affairs of Canada are very important, that is as connected with the Boundary Question & the Province of Maine, which ought to have been finished 30 years ago. God forbid it should lead to war between the two countries ; but nothing is certain.

2d April. Hd H.

We have the Lansdownes as inmates. He is already better, walking without a stick. She is more cheerful, much relieved from her anxiety of yesterday, as Henry [2] went to join his Yeomanry at Devizes to be in readiness in case the meeting of the Chartists proved tumultuous. On the contrary, the numerous mobs were objects of ridicule & obliged to apply to the Mayor & civil authorities for protection themselves against some of the scoffers. So all went off charmingly. They remain a few days longer.

[1] Later Czar Alexander II (1818–81).
[2] Henry, Earl of Shelburne, later 4th Marquis of Lansdowne. His brother Lord Kerry died in 1836.

We had a most agreable party yesterday at dinner, not one person who was not remarkable for sense, wit, acquirement or some distinguishing quality. George [Ld Morpeth], who occupied your apartment, was much struck. We have Luttrell & Rogers for permanent guests. Macaulay staid over breakfast ; & Ld Jeffrey came for that meal. Today we shall have Ld Clarendon, who has been on a visit to his *future* parents at Gorhambury.[1] The story of Lady Flora is not allayed. A prosecution is half determined upon in her name for defamation & conspiracy, but not decided against whom, whether the ladies or the Doctor. Sir Wm. Follett [2] advises *strongly* against it, saying that much pain may be inflicted by calling evidence into the witness box, but *no* verdict can be obtained. Ly F. by her letter to Mr Fitzgerald has done herself no good. It is a gross, indelicate disclosure which shocks people. The mischief is to her ; but the rebound is bad for the Court. The young, innocent Queen should never have had her ears polluted by such filthy stories.

Lord Brougham arrived in the diligence at Paris with young Montgomery (Ld Wellesley's son).[3] They occupied the coupé ; Mr Leader & Ld Ossulston the body ! He is in high force, very amusing, laughs at the Committee of the H. of Lords, who will probably find good reason for the liberation of the prisoners whom Ld Normanby had let loose. He wickedly tells a ridiculous story about Normanby, which he probably invented himself, that on one occasion the post boy of the carriage turned out of the direct road on which Ld N. was travelling, & being asked why, he turned towards a town which the Lord Lt. intended not to visit, & answered, " Why sure, have not I a brother in prison in that town ? " This is all nonsense, which however may divert your Aunt, if not you. Before he went to Paris he sent me a view of his *château* at Cannes, a strange, ugly building. Lord Plunket's eldest son is to be the new Bishop of Tuam. The former Bishopric ought to have been his ; however, better late than never. Lord Plunket was here yesterday, quite young & renovated at this event.

[1] George William Villiers, Miss Theresa Villiers's brother, succeeded his uncle in 1838 as 4th Earl. He was Ambassador in Madrid 1833–9. He married Lady Catherine Barham, widow of J. F. Barham who died in 1838, and daughter of 1st Earl of Verulam. Mr. Barham was a cousin of Lady Holland. " She is admired," she wrote earlier, " but not by me."

[2] Attorney-General.

[3] Alfred Montgomery (1814–96). Charles Greville mentions that Montgomery took a hand in the hoax of Brougham's supposed death later in the year (IV, 214). J. Temple Leader, M.P., was a Radical ally of Lord Brougham.

Some admirer of the Duke of Wellington told him they were
certain, if he was in India, all difficulties would be settled in two years.
"Two years ! Why two months you mean ; but then what would
become of the Maids of Honour ?" Tho' he can be jocose, I much
fear he is shattered greatly. He has taken Ld Carrington's house in
Belgrave Square for the new married couple, who are to be married
on 15th or 16th.[1] Our weather is severe : Easterly winds & black
frost, paying for the mildness of the winter.

April 26th, [1839].

. . . No sooner the Govt are out of one scrape, but another arises.
Such for instance is the Jamaica Bill on Monday, to which Sir Robt
Peel has announced formally his opposition. He will make it another
trial of strength ; but the Govt will have all the *Saints* & the feeling
of the serious public on their side. This & the Canada Bill are the
most urgent points this session.

The dinner went off admirably at Lansdowne H. The Queen,
Papa described, as being so prettily & naturally pleased. She looked
about her quite like a girl at home for holidays, examined the silver
plates, ceiling, & all that was new to her eyes. She laughed, & was
excessively merry. The lighting & increase of chandeliers in the
great room had a beautiful effect. In short, nothing could succeed
better than the whole affair. Louisa looked, they say, really very
pretty ; & thank God ! Shelburne is in good plight. Ld Hd sat next
to a pretty woman with whom he was much struck, Lady Bruce.[2]
She has one unmarried sister whom they describe as even handsomer ;
the other is quite ugly. Ld Hd was very unfit to partake of the
festivities, as he is overcome with one of his dreadful choaking colds
& cough ; so, after fairly seeing her Majesty established in the concert
room, he came away.

The outset of Lord Douro's marriage scandalized the world. The
bride fainted away in her return from church ; he went riding in the
Park, & played a game of tennis. Returned at 4 to accompany her
to Strathfieldsay for the honey moon. On the Queen complimenting
him on her beauty, he said she was all head, hands & feet (they are
large), that she weighed 11 stone, & more than he did. Some say
all this is bravado ; for he is in reality much in love.

---

[1] Arthur Richard Wellesley, Marquis Douro (1807-84), 2nd Duke of Wellington, married Lady Elizabeth Hay, daughter of 8th Marquis of Tweeddale.
[2] Lady Mary Caroline Herbert, daughter of 11th Earl of Pembroke, married
Lord Bruce, later 2nd Marquis of Ailesbury, in 1837.

The Government majority sank to 5 in the Commons on the Jamaica Bill early in May.   Lord Melbourne resigned, but owing to the refusal to Peel of the Queen to part with certain of the ladies in her household, he was recalled to office.   Lady Holland commented : " Had the D. of W. conducted the negotiation it would probably have gone well ; but Peel's vulgarity, stiffness and grasping, wounded the feelings of the high spirited Princess."

28 *June*, 1839.

The concert at L.H. was very perfect : the Grisi & Garcia, who overstrained themselves to out do each other.   Upon the whole the male singers carried off the palm, at least to my taste.   I have rarely seen a greater assemblage of pretty women than there was that night ; & there is a surprizing improvement in the dressing of the women. Really they are as well equipped as even the French, but there is still a sad gaucherie in the maintien, swinging of the arms & entering a salon, which they have not conquered.   We have had, & have still Henry L. Bulwer [1] as an inmate.   He is very agreable, besides being well informed & very sensible.   Ld Granville writes only today how very much he is pleased at having him for a successor to Aston, tho' parting with him is a severe pang ; but of course as his sincere friend he cannot but rejoice at his great elevation.   Bulwer is remarkably conversant with France, its politics & intrigues, & quite steady enough to make this Govt feel satisfied he will do well in the event of Ld G.'s absence, an event quite desirable for his health for a few weeks, tho' he is afraid in the present posture of affairs it would not be right to ask.   He wanted to go to Baden ; but the overflow of visitors deterred him.   So altogether, I fear, he will be obliged to content himself with Paris & its environs.

So *Thiers* has renounced his *History* of Florence, & arranged with booksellers to continue on his own *History*, including the Consulate & Empire.   For this he is to receive five hundred thousand livres. He is gone to the Pyrenees to write the *History*.   Previous to leaving Paris he became an ally & warm friend of Molé's ; so that will probably be a Ministerial combination for the next session.   We shall be sorry to lose Soult, who is much inclined to *peace* & to maintain the English alliance.   The reception he met with in this country has left a very strong & favorable impression on his mind, & also of the power & magnitude of the resources of the Country.

[1] William Henry Lytton Bulwer (1801–72), created Baron Dalling and Bulwer in 1871. He succeeded Sir Arthur Aston (who had been appointed Minister in Spain) as First Secretary in Paris.

Did you hear of the strange & cruel delusion, if such it was, of Ld Brougham ? The first days of Ly Flora's illness, it was supposed she would sink immediately. Accordingly Ld B. was determined to be in time for the catastrophe, & selected Ld Harewood, Ly Portman's [1] father, to impart the intelligence : said when she had died, & gave a very detailed report of the surgeon's *post mortem* examination, & made a dying speech for Lady Flora against the Queen ! ! This is, I assure you, a *fact* ; nor was it till the next day Ld Harewood was undeceived. Some think it was a real aberration of mind ; others sheer malignity. As he likes to have a finger in everything, he is plunged into the confidence of the Hastings's, and much vexed that his interference to effect a duel in these instances has failed : but he says still there *must be blood*. Were he not already so well judged by all men, he might be seriously dangerous. It is lamentable to see such transcendant abilities thrown away, as upon him.

The departure of Conroy [2] has, I am told, already been productive of some good, by producing an encrease of cordiality between the Mother & Daughter. If this is so, it will be a very happy result for both parties.

I have got acquainted with a very remarkably clever, distinguished woman, reckoned by many extremely handsome, Ly C. Guest,[3] nobly born, married to an immensely rich man, who wanted what the Spaniards call *Sangre Azul*, & gave her wealth which she wanted. They seem perfectly happy ; his riches are in Wales. She has learnt the Welsh language & translated an ancient poem of romantic chivalry into English. I have only just got it, so cannot, if ever I should, judge of its merits. Did they ever fall in your beat ?

Tuesday. Hd H. [*August 27, 1839.*]

. . . The loss of Mr Rice [4] is felt by all his colleagues. His inflexible good temper, knowledge, readiness and conciliation were qualities which he possessed in no ordinary degree. He unluckily

---

[1] Lady Portman was one of the Queen's Ladies-in-Waiting.

[2] Sir John Conroy, Comptroller to the Duchess of Kent till 1739.

[3] Sir Josiah John Guest (1785–1852) married, in 1833, as his 2nd wife, Lady Charlotte Bertie, daughter of 9th Earl of Lindsey. Ivor Bertie, created Baron Wimborne, was their son. Lady Charlotte married, 2ndly, Charles Schreiber, and died in 1895, leaving much of her collection of porcelain, etc., to the Victoria and Albert Museum.

[4] Thomas Spring-Rice (1790–1866) had been created Baron Monteagle of Brandon on retirement from the Chancellorship of the Exchequer. Lady Holland wrote of him elsewhere : " He was always ready to speak and assist ; clear, well-informed, with a winning faculty of never losing his temper."

was soured at being disappointed of the Speakership, no fault of his own friends, but faithlessness among the Tories on whom he had *personally* reckoned. It is foolish, but so it is.

The Coburgs, who are here, are said to be the dullest of the dull. Yet one, the youngest, is talked of for the Princess of Brésil, the little Emperor's sister.

7th October, Tuesday, [1839].

. . . The *public* are quite satisfied the Queen is going to be married. The young Coburg arrives on Saturday ; but certainly nothing has transpired to the members of the Govt ; & for *one*, I much doubt the truth of the report. It is a sad chapter, the *Greys* ; but I trust there will not be much more hostility on the part of the Eldons than there has been all along. The Howicks are very friendly in language. It was an unlucky affair, & is one among the many instances of the mischief of *writing* instead of speaking.[1] Ld John was in the country & ill, & wrote, as he always does, par parenthèse, *tartly*. The other was nettled, & so parted company in a pet, each party very sorry. Lady Howick also was absent ; had she been at hand, it would have been prevented. In short, it is a bad, unlucky affair ; & the loss of Mr Wood incalculably mischievous. *He* is quite overset by it, but says he must have hanged himself had he not followed Ld Howick. He could not have stood the brunt of the family indignation.

October 10th.

We have had the Granvilles. They are now at Windsor, & go on Tuesday to Paris, where his sound head & knowledge is required. Bulwer is most restless for his arrival. However, I have no doubt all will be adjusted à l'aimable and all the five Powers agree more or less. Bülow writes to me in excellent spirits about himself, & will be here about Xmas time. Alas ! for poor Pozzo, who declines mentally & physically every day. His imagination is frappée that after his death his *héritiers* will try to exterminate each other by litigation & his whole fortune be squandered, & none of his family be bettered by him. The Sebastianis dined here yesterday. He was in a state of great depression, as his old attached valet-de-chambre had fallen dead from apoplexy the night before, an old faithful friend

---

[1] Lord Howick, who had for some time been dissatisfied with the measures of the Government, tried to obtain the Board of Trade for Charles Wood, later Lord Halifax, and resigned on his failure to do so.

who had lived & campaigned with him 36 years. He was sensibly affected by the blow.

The *soi* disant prétendu of our little Queen is arrived. Only last night; so nothing has transpired of the effect produced by his presence. He comes of an aspiring family, who talk, I hear, as if this Realm was his inheritance; but he may be modest & unassuming. Nous verrons, but *certainly* nothing is fixed.

November 8th, [1839].

. . . Our Princes go away on 14th; the question is when to return? The general belief is that the Great Lady has made up her mind, & only waits for the convenient moment to declare it. He pleases greatly, & the same said of him that used to be said of Mde de Coigny, " Qu'elle n'avoit qu'une voix contre elle, c'etait la sienne," for his *organe* is reckoned very shrill & displeasing.

South Street.   *November* 19th.

We came last evening. I dined with Papa at ½ 4, he to go to the first Cabinet dinner this season : Allen & I to the play, Ly Cowper, Ld Ebrington & Stanley. What I am going to add is for the moment a secret, tho' on Saturday will be made public. The marriage is settled, & will be declared to the whole Privy Council on Saturday. People in general are pleased ; but when more particulars are divulged we shall all know more. En attendant, be discreet and avoid giving the news as a well known *fact*.

The last sad rites have been performed at Chenies.[1] Every mark of respect & attachment was shewn to his memory, as it is about Woburn, where everybody above the condition of labourers are in mourning. He has left £5000 to poor Adair, a most opportune gift, he having just lost £20,000 by the dishonesty of the Portuguese Govt. £1000 to Lady Wriothesley [Russell]. These are the only legacies in money.

November 26th.

. . . The Queen went through her trying scene at the Council with great propriety. Her voice was firm, tho' in some passages it faltered & betrayed great emotion. Her dress was remarkably simple ; the only ornament a bracelet with her futur's portrait. She is to have 10 bridesmaids, after the model of Queen Charlotte. The Prince's establishment will be after that of Prince of Wales's, George IV.

[1] The Duke of Bedford had died on October 20, at the age of 73.

December 10th, [1839]. Hd H.

Lord Clarendon may perhaps find himself better off as a member of Govt than according to his language he seems to expect.   Certainly there is a favorable change in opinion latterly ; the Foreign affairs, India, & Canada have all had an influence.   Lady Cowper's marriage will take place immediately.[1]   They have taken a spacious, handsome house on Carlton Terrace, belonging to Ld Caledon.   Her own house in George Street will be occupied by the Tankervilles, who are on the pavé, not liking the high rent of theirs in G. Square.   Ld Palmerston's will be let in Stanhope Street.   It will be the union of the best-tempered persons in the world.   *Never* did I see a man more in love & devoted ; so there is every prospect of happiness for them, as her family on both sides are friendly & kind upon the subject.

[*January,* 1840.]

The Tories have fixed the 28th for the downfall of the Whig Govt. Our friends are confident, yet to me it is always better to have a crisis *over*.

Scandal says Dsse Dino proposes making a long séjour in Germany : but in reality to conceal what others display.   The favorite is a very young, handsome employé ; his name I have forgotten.

The fate of Frost [2] is not decided ; but it is evident the public feeling is strong that an example should be made of one who was the ringleader of desperate men who caused so much bloodshed & havoc, and against whom the proofs of guilt are abundant.   I am glad that it is not my province to decide ; as feeling & reason might be at variance.

The Dunfermlines, *alias* Crusty, are in town.   He has an occupation in settling the Household of the Dss of Kent, and has made an admirable appointment of a successor to Sir John, a Col. Cooper.   The King of Hanover threatens loudly, should any attempt be made to take his apartments [3] ; so for the present, to avoid an esclandre, the Dss will be obliged to live in a hired house, as the young couple do not like to have a *tiers* in their connubial felicity.   Already the Queen has notified that the Women of the Bedchamber will be dispensed

[1] To Lord Palmerston.

[2] John Frost, Chartist, Major, and J.P. of Newport.   Tried for High Treason in 1839, and sentenced to transportation in 1840.   He served his sentence in Tasmania, but was pardoned in 1856.   He died in 1877.

[3] His apartments were in St James Palace.   The Duchess of Kent would not go back to Kensington ; and the Queen finally had to hire a house for her at £2,000 p.a. (*Greville Memoirs,* IV, 258).

with, except upon State occasions, and probably soon the same measures will be adopted about the Maids of Honor : salaries continued the same to all.

Lady Palmerston gave her first soirée last Saturday. It was highly approved.

February 4th, [1840]. S. St.

. . . You will have heard all the vexations about precedence that the Tories have raised merely to annoy the poor little Queen. The Dss of Cambridge is supposed to give her aid to the King of Hanover. *He* has absolutely refused to give his apartments for the use of the Dss of Kent, even threatened to resist vi et armis. Monday will be a busy day for the Dss of Sutherland. First the attendance on the Queen in Palace & Chapel : then to preside & represent her at a banquet at St James's to all the Household, with their respective wives & husbands. The Lord Steward heads the table. She is then to give at her own house a party to all the Town. I am sorry ; as she is not very strong, & fainted away at dinner the other day at the Palace. Lord Carlisle is remarkably well. George distinguished himself very much in his speech the other night. It was useful, & will, I hope, be published. John Wortley is laid up by a severe fit of the gout. Miss Conyers, the great heiress of Copt Hall in Essex, is to marry that ugly, but sensible young man John Ashley.[1] They say the Ashleys are as lucky in marriage as the Coburgs.

February 18th, [1840]. S. St.

. . . I wish the wedding cake, which is now opposite to my eyes, could with safety be conveyed to deck your board ; but the materials are so fragile that it is impossible. So instead you have a drawing, which gives the form but hardly the brilliant snow-like appearance. When it is cut, you shall have a slice, for the English colony will be charmed to possess a bit : especially the young ladies to place a morsel under their pillows & indulge in visions of lucky marriages.

Papa was unable to dine at Stafford House to meet Jerome.[2] I liked him, & did not perceive any assumption of Royal airs. He spoke of you with *great* affection, & claimed Lady Augusta for an Italian solely. He spoke doubtingly of sending for his daughter. He

---

[1] 4th son of 6th Earl of Shaftesbury, a lawyer and Q.C. (1808–67).

[2] Jerome Bonaparte (1784–1860), ex-King of Westphalia, known at this time as Comte de Montfort. He was a friend of the Foxes, living and entertaining largely in Florence.

will perhaps act more wisely in not doing so. You will be glad to hear that Prince Albert intends to receive him, should he express any wish to that effect. They have been well acquainted. The gout, & this small house, has prevented Papa from seeing him yet. But should he not be able to meet Jerome next Friday at D. House, we *must* for your sake fix some day, even here.

The Duke of Wellington is today remarkably well, fretting at his confinement.[1] Even yesterday he felt so well that he put on his boots resolved to ride ; but the rain made him listen to advice. The attack was the severest he ever had. . . . However, the character of the Duke is much changed by these attacks. He is irritable, violent, & has no control whatever of his temper. It is lamentable.

March 3*d,* [1840]. S. St.

Bülow is returned looking thin, & shewing he has been shattered. He saw dear Falck at Bruxelles since his attack, gives satisfactory account of him, seeming really to credit the hope of his complete recovery. What a painful period these last 8 or 9 months has been to me ! Lauderdale,[2] the D. of Bedford, my own perilous excruciating illness, Papa's gout, Aunty's uncomfortable state of health, alarm about Falck, & various other minor annoyances. Some however are the natural condition of long life, but nevertheless acutely painful when encountered. Guizot [3] has hitherto had great success. He is agreable : was much so here the other night. The Queen in her audience told him she had read his work on England with very great pleasure, & derived instructions. It is really one of the few books since her accession, & Hallam's is the other, that she has read *through.*

Sydney Smith has had put into verse a very *excellent* receipt for a salad. Jerome has been endeavouring to persuade his brother, Joseph,[4] to return with him to Florence, urging that it is a better séjour than U. States ; tho' he slily adds, it is more a place to die than live in, from its tameness. Joseph reckons this climate as remarkably salutary to his health. Goodbye.

[1] He had had a severe stroke five days before this letter was written.

[2] Lady Holland's old friend Lord Lauderdale (*see ante*, p. 8) had died in September, 1839. The family were also very worried about Miss Caroline Fox's health (" Aunty "), which was breaking down.

[3] Guizot (1787–1874) had just arrived in London as Ambassador, appointed by Thiers's Government.

[4] Joseph Bonaparte the ex-King of Spain, known as the Comte de Survilliers. He had visited England in 1832, when Lady Holland seems to have taken a dislike to him. He did return with Jerome to Florence, and ended his days there.

May 19th, [1840]. Hd H.

Young Mackintosh with his rich, pretty Yankee wife is just returned to England, not yet to London. He is very clever, but strangely crotchety, & without being pleasing. He did, however, behave very handsomely to Macaulay, by lending all his father's historical materials, but which I fear at present there is little chance of his using. You admired, as it deserved, the review of Lord Clive's *Life*. This success has determined him upon taking another Indian character ; so you will read the justification of Warren Hastings, a remarkable man, cruelly traduced by the splendor of Mr Burke's eloquence. Macaulay has done very well in the House of Commons, but people are determined to express disappointment. Some one said, truly enough, that the H. of Commons is a most aristocratic assembly ; so that Macaulay is really weighed down by his want of *pedigree* & his immense reputation. For no speech can ever attain the expectation formed upon that ; & his want of birth does not commend the opinion of the House in his favor.

May 22d. Hd H.

You will be sorry the Ministers lost an important question *solely* by the votes of friends, Ld Howick & Mr Wood.[1] The latter really pains me to have fallen off. He is a sprightly, clever man, excellent as an *administrateur*, with much practical knowledge & *tacte*, extremely beloved with all who have had to deal with him. But unluckily domestic affections warp his own better judgment & lead him to follow in the wake of one to whom he is much superior in judgment & ought to lead. Ld Howick is of a much higher cast of intellect, indeed, in mental power few equal or excel him : high principle & great moral worth, but deficient in temper & discretion. Altogether it is very painful ; & there is much to fear that the over-zealous of the Party will shout & hurt them, & determine their hostility to the measures of Govt. Few things have vexed me *personally* more.

Poor Landseer [2] has fallen into a very distressing state. The fatigue & mental anxiety of having been on the *hanging* Council of the Royal Academy, where there are so many jealousies & bickerings, & then the shock of the murder of poor Ld William [Russell], with whom he was very intimate & had seen frequently just at the time, has quite

---

[1] On the Registration Bill.

[2] Sir Edwin Landseer, the celebrated painter (1802–73), a frequent visitor at Holland House. Lord William Russell, brother of the late Duke, was murdered by his valet, Courvoisier, early in May.

overset his nerves. He is attended by Chambers & Hammick ; they say much depends upon extreme quiet. He is full of terror & horror, expecting an assassin to destroy him. It is really very shocking.

May 26th, [1840]. S. St.

. . . Without croaking, there is really much to fear. The want of numbers make the Govt gradually sink ; the defection of several is important now, where every nose tells. There is an alarm about Cockermouth, a borough opened for the new Lord of the Treasury, Mr Horsman. If this should be lost, it will be nearly fatal. Landseer is better. His horrors are lessened ; he can bear light with less suffering.

I know not which of the two deserters remarked with some compunction that it certainly was unlucky their two votes decided the question against the Ministers. You know how much I feel about Mr Wood. He will be hurt at the Halifax remarks ; his father will both be angry & *hurt.*

It will divert you to hear that Papa has taken a strong fancy to see the *Derby.* He has never been in his life at Epsom. Accordingly, we have put off two very agreable dinners, at Ld Radnor's & Cowper's, to go to Cheam,[1] to be near at hand for the race. This sport is not tempting to me ; therefore I shall not partake of it, but remain quietly in the gloomy shades of Cheam. It is pleasant to see him so eager. Yesterday, the Queen's birthday was honored by great dinners. At Lord Melbourne's, the table was decorated by some magnificent silver candelabra, beautifully worked, a gift from Her Majesty as a token of her regard & friendship to Ld Melbourne.

June 6th. [1840]. Hd H.

. . . Papa's trip to see the Derby answered very well. The day was bright, windy & cold*ish.* However, tho' he went in an open carriage, he escaped without any suffering beyond a smart burning of his face. My share of the expedition faded, on account of the illness of Mr Smith's little girl, and Mr Smith did not like company in his house without her. I got Woolryche [2] to accompany Papa ; for tho' I had asked Charles & he had accepted, yet knowing his loco motive pranks, it was as well Papa should not be perched alone on the racecourse ; so Woolryche saved him that annoyance.

[1] The " Bobus " Smiths had a house at Cheam.
[2] Lord Holland's doctor.

Guizot maintains his ground, & is very popular still. He is here a good deal. The accounts of Pozzo are deplorable, distressing from his state of irritability & distrust of all his entourage. . . .

June 12th, 1840. S. St.

You will in common with us all have been horrified & shocked at this dreadful attempt upon the life of the poor little Queen.[1] You will see the details amply in the papers ; so shall spare the repetition. Lds Melbourne & Normanby went to her immediately on her return to the Palace, & found her well & tolerably composed. She told them she saw the man distinctly take aim when he fired the second pistol, adding, " It was not at all pleasant, I assure you." Her first impulse of going to her Mother, to spare her the fright of hearing it from others, was very amiable. She was to have gone to the German Opera, but very properly did not ; even if her own state of mind could have borne doing so. There are many conjectures as to the motives which actuated the wretched man, such as whether he belonged to a Secret Society, either of Chartists or fanatical Protestants, or if a political tool for change of Sovereign. Nothing has transpired as yet.

Mr Wood made a very useful amendment in a friendly spirit, to atone for the mischief he had done before, but ineffectually ; as it was lost by a majority of 11. It is a *blow*, but, I hope, not vital.

Is it not an extraordinary *fact*, that the pistol case had outside the initials in silver, E. R. ? It is a singular coincidence, but not more one should hope ; only it sets people talking.

June 16th. S. St.

. . . Well, we are again upon almost the eve of another very serious crisis. On Friday, there will be a *pinch* upon Ld Stanley's motion, on which twice the Govt have been in a minority.[2] Ld John's meeting of his [supporters ?] proved very satisfactory. They all promised better attendance in future. The Tories are so very sanguine that already they have allotted the destined offices to their partizans ; & a great Tory personage has suspended his arrangements for going abroad, which he would have done otherwise next week.

[1] Edward Oxford, a youth of 18, fired two pistols at the Queen, as she was driving up Constitution Hill in a low carriage on June 10. He was found guilty, but insane. No bullets were ever found, and there appears to have been a reasonable doubt whether the charge contained ball.

[2] On his Irish Registration Bill.

All the world is at Ascot.[1] The Queen has a numerous party at
the Castle. She has very skilfully divided her invitations from Monday
to Wednesday to some, who will on that day be succeeded by another
set to Friday. She is in good spirits, but looks very pale, showing
visibly her *interesting condition*.

June 30th, 1840.

One is half inclined to believe this ugly postage,[2] which is so inconvenient on many accounts, is likely to be a failure ; but at present
it maintains its popularity, altho' the financial part is very deficient.
However, the individual finance is better, as our porter's book, for
the item of letters only, is reduced from *upwards* of £1 weekly on an
average, & is only a shilling or two.

Why does Galvani wear mustachios ? Surely it is ridiculous for
a civilian ? Albert has cut off his ; so the dirty habit will soon drop.
Already the young men of fashion have renounced *black* cravats for
evening. The coloured are only used in the morning. At this I
rejoice, never having been able to reconcile myself to them for dinner.

The Queen will be confined in December. The three accoucheurs
are named, Drs Blagdon, Lacock, Fergusson. The nurses also are
secured ; but Her Majesty will not see one of the whole set till they
are *wanted*. This, the wise ones do not approve ; as symptoms may
occur that a medical eye might judge of better than so young a wife.
She has *never* spoken to any of her Ladies as to her condition, not even
those she is most intimate with. The Abercorns dined here for the
first time on Sunday.[3] It is pleasant to see people so happy & so
handsome. I confess I see *him* with most affectionate eyes ; for his
behaviour to the family of the late Duke [Bedford], & to the poor
Duchess, is quite admirable, proving a warm & grateful heart. Lord
Claude as a boy was better looking ; but as a man Abercorn has
greatly the advantage over him, & I am told also in understanding.

Those verses of Mrs Norton's are very pretty. She is in greater
beauty if possible than ever, but very cross & touchy they say. She

[1] Lady Holland wrote three days later : " Mde de Lieven would not arrive
in London during Ascot week, well knowing how empty of her friends it would
be. So we must look to her only on 21st."

[2] Rowland Hill's system of adhesive penny stamps, which had been put up to
Lord Melbourne in 1837, and was rather unwillingly accepted by Government
early in 1840.

[3] James, 2nd Marquis of Abercorn (1811–85), later created Duke. He succeeded his grandfather in 1818, and married, in 1832, Lady Louisa Jane, the
Duke of Bedford's daughter. (*See also* p. 33 *n.*)

expected her reception at Court would open all arms & doors to her. Not finding this or much beyond great civility for routs & balls, she is angry.

Richmond. 18th August, [1840].

You always smile at hearing we are at Richmond for change of air ; but this time it is to accommodate Papa, by shortening his trip to St Ann's, where he went this morning, to return the evening. I have been so often told that our going to St Ann's for a day or two is injurious to Mrs Fox, that we do not go as inmates.[1] I must say it is quite contrary to my observation, as she always seems perfectly happy when we are there, only complaining of our short visits, & only regrets that we go. But wiser people say that she is over excited, so we comply, quite against my judgment however.

Guizot dined with us on Sunday, the day after his boisterous voyage. His manner was not so full of satisfaction as might be wished, were he the depository of very good news. However he met La Psse,[2] which was enough for him. He really is childishly in love ! Lady Keith dined at the Château D'Eu with two younger daughters, one rather pretty. Flahault & Emily remain in Paris. I hope A. de Morny[3] has been discreet in his language upon this frantic expedition of his *Brother's*, which the French love of plaisanterie call, " L'affaire *des Tritons*," from their being half drowned. Imagine the silliness of the young man with his live eagle, which was taught some trick to play off upon the Column ! He would not quit the Citadel at Boulogne, till a hairdresser put his hair in order for the voyage à Ham.

---

[1] Mrs Charles James Fox had reached the age of 90, and died just two years later. Miss Caroline Fox wrote of her in July : " Mrs Fox is still a standing wonder, retaining as she does clearness of head and tenderness of heart ; but the eye grows dim from day to day, the ear more dull, and the limbs more painful and feeble."

[2] Mde. de Lieven.

[3] Auguste de Morny, son of Queen Hortense and Flahault, and consequently a half-brother of Prince Louis Napoleon. The latter seized upon the occasion when the Emperor's body was in transit to Europe from St Helena, to make a landing at Boulogne, in order to start an insurrection, which failed dismally. In the result he spent the next six years in captivity in the Château de Ham.

Five daughters were born to the Comte de Flahault and Lady Keith and Nairne, who married in 1817. Two only grew up, Emily Jane, who married Lord Shelburne in 1843, and Georgina, who became wife of Marquis de la Valette in 1871.

CHAPTER XII

1841, 1842, 1843

Many things had come to pass before the penning of the next letter which we print. Lord Holland, to the dismay and heart-felt regret of all his friends, died suddenly on October 22, after two days' illness. " This wretched day closes all the happiness, refinement and hospitality within the walls of Holland House," wrote Lady Holland in the "Dinner Books." Within a month of a hundred years later, on the fatal night in September, 1940, a shower of incendiary bombs closed the portals of the old house for ever.

The Foxes hurried home from Florence, to find, on their arrival in December, that his mother was established by his father's will in complete control of most of the properties and of all his personalty : and that he had been left extremely badly off. Constant bickerings ensued ; as the new Lord Holland was not in agreement with the policy of sales of property and works of art upon which his mother insisted. Consequently the date of Holland's departure to return to his post in Italy, early in April, came as a relief to all parties.

Lady Holland's letters do not recommence till the end of May, 1841 (with the exception of one in March), after the Government had been defeated early in the month, during the Budget discussions, on Lord Sandon's motion condemning the proposed reduction of the Sugar Duties, by 36 votes. Melbourne and his colleagues, however, braved out the situation, and still did not throw up the sponge, even after the defeat of the Ministry on June 5 by one vote on a direct Vote of Confidence. The debate lasted for five days. Parliament was dissolved ; and the Tories were returned with a majority of over 70. Melbourne finally resigned at the end of August, after the loss of a further Vote of Confidence by 91.

[*March 25th, 1841.*]

Prince Albert escaped narrowly being run down in the middle of the Thames, when going to visit the iron vessels preparing for the expedition to the Niger. Ld Minto & other Lords were with him in the Admiralty barge when this almost collision occurred. They were quitte pour la peur, but Ld Minto says it was very near. This & the Queen's toilette were the topics at the Levée. She appeared for the first time with a change of coiffure, her hair dressed à la Sévigné with ringlets. She was described as looking beautiful, so improved that she was *truly* admired.   Critics say, tho' it may improve her face, the figure will lose by being diminished extremely.

This day I am seventy years of age !   What a contrast is the passing of it to those of almost half a century back, when I was greeted with cheerful tenderness at passing another anniversary together.   Little did it ever occur to me that the severing would be as it has befallen. Let me look forward to the only glimmering of peace now left, that the scanty period of my life may pass with the kindness & protection bestowed by my children.

May 23d, 1841.   S. St.

The reception of some of the Ministers by the assembled crowd on their way to the Birthday Court was highly flattering.   To Ld John, whom they cheered warmly, one or two cried out, " Go it, Johnny, go it."   Ld Melbourne was much applauded, also Ld Palmerston, tho' several cried out " 36."   When Ld John in the last debate announced his intention of moving for the Sugar Duties, Ld Lyndhurst, who was in the H. of Commons, sitting next to Ld Abinger, said, " One must admit that they have *pluck*."   Some of the violent, hot, rash Tories wish to resist the Sugar Duties, but Peel, more cautious & politic, will not allow them.   However, all this is idle to tell you, because before this letter quits our shores, this matter will be one of public notoriety.

Ld Lyndhurst remarked to the Attorney-General, " that *this* was a crisis without a catastrophe."   I hope his phrase may be verified, mais j'en doute.   Ly Mary Stanley[1] has written to me to announce her pretty daughter's marriage with Ld Cremorne, a very delightful young man, full of good sense, intelligence & information.   He is besides very remarkably good tempered, great ingredients with abundant love for happiness.   His fortune is large, but his home is Ireland.   I ought to have added that among the good qualities of Ld Cremorne he is a Whig : was educated by his step-father, Col. Rawdon, in very liberal principles.

The Greys are all remarkably well, & as kind as possible to me. On Friday I am to dine with them, which is a pleasure, tho' a gulp at first from sad recollections.   But these over, I know I shall be better for it, as it gratifies me to receive protection & notice which

---

[1] Daughter of James, 8th Earl of Lauderdale, and wife of Edward Stanley, of Cross Hall, Lancashire.   She died in 1877.   Their daughter, Augusta, married Richard Dawson, 3rd Lord Cremorne, later created Earl of Dartrey (1817–97), the grandfather of the editor of these letters.

I know are devised chiefly, if not solely, from reverence to the memory of one to whom I owe all that is estimable in life—and all that constituted my happiness in it. For many years he had wanted to go to Epsom Races, saying that is was stupid that an Englishman should not see what all foreigners admired as unique : saying he must go before he died. So it was arranged that he should go to the Derby, which he did, enjoyed it much, & also had his wish. This is the anniversary !

Lady Tankerville is returned from Paris much disgusted by the ton of the society : the young, pretty women smoking cigars & talking slang ; the men covered with hair, ill bred, and low in manners & conversation.

June 1st, [1841]. Richmond Hill.

. . . The appearance of Lord Clanricarde is alarming. He is quite emaciated, feeble & sickly, oppressed by constant cough & evidently uneasy. She is extremely so, & with but too good reason I fear. Never was man more pleased than he is at quitting Russia. He describes Court & society as detestable, pomp & show with such a mixture of meanness that altogether is unsuitable to persons who have enjoyed the polish & ease of refined society. The young new Grand-Duchess is not liked, as her education & manners have been more carefully attended to. She is grave, relishes books & correspondence ; whereas all the other Princesses, beginning with the Empress, are very great hoydens full of practical jokes & gigglings.

Tomorrow the H. of Commons will begin its discussions.[1] John intends speaking, which will shorten the duration of the debates. So a division may take place that night, tho' most probably not till Thursday, as there are several persons to be heard who have not yet spoken upon this important point. The most expert calculations are doubtful how the numbers will go, each say 2 only will be the majority. Many think that will be on the Ministerial side, nous verrons. . . .

June 5th. S. St.

. . . The debate has been prolonged on to this day, partly from the Queen's Ball, & chiefly from John having a severe feverish cold which confines him to his room & prevented his attendance in the House last night. How your dear, dear Father would have rejoiced at the progress, tho' very slight, only one vote, in favour of

---

[1] The debate on the Vote of Confidence.

the Jews.[1] Toleration was his darling object. Peace, amity &
indulgence to all mankind were the predominant feelings of his heart.
He would indeed have been gratified and hailed this slight advance
as an omen of future liberality. It is still doubtful whether or not the
division will be in favour of Sir Robert. If it is not, he will have
made a very false move in trying a Vote of Censure. It is still uncertain
how the result may be of the dissolution. Some think each side will
remain much as they are ; but I am afraid that is rather a sanguine
view of the case.

June 11th, [1841].

. . . Our friends are in high spirits at the Election prospects.
Certain it is the Tories are far from being elated. But speculations
of this sort are not worth attention, when nothing positive can be
known till the event occurs. The meeting of the new Parlt will take
place in August, when the question on the Address will be the test
whether the old Ministry remain, or if a new Ministry will be formed.
Some suppose the high character of the Speaker [2] is such that there
will not be an attempt to make him quit the chair. He is universally
esteemed. The truth is he is an excellent man & much beloved.
Lord Brougham lost no time in appearing in the H. of Lords. He is
disposed to great activity, & has selected Ld Ashburton as his mark,
picking out ingeniously all his inconsistencies on the Corn Laws.
This leads to recrimination, making a disagreable wrangle to the
audience. Your Aunt is certainly very fragile. Life hangs on a
thread, which any bodily exertion over the common routine may
snap suddenly.

June 15th, Tuesday. Dulwich.

I return tomorrow to my pretty but stifling Nutshell. The Elections
are such an engrossing topic, that rational conversation must not be
expected ; & I shall try to get out of town soon again. One cannot
but admire Ld John's stout heart & spirit in engaging in the arduous
undertaking of representing London City. From his acceptance one
must feel pretty confident that he has good hopes of success ; otherwise he would hardly renounce his steady friends at Stroud. Ld
Melbourne has a touch of gout in his hand. He did not follow the
Royal party to Oxford. Perhaps his reception there might not be

[1] The Jews' Civil Disability Bill passed the Commons, but was defeated in
the Lords on 3rd Reading.
[2] Charles Shaw-Lefevre (1794–1888), Speaker 1839–57, when he was created
Viscount Eversley.

flattering ; nor does the Queen herself, I believe, go *in* to Oxford, but remains at the Archbishop's at Nuneham.[1] What a immense house it must be to contain the Queen, her suite & many visitors, Lansdownes, Sutherlands, besides various others ; yet *none* but Ld & Ly Norreys sleep out, & they are to be at the clergyman's close at hand.

Dickens is going to Scotland, where at Edinburgh he will be honoured by a public dinner. His present work,[2] which is in progress still, is very intriguing ; & even you who dislike his Pick Wick style might approve this, tho' occasionally he relapses into *slang*, which is to me as well as to you offensive.

July 2d, [1841]. S. St.

Charles is triumphant.[3] His well-deserved success gives a fillip to my heart ; for it would have caused such delight to one, from whom he inherits *all* his virtues & goodness. It is a reward to his frank, manly, straight forward conduct. His health has not suffered in the least by his indefatigable exertions and exposure to weather. The Jews in his case did what was never done before. The Rabbi, one of the chief, canvassed on his behalf. Let no cynic say gratitude is not felt. His name, as his Father's son, gave the impetus to their zeal. They remembered how warmly their cause had been advocated by him, who lived but to promote peace & amity among mankind. These thoughts please, tho' they overcome me greatly. The Elections have not come up to the general expectations of our friends. Several places considered as secure are lost ; on the other hand, many not looked for have turned up trumps. The system of bribery & intimidation has surpassed any ever known before, the latter quite appalling. Mr Brodie nearly lost Salisbury, by the excess to which it was carried among the tradesmen. However, fortunately, it failed ; as by this day's report he is re-elected. The Tories threaten a Scrutiny for the City. They are incensed at Ld John's success ; but when the enormous expense which must be incurred by such a proceeding is considered, they may think twice before they proceed. Ld Palmerston had famous success, as you will see, at Tiverton ; & Ly P. to have been as popular there as she is, & deserves to be, go where she may.

---

[1] Edward Vernon-Harcourt (1757–1847), Archbishop of York, who added Harcourt to his name on succeeding to the family estates.

[2] A serial, known as *Master Humphrey's Clock*, containing *Old Curiosity Shop*, etc.

[3] At Tower Hamlets.

July 10th, [1841].

. . . Leopold has left his Queen & child at Windsor. As he has
a camp of 28,000 men collected to be reviewed by him, & for that
period *maintained at his charge*, he was eager to go & dismiss them.
The child is better, & may it is hoped be able to travel shortly. This
contre-temps has altered the period for the Royal visit to Woburn,
which now stands for Monday week, 26th, I believe. The Villiers
& Peel wedding [1] was numerously & brilliantly attended, not only
by relations, but by half the expectant new Govt. Sir Robert, in
returning thanks for the young couple, made a *speech*, which people
said was to keep his hand in during the summer months. There was
a proper degree of fainting & hysterics ; but poor Ld Jersey really
bona fide sobbed & cried long after like a child. The Elections daily
become worse & worse. It is most provoking to have been misled
in the calculations upon the result—to the extent which is apparent
now.

Yesterday Bülow took leave of me. He goes today for ever. It
was a pang to separate from a real galant homme, with whom for
upwards of 10 years I had lived on terms of complete friendship &
intimacy, & who has been invariably the same in weal & woe towards
me. A tie less in life. S[ydney] Smith is in a precarious state of
health, alarmed about himself, unfortunately with reason. The fifth
act of this strange life is, as Mrs Smith calls it, a woeful concern.

July 13th. S. St.

The Elections have been a dismal failure, that of Yorkshire & Northumberland severe blows politically, & extremely painful privately,
from the merits & virtues of the defeated. To the Howicks, it is a
complete break up of their plans for life. They will go abroad for
two years, & do what they have long wished, make a journey to the
East. She is grievously affected, & feels acutely the discomfiture
which was produced by acts of treachery quite unparalleled even in
election contests. As to George [Morpeth], his natural buoyancy of
spirits & the many advantages of his domestic position will temper
the blow as to his personal feelings. One good effect to the Greys
has been the bringing them together more amicably than they have
ever been since the unlucky disunion upon politics between father
& son. So out of evil springs good ; & this may be a mitigation.
Cheshire is also a discomfiture, & will, I fear, compel Stanley to

---

[1] George Augustus Frederic, Viscount Villiers (1808–59), for 3 weeks 6th
Earl of Jersey, married Julia, eldest daughter of Sir Robert Peel.

accept the vacant post at Bombay, an expatriation & separation from
their children ; as it will be a divided feeling to choose between
husband & her children, for she is very warmly attached to both.

The Queen, you will have heard, is to make visits to Woburn and
to Panshanger. The choice of the latter place is chiefly, I suspect, to
get a peep at Brocket,[1] where she has a fancy to go, but was not much
encouraged. She is in a sad state of annoyance, as to the *certainty*
of her change of counsels & companions. Poor little thing, it is hard
upon her to be so compelled ; but in this world of vexations Princes
must submit to the perverse decisions of Fate.

The small house & London air disagree with me ; but I have no
energy to stir. Hd H. is kept ready, & I am trying to go ; but my
courage sinks at present.[2] Indeed that horrid emblem of my misery
staring me in the face is a check ; but I will try. I have had the
gardens near the house put in good order, to take off the air of desola-
tion which struck me to the heart when I was there last. Goodbye
my love, this theme overcomes me too much to pursue. Your aff.

December 28th, [1841]. S. St.

. . . What you say of Ly Beauvale [3] is by all convincing testimony
quite just. She has had equally friendly hints with yours, not exactly
upon language, but advice to conceal the tone of high sentiment,
which, however admirable in Germany, is but ill suited to the English,
& more especially little adapted to the new family with which she is
united. She has so much *tacte* that she will adopt, has adopted already,
this suggestion. If she has softened her husband & made him good
humoured, she has achieved a miracle. It will give pleasure to hear
that she is likely to have an heir.

[1] Lord Melbourne's.
[2] Lady Holland only twice passed a few days at Holland House after her
husband's death.
[3] Sir Frederick Lamb, Henry Fox's former chief, was created Lord Beauvale
in 1839. He married early in 1841, in Vienna, a daughter of Count Maltzahn.
The new Lord Holland had written to his mother from Florence : " Lord &
Lady Beauvale are here. I never saw any one so improved in health, spirits &
good humour as he is by his young wife. She is a pleasing person, & has the
greatest wish to please. She has no beauty of face, a good figure, and a very
distinguished lady like manner. She talks English so very well that I ventured
to correct one or two little things that she said, tho' I did not venture to tell
her that she must be careful not to use some of the expletives her husband has the
habit of bringing out ; for she will scandalize Lady Ashley & the Jocelyn family,
if when they tell her some fact that slightly surprised her, she were to say
to them as she did to me, ' Christ God, you do not say so.' "

[No date. *December* 30 ? *Last days of 1841*. To Lady Augusta Fox.]

Mr Dickens has just been to take leave of me.   He goes on Sunday
to Liverpool, embarks on Tuesday, expects to be at Boston on 17th.
He leaves his children, a pledge of his return in six months.   They are
under the care of his friend Macready, living in an adjoining house.
He is resolved to go into the slave districts, determined to ascertain
by personal inspection the condition of the poor slaves.   He should
not divulge this on the other side of the Atlantic : his life might be
endangered.   Sancho, the Spanish Minister, dined with me yesterday.
He is an amiable, dull man, understands French very imperfectly,
English not at all ; so he will pass his time but ill in this country.
Lady Keith was very amiable to him ; but it was uphill work for her.
She is not valiant, & intends to go, as I returned, by land, not iron.

January 7th, 1842.

. . . Strong minded as is our little great Queen, she was during
her first pregnancy towards its close dreadfully nervous : & now she
derides those who complain or fear.   The preparations for the
Xtening are extensive at Windsor.   87 are to be lodged ; only 3 or
4 ladies, Sutherland, Northumberland, Lansdowne, perhaps Somerset ;
no Ministers' wives : two ambassadors, & four family envoys,
Hanover, Flemish (Van de Weyer), Portuguese, & Saxon.   King of
Prussia stays four days ; [1] the other four he will devote to Oxford,
Cambridge, perhaps Liverpool.   I hear Ld Melbourne's visit pleased
all.   *His* chair, they say, was replaced by the Queen as usual adjoining
her own as in former days ; but this is only from hearsay.   It is said
he is to be at the ceremony ; but as yet he has not, they say, had any
notification of it.   He is now at Broadlands, where there is a pleasant
party, which, but for the weather, I should like to join.   The parties
at Bowood this season have been delightful.   All that had never been
there before are astonished at the splendid comforts, and seem really
to have enjoyed their séjour : some *severe* critics, such as C. Greville,
& Lady Harriet Baring.

It seems a formidable undertaking for Ld Ashburton to cross the
Atlantic this stormy season, when on the score of health he declined
office. [2]   From the indecision of his character he may not be the best
fitted for this reorganization.   One of the objections raised against

---

[1] Frederick William IV, who came over to be Godfather to the Prince of
Wales.

[2] He had been sent to Washington as Commissioner for settlement of the
Boundary dispute.

it is his close connexion with that country ; but there is not much in that, for his stake & importance is *here*, which he would not sacrifice for other interests.   He is very able, well informed & full of ingenuity : so candid that the arguments against him have always much weight with him & neutralize his opinions.

January 25th, [1842].   S. St.

. . . The town is full of the events at Windsor & the agrémens of His Prussian Majesty, who is very frank & affable, pleasing all.   He went into Westminster Hall, after seeing the Abbey yesterday.   He would [not], as the Courts were sitting, disturb the progress of business, but begged to speak to *any* lawyer who might chance to be in the Hall.   There was one, perhaps a briefless barrister, walking about. He had him called, shook hands with him, enquired much about our jurisprudence, etc., to which very apt, pertinent replies were made. The lawyer was Serjeant Ludlow, not a person of any great eminence, but quite competent to make good replies.   This day for the Xtening is very brilliant.   Ld Melbourne is less well this morning ; his gout has been extremely severe.   There has been a long talk of his having the Garter.   I know nothing of it, but rather hope it may not be true.

February 22d, [1842].

. . . You will have heard, tho' perhaps not have read, of the tedious debates on the Corn question ; the good speeches were Ld John's, Mr Gladstone & Palmerston, the latter super-excellent.   Another branch of the same question is now under discussion ; but I have not had any particulars of the merits of the speakers.   Charles asked a pertinent, useful question concerning Spanish affairs, which was very satisfactorily answered by Peel, that is as far as good will being ex-pressed towards that unhappy country.

Lately Ld Hertford requested an interview with Sir R. Peel.   He went to his house accordingly, was assisted into the room & placed in a chair.   He began uttering : for speaking, poor man, it could not be called.   At length Sir Robert very civilly protested that he did not understand his meaning, therefore requested him to signify by writing his wishes.   Accordingly they were manifested to the astonishment of Peel, a Mission !   You might guess Paris.   Not a bit of such soaring ambition—the humble post of Naples !   This is strictly true, as Lord Aberdeen told me ; Peel desired him to write the answer. Could anyone have imagined such a request from such a man possible ? The interview of course was generally known, but everyone imagined he had asked for a Dukedom. He is in a wretched state of health & disgusting depravity.

March 4th, 1842.

You will have heard of the death of my great neighbour, Lord Hertford; tho' he had long been in a bad state of health, it was sudden at last. A day or two previous, he had made a partie *fine* with some of the worthless women whom he had admitted into his house after the *expulsion* of the Zichys,[1] whom he had expelled for that purpose. He took them to Richmond, dined at an inn without attendants. On his return he was violently sick, & shortly, after three days, expired. His son will be here on Monday. Till then the contents of the will will not be accurately known. As he never loved anyone, his loss is not likely to be much lamented. His wealth is calculated to be equal to that of the Duke of Cleveland.

At Belvoir the quarrel between Ly Jersey & Lord Londonderry was ludicrously violent, as to the *precedence* of Psse N. Esterhazy.[2] Ly J. contended that she would take rank of all Duchesses. Ld L. said she should not of one Marchioness, at least. Such discourteous language ensued, that Ld L. declared, were *she* a man, he would know how to treat her.

March 15th.

. . . The Income Tax is come.[3] The effect can hardly be known upon public opinion yet, nor do I feel competent myself to form any. Sir Robert, by general approbation, acquitted himself with great ability & perspicuity, with powers equal even to those of Mr Pitt upon similar statements. But should the pressure of the Tax prove too great, eloquence will not avail or reconcile the impoverished to the griffe (?).

Ld Hertford's will offends & shocks. It is heartless and wrong. It reminds one of the Duke of Würtemberg some 60 years ago, who insisted that all the ladies who had been his *favorites* should wear blue satin heels to their shoes (in those days women wore high heels) whenever they appeared before him at Court. To this compulsory

---

[1] Charlotte, daughter of Sir Richard and Lady Strahan (Lord Hertford's mistress), was married to a Hungarian, Count Emanuel Zichy.

[2] Lady Jersey's daughter, Sarah, married in February, Prince Paul Esterhazy's son, Nicholas.

[3] Seven pence in the £ Income Tax on incomes over £150 for three years. Any similar tax had only previously been imposed in war-time.

etiquette all were obliged to conform.   Accordingly, in that spirit he has by legacies stigmatised his favorites.   One is very cruel, lapsed however.   The others are all alive, & will enjoy their *immense* bequests. The legacies are to the extent of absorbing more than the personal property.   The wealth of the present Marquess is however quite enormous. . . .   His dinner Star & George he had left to Sir R. Peel : but on being refused the Mission at Naples, he scratched out his name.   What a man !   He lived & died without inspiring one sentiment of esteem or some regret.

April 19th, 1842.

The Committee for the Houses of Parlt are sitting to decide upon the decorations of them.   Prince Albert presides, & shews not only taste but considerable knowledge.   One great question is how the walls are to be treated.   Fresco paintings are proposed : then the subjects for them, historical incidents in our own history.   Some were for poets also, Milton.   Albert addressed, sotto voce, Ld John, " Perhaps you would approve of passages from *Paradise Regained* " ? [1] This was very well for a Royal joke, & in a foreigner.   It was rather like Leopold, tho' better ;   for with him one may apply the line of,
" Gentle dulness ever likes a joke,"
a line either of Genl Fitzpatrick or Sheridan's.

The ladies are all in a fuss for costume for the Fancy Ball at Court.

April 22d.

I must begin by correcting a blunder made in my last.   The quotation, which I ascribed either to Sheridan or to the General, is in the *Dunciad.*   This you will think an egregious blunder ;   but so it is. It is remarkable how puzzled people are about the most common quotation, such for instance, " The feast of reason, the flow of soul." Well read persons give it to various authors, except the right one. [2]

On Monday I am going to make your dear Aunt a visit for a night or two. [3]   She has not been as well as usual, but has rallied, by cautiously keeping within doors in this dreadful weather.   A little society without fatigue or emotion does her good and amuses her ;   for she passes many solitary hours, which few endure with impunity, still less those who like her have always been blessed with connections constantly about her, as she enjoyed all her life.   Occasionally, I know,

---

[1] An allusion to Lord John's second marriage in July 1841, to Lady Frances Elliot, daughter of 2nd Earl of Minto.

[2] *Pope's Satires.*   [3] Little Holland House.

E.L.H .   O

she is quite alone. This has readily reconciled me to her school,[1]
as that furnishes occupation ; & both school master & mistress are
persons she can converse with. You will be glad hear how well
Shelburne [2] keeps his plump, good looks, even in London. He seems
perfectly happy, & is installed in charming rooms under the paternal
roof, which is a great enjoyment to his family, and made better for
himself as to space & frequent meetings with his little sister, who doats
upon him. There is no rumour of his selecting any fair lady. It would
be better if he did ; & I am sure his good temper, cheerfulness & very
agreable conversation would make any young woman fond of him.

Yesterday I dined with Baring Wall [3] in his beautiful house, which
he shews off to every advantage by lighting well, good company &
bonne chère. I was gratified by meeting at their own request Mr
Baring, the late Chancellor of the Exchequer, & his plain, but very
agreable wife, Lady Arabella. This might be considered a tribute of
esteem for the name I bear, & as such was deeply valued ; for God
knows what even slender agrémens I might have had are now gone,
& leave me only a dispirited, melancholy being, but *nervously* grateful
for any kindness bestowed.

Wilkie's drawings are exhibited at Christie's. They are very beautiful, and will I hope sell well for his sister's sake. But nothing sells
well since the income tax has been enacted.

April 29th, [1842].

London is now so full & busy, that it keeps all my quiet friends
in a bustle. The rebound falls on me ; so that I long for the calm
of being out of town. What a change ! Formerly the fullness of
the town & occupation of Parlt were all agreable, amused *us* both,
& gave us the enjoyment of the élite of society *quietly* within our own
walks. And how he used to enjoy his H. of Lords & anecdotes : &
told stories so well & full of point of the little incidents of the day
which diverted him, & was so relished by his hearers. All this is as
fresh as if it was going on, so that at moments I am puzzled before I
wake to the cruel reality.

[1] Miss Fox had bought a quarter of an acre from her brother's estate in
Kensington, probably on the North side of the present Holland Park Road,
in order to erect a school, in which she took great interest.

[2] Lord Lansdowne's eldest surviving son, who married in 1840 a daughter of
11th Earl of Pembroke. She died six months later.

[3] Charles Baring Wall (1819–53). Sir Francis Baring (1796–1866), the ex-
Chancellor of the Exchequer, was created Lord Northbrook in 1866. His
second wife, whom he married in 1841, Lady Arabella Howard, was daughter
of 1st Earl of Effingham.

Wilkie's drawings are fetching immense prices, out of respect to him & regard for his sister. I have begged a friend to buy *something* as far as £10, but nothing goes so low. Per contra, Strawberry Hill yields less than was expected.

[*May 3d,* 1842.]

The appointment of Lady Lyttelton [1] to the superintendence of the Royal infants is much approved. She is an excellent woman, & tho' very strict in religion has not given in to any of the extremes which divide society so much—indeed to an excess that makes it irksome to those who have no strong turn for theology.

What a world we live in ! How daily is the exemplification of the fable of the man & his ass. The Queen yielded to the supplications of the tradesmen to give a fillip to trade, so had the Fancy Ball. Another part of the community now abuse the levity of such shows when the people are starving. How hard, with the best intentions, to be so treated. The squabbles about the costume are very great among the ladies. Lady Walpole [2] goes as Lucrezia Borgia ; her partner, Shelburne, will be Ludovico Sforza il Moro. What detestable characters for such good persons to personate. The Queen is to be Philippa ; Albert, Edward III. I believe Ld Abercorn is to be David Bruce, 2d King of Scotland, the captive of Philippa : Dss of Sutherland, Sibilla, Dss of Saxony.

Ld Lauderdale & Anthony [Maitland] [3] dined here yesterday. They are only just arrived. They hear Ly L. had a cold, & by an accident of illness would be alone two days ; so Anthony is off to Scotland to join her, tho' he came to pass a month. They are most devoted sons ; it is quite pleasant to see the continuance of affection & tenderness to such a degree as exists in both of them towards her.

Lady Seymour [4] has not lost a jot of her beauty ; they both liked Italy. There cannot be a more estimable & agreable man.

---

[1] Sarah, widow of William Henry, 3rd Lord Lyttelton, and daughter of 2nd Earl Spencer.

[2] Lady Holland's grand-daughter, Harriet Pellew, who had married Lord Orford's son in November, 1841.

[3] James, 9th Earl (1784–1860), and his brother, who succeeded him as 10th Earl (1785–1863), sons of Lady Holland's old friend James, 8th Earl and his wife Eleanor Todd, who survived till 1856. Neither of their sons married.

[4] Later Duchess of Somerset, and formerly Miss Sheridan (*see ante,* p. 76).

May 6th.

Lady Abercorn, who is quite an angel in disposition, has been twice
to see Ly H. Russell since her loss,[1] & will I am persuaded always fulfil
every sisterly duty towards her.   This calamity will be a loss to the
splendor of the Fancy Ball, the brilliant toilette of the Dss of Bedford,
& all the grace & taste of Ly Abercorn.   The Dss of Roxburghe
takes the jewels, & the Duke will be the captive King David Bruce.
But all these matters must be as indifferent to you as they are to me.

Washington Irving [2] came to see me the other night.   He is looking
better than formerly, much delighted with his appointment to Madrid
which really seems to be judicious on the part of the American Govt.

May 17th, [1842].

. . . The only joke or repartee of any merit at the Ball, was by a
person who went as the Pretender.   Sir Robt Peel said to him, " You
are a bold man to venture here, as there is a reward of £40,000 for
your person."   " Oh !   I knew there was no danger, as you said
the Whigs had not left so much in the Treasury."

July 8th.

Curious to hear the fine *Stabat Mater* of Rossini, I ventured to
L[ansdowne] H., placed myself in a dark corner of the semicircle, &
slipped behind a curtain : so avoided all the throng, but I was a good
deal overcome and could not stay it out, by which the fine finale was
lost to me.   I will try again at one of the theatres.   It was extremely
fine & touching.   The room is magnificent & admirably adapted to
music.   Is the *Stabat Mater* of Rossini much admired in Italy ?   In
my early days that of Pergolese was considered perfect.   Is there any
good translation into Italian ?   The original is said to have been
written by Pope Innocent III or IV, a co-temporary of our King John.

People are dispersing rapidly.   The John Russells had their last
dinner with me yesterday ; they go to Minto immediately.

Tuesday, October 12th.

. . . Poor Lord Wellesley has not left a sol in the world, no debts,
& no money or chattels.[3]   Ly W. has only an old pension of £300

---

[1] Henrietta Maria, daughter of Admiral Hon. Robert Stopford, married Lord
Henry Russell, son of 6th Duke of Bedford, who died a few days before.

[2] American writer and diplomatist.

[3] Lord Wellesley had died in September : his widow in 1853.   She was his
second wife, a native of Philadelphia, and earlier married to Robert Paterson,
brother-in-law to Jerome Bonaparte.

pr am, suspended during his life, & her salary of £500 as Lady to the Q. Dowager. Her health & habits make this but a sorry pittance for her. The family naturally enough were mortified & offended that Downes, the maître d'hôtel, was left sole executor, & walked with them at the funeral. The D of W. was very wrath at being kept two hours for the ceremony : & shewed his displeasure in a marked manner at Eton to those who conducted the cortège. The private papers are left to Alfred Montgomery.

In October, Lord Melbourne had a stroke. Lady Holland wrote a few days later : " The great dread of Lord Melbourne's family was that any sinister report of his illness should get into the newspapers. This has been avoided, which is lucky, as he reads them as usual. It is strange to say, but nevertheless true, that he is *not* aware of the nature of his attack, talks of lumbago and suppressed gout, in which a fit of the gout in the affected limb has been a corroboration."

December 20th, [1842]. S. St.

My visit to Brocket was very satisfactory. Ld M. is going on in a progressive state of amendment. His spirits are good ; a little society cheers him. He is very happy in his entourage ; nothing can be more affectionate & comfortable to him. He made me promise another visit. . . .

Tuesday. [*Late in December*, 1842.]

. . . The snow came on very formidably, the falling of the barometer indicating something extraordinary ; so I abridged my visit by a day at Brocket, to avoid the chance of being snowbound, & returned yesterday with Mrs Lamb here for a day or two. Ld Melbourne is greatly improved in bodily vigor, moves with freedom without assistance. He was more serious than before, his mind evidently engaged upon the subject of coming or not to Parlt. However he has left the decision entirely to his physician ; for he says he feels like the captain of a ship when he has the pilot on board, free from all responsibility. Indeed, he is an excellent patient, abiding entirely by his doctor. I know Dr Holland is very distinct in his opinion, that any such attempt would be rash at present, for he is not equal to the excitement. I expect your Aunt tomorrow & long for her arrival. She is a great comfort, tho' it will be but for a short time. I shall make her a visit frequently at Little Hd H. I have not had courage to go *there* these 3 months ; it oversets me for many hours afterwards.

You will enjoy Brougham's society much, if he is in good trim ; but he is always restless & full of speculations when the meeting of Parlt approaches.

March 3d, [1843]. S. St.

. . . Ld Brougham has furnished many topics to the town from his sayings & deeds. There is a caricature, quite excellent, of him as a *pantin*, the strings of which are pulled by D. of W. The figure jumps & skips all ways. To have been more correct, the string ought to have been pulled by the Chancellor, who entirely directs his proceedings as far as is convenient for the purposes of Govt. His answer to Mr Charles Philips, an Irish lawyer, who was lamenting his whiskers were growing grey while his hair was still brown. " My dear fellow, how can you wonder. You have been working your jaws these 30 years ; & your brains have done nothing all the time." *He* set Roebuck upon the business of the policy of the Indian war the other night, who executed his scheme with as much vituperation & malignity as possible quite to content him, to annoy both Lds Palmerston & Auckland . . .

The Queen has been so horror struck & terrified since the murder of Mr Drummond,[1] that she has never taken air or exercise out of the Palace Gardens. No wonder ! Should the assassin not be committed today, she & all public characters may expect a fate similar to poor Mr Drummond's. There is a great dread the verdict will be insanity : very mischievous indeed, should it be so.

9th May, 1843.

. . . This overwhelming blow affects my thoughts & habits so much, that when I write there is nothing occurs to say, but I will try to gather what my memory may rake up.[2]

People are so much distressed & pinched in their means by the income tax & the probability of great reduction in rents this autumn, that there will be few purchasers for the Duke of Sussex's library & rich plate.[3] It is quite singular how people are saving all expenditure : no balls, or fêtes, or gaieties of any sort. Covent Garden is closed ;

[1] Edward Drummond (1792–1843), Private Secretary to Ripon, Canning, Wellington and Peel, was shot, in mistake for Peel, by Daniel Macnaghten.

[2] Dr. Allen had died in April.

[3] Augustus Frederick, Duke of Sussex, died in April. Lady Holland wrote : " His excellent little wife is scarcely provided for." He was twice morganatically married. His 2nd wife, Lady Cecilia Underwood, was created Dss of Inverness.

& bankruptcies occur daily. Wm Cowper [1] is going to marry a lovely girl, Miss Gurney. She is not of the Quaker branch, but most of her relations are of that persuasion. They will not be rich, but in love, & good qualities.

May, [1843].

It is difficult to answer your enquiry as to the probability of Mr Ellice's marriage. [2] He denies it stoutly to those friends who are most intimate with him. Yet his son & daughter evidently believe in it ; & the purchase of a small house in this quarter gives weight to the story, as it seems destined for them. He is so perfectly happy in his little domestic circle, and she seems to suit him so perfectly, that any change must be deprecated, *le mieux est l'ennemi du bien,* a maxim my poor old friend Dumont used to be shocked at my maintaining. In the meantime Mr Ellice announces his plans as being settled for the shooting in Scotland, & then a winter at Naples. He is so friendly & warm hearted, that it is impossible not to be much interested in his welfare ; so I sincerely hope all he may do will prove conducive to his happiness. Genl Ellice & his wife are very useful members of society, and I am not surprized at your being glad to have them back again this winter. A wild son has been troublesome to them ; but Mr Ellice has been very sensible upon that occasion, as indeed upon all where his friends & family require assistance.

There has been a breeze between the Dss of Buccleuch & Prince Albert, which ended by her resignation & his making an apology— this at least is the on-dit. It was occasioned by his dismissal of the Dss from the Director's box at the " Ancient Music," as the Queen was not there. He is accused of greater assumption than is quite relished ; enough, it is said, to make it necessary the Queen should *herself* hold Levées in future. This will be seen soon, if true.

Ld Melbourne really is astonishingly recovered. He hardly shows any remains of illness. He is tolerably discreet in his proceedings. He is more amused in London ; & as he takes it moderately, it is as well he enjoys the variety. The Beauvales are inestimable to him.

---

[1] Hon. William Francis Cowper (1811–88), later created Lord Mount-Temple, son of 5th Earl Cowper.

[2] Edward Ellice, sen. (1781–1863), known in London society as " Bear," being connected with the Canadian fur trade, married Dowager Countess of Leicester, " Coke of Norfolk's " second wife, in October. His brother General Robert Ellice resided in Florence, and was largely instrumental in introducing G. F. Watts, the painter, to the Hollands. The picture of his three daughters, painted by the young artist during that year, was given to the Hollands.

They square all their motions to his advantage & comfort. There never was a greater change in a man's character made by matrimony than has been effected in Ld B's.

23d May.   S. St.

I slept two nights at Richmond at *Sir* Henry & Lady Webster's, at a charming villa on Richmond Hill. They were very kind & did all they could to make the time pass lightly ; but Richmond affects me too much. We used to go so often either to Ld Lansdowne's or the Castle Inn for change of air ; so that every object is replete with painful recollections.

The Misses Berry are established with Ly C. Lindsay for the summer. They occupy the house which Princess Lieven had for some years. They are very hospitable always, & one day, Saturday, have luncheon at 4 to *all* their London friends, who flock in numbers, as it is a vacant Parliamentary day. The D. of Devonshire gives a morning affair at Chiswick on the Wednesday. The weather has been so wretched that the gardens are not available at all ; the guests being crowded into the house, not very champêtre.

The Royal visit to Ireland is renounced on account of the unsettled state of that country ; people seem really to be alarmed. The little Princess is to be Xtened Alice Maud Mary ; the latter name because she was born on the Dss of Gloucester's birthday. I have just been sitting with Ld Carlisle, who is much better. If the weather ever mends he will rally, & if he gives up Castle Howard for the winter, may enjoy much comfort still. He has every blessing in life in a numerous and devoted family.

May 26th.

Upon the strength of Lord Carlisle's & Miss Berry's praise of *G. Selwyn's Correspondence*, I despatched it immediately, in the hopes it might be in time for a messenger going to Naples. I did not even keep it to read. I am assured the letters are amusing. The editor's [1] connecting links are not reckoned good. Ld Carlisle says he could have supplied much matter, had the editor applied to him, not only letters but curious anecdotes of G. Selwyn himself. The not doing so makes me afraid it is not a very excellent work. *Gilly Williams*, the lively writer of the best letters as I am told, I knew pretty well in my early life. He was very gay & agreable to young & old, the brother of Lady North, wife of the Minister, & consequently uncle to our friend Ly Charlotte Lindsay. [2]

[1] John Heneage Jesse.   [2] Daughter of 2nd Earl of Guilford.

I am going on a visit to the Master of the Rolls & Lady Langdale at Roehampton.[1] It is very kind in them to ask me, as a change of air & scene is beneficial both to health & spirits.

May 30th.

. . . Large parties are gone to stay in the neighbourhood of Epsom for the races ; the Derby is tomorrow. One horse belonging to Ld G. Bentinck may win £98,000. His name is Gaper.[2] Lady H. Baring has a large party at their cottage ; Mr Ellice, his annual party at Banstead, of D. Dss of Bedford, Ld Spencer, Duncannon, etc. They have enlisted Ld John for the first time. They are sure at least of good company & cheer, if not of good sport.

The book I sent, upon Ld Carlisle's approval of it, has disgusted me much. The editor in his biographical links has given a most abominable view of the character of Mr Fox, under the specious hypocrisy of the moral cant of the day.[3] All that is derogatory & *false* is said, a few sugared words to cover the base, insidious falsehoods. Ld C. had not read that volume, & will be as much disgusted as I am. Indeed he is not overpleased by what is said of his father, whose memory might have been spared the revival of the Byron differences & other matters of levity, not very pleasant for his descendants. However, these are points of less importance than the slander on Mr Fox. I quite regret having sent you the book, or given a mite towards its success.

The prudish ladies who attend the " Ancient Music " are scandalized at the *immoral* life of Grisi ; & have remonstrated with Prince Albert & Duke of Wellington at her singing here. Can you believe such canting folly ?

An agitation for the Repeal of the Act of Union with Ireland was brought to a head, by the dismissal by the Lord Chancellor of Ireland from the Magistracy, in May, of Lord ffrench, O'Connell, and 32 other justices. Troops were moved over to Ireland ; and in October, O'Connell was arrested on a charge of conspiracy. An adverse verdict, however, was reversed by the House of Lords in 1844.

June 2d. S. St.

. . . People are beginning to be serious about Ireland. Wm Lascelles, a friend of Peel's and supporter, considers the question of

---

[1] Henry Bickersteth (1783–1851), raised to the peerage in 1836.

[2] Cotherstone won the race.

[3] Charles James Fox. These passages appear in Vol. II, as well as a comparison between Lord Byron's and Lord Carlisle's poems, on Rome, etc.

Repeal carried, if persevered in ; for it seems the Irish Bar are going over & many calm persons changing their conduct. This would not have happened, had the Govt pursued the measures of their predecessors. The dismissal of the magistrates taking away O'Connell's Commission of the Peace has been impolitic to a great extent ; for it does not appear at any of the meetings they exceeded the law. The Tories are very much discontented, & complain of Peel to an absurd degree.

June 9th.

. . . Shelburne arrived suddenly after a rapid journey of 6 days from Vienna. He went immediately to join his father at Richmond. This may be inferred to be a proof that all is concluded with Emily, which I know will give great pleasure to all their friends.[1] She is a lucky person ; as he will make an admirable husband, a sweet temper, gay, & *amusable* which is a great quality en ménage, and very entertaining. I hope she likes him enough to appreciate all these merits. There is a great feud between Lys Londonderry & Jersey, aggravated by two rival parties last night, a contention for the K. of Hanover's presence. Ly L. carried it by the *substantial* charm of the dinner. One of the offences was Ly Jersey saying that Lord Blandford [2] was one of *Sarah's cast offs*. In short, the tongue has been very active with both ladies against each other.

July 3d, [1843]. S. St.

. . . The cartoons exhibiting in Westminster Hall are considered much superior to anything ever expected from native talent, all executed by unknown young men but one, who is your friend Severn.[3] His is reckoned the best & obtained the prize. The whole is in the grandiose style. This exhibition will improve the drawing of our artists, in which they are accused of being far inferior to foreign artists. Lady Davy is quite well, tho' somewhat *thinner*. She talks

[1] Lord Shelburne's second wife was Emily de Flahault, daughter of the Comte de Flahault and Baroness Keith and Nairne. The wedding took place in November.

[2] John Winston Churchill, later 7th Duke of Marlborough, who married in July, Lady Londonderry's daughter, Lady Frances Anne Vane-Tempest.

[3] Three £300 prizes had been awarded in 1843 in a competition for frescoes for the decoration of the new Houses of Parliament. Two of the successful artists were Joseph Severn (1793–1879), who had just returned from Rome with his family, and George Frederick Watts, who became so closely associated with the new Lord and Lady Holland in his visit to Florence on the proceeds. (See *Chronicles of Holland House*, p. 320.)

decidedly of pitching her tent here, is doing up her house, & will compete with the Berrys in her soirées. She is goodhumoured, gay, & always kind hearted. She is now living with her sister, till her house is ready for her reception.

The Parlt is dragging on, nor likely to be finished before August. The Irish Arms Bill is tedious ; & every clause contested by very tiresome speakers, Lord Clements especially, of whom Serjeant Murphy says, " the penalties are bad enough, but the *Clement*cy worse." Lord Grey is really getting over this unpleasant, serious attack.[1] Yet his *sight* is no better ; he has seen all his family without being too much excited.

The next letter again refers to the overwhelming shock which the writer had received by Dr. Allen' s death on April 8.

Friday, [*July*] 21*st*. S. St.

. . . The close heat of this little residence was impossible during the bright days ; & alas ! I cannot stir from it. Hd H. is out of the question. I would & might have tried it, but for this second loss, which has deprived me of my prop & companion, friend & protector. I cannot travel, to pass solitary, dull evenings in an inn. My health is greatly affected by the confinement. I dine out a good deal, & with persons I like who give me agreable society ; so that a few hours are thus beguiled away. But the others are sad enough. The *return* to what is called *home* !, that dear word which comprizes all that is valuable in life, affects me dreadfully still. Charles & Ly Mary are much occupied in settling their house, which is really very pretty ; so that He is rarely to be seen, & unfortunately offered me no resource.

Another great marriage is declared, Ly Blanche Cecil & the rich Balfour & Ly Eleanor's son.[2] They say he is gawky ; but they are all good people, & it will do well without doubt. There is another alliance on the tapis which is not very promising, nor as yet quite certain, between Hastings Russell & Lord Delawarr's daughter, Ly Elizabeth West. The father is an easy going, weak man ; the mother is reckoned scheming & interested ; the whole family high Tory & Puseyites. These principles will not do with the domains & departed shades of Woburn. You will say the possible want of

[1] Lady Holland wrote on June 20 : " Lord Grey is a state of health which causes much anxiety, a sudden loss of sight, at least for all purposes of *reading*, attended with headache & debility."

[2] James Maitland Balfour, of Whittingehame, son of James Balfour and Lady Eleanor Maitland, married the daughter of 2nd Marquis of Salisbury.

beauty does not concern others ; yet it is a merit the less.   No answer is come from Ld Wm.   It is said Ly Wm is well disposed : perhaps she would not object to what must annoy the family on that very score.

August 5th.

I returned today from Richmond in a *thunder storm.* . . .   I cannot say my alarm of thunder is conquered because I sat still & let the carriage proceed ; but life is less valuable and need not be clung to as formerly.   You will see one of these days, when H. Walpole's *Memoires* are published, what he repeats as having been said of Richmond.   He had called at Holland House & seen your G. Grand-father [1] in a state of alarm about his son Stephen, who had St. Vitus's dance in consequence of a fever at Eton.   He had tried sea bathing & all that was recommended, & finally was going with him for change of air to Richmond ;   upon which Alderman Beckford exclaimed, " That is the most unwholesome place in England. Why I lost in the course of one year 12 natural children."   Said *Memoires* will not appear yet.   Sir D. Le Marchant is the editor, & is supplying notes.

London is dispersing.   There is a new epoch in the day chosen for diversions, a *ball* by daylight from four to seven, with substantial breakfasts.   Many of the young fashionables go afterwards to dinner & other balls or concerts in the evening.   Chesterfield House began this frolic, followed by Lady Londonderry ;   & Mrs Damer gives her first next Saturday.   All the foreigners are astonished at the physical strength of our fine ladies.   They are quite knocked up by the pursuit of what is termed pleasure !   The King of Hanover has issued cards for a great party at his apartments in St James's, under the title of *Duke of Cumberland.*   This is rather unintelligible etiquette.

Sunday.   [*August* 1843].

Mr Motteux has left *Spencer* Cowper[2] heir to all his immense fortune. I am not surprized.   He was so like his father, Ld Cowper, who was Motteux's greatest friend, & the young man was also a great personal favorite.   The wealth is very great.   Spencer is charming.   You

---

[1] Henry Fox, 1st Lord Holland.

[2] Charles Spencer Cowper, son of 5th Earl Cowper, and nephew of Lord Melbourne.   John Motteux was owner of Sandringham, in Norfolk, said to have been originally an Italian mountebank, who became a favourite everywhere in London society.

must remember how much he was at Hd H., & how much we liked him. This gives me great pleasure.

October 27th.

. . . I believe in one of my letters I must have mentioned that the Emperor of Russia had sent for Balzac from Paris to answer Custine back. This is confirmed by Balzac going to Petersburgh, which he has already done.[1] Probably Psse Lieven suggested the measure, & was the intermediary. Any contradiction will be vain ; so many can warrant the truth of his facts. Mrs Austin,[2] who knows from a long residence at Berlin, says an addenda might be even fuller of atrocities than Custine has given. The two first volumes were as much as I could accomplish ; the others tired. Mrs Trollope[3] is spoken of by those who have met her often very much in the terms you use, great quickness, ready perception of the ludicrous, with remarkable clearness o expression, altogether making her a very agreable companion. Her son is dreadful, very nearly got his nose pulled at Rome at some soirée there. I hope you will be well with her ; she has a powerful pen.

Ld Brougham pretends to be very violent against Lord Aberdeen, for the appointment of what he chooses to call a *Whig Radical*, Hy Bulwer, to Spain,[4] by which 50 votes were lost to the Tories in the City. B. is on his way to Cannes. He is cheerful, not wild as he is often.

October 30th, 1843. S. St.

. . . Dickens unfortunately has written himself down. Your friend Mrs Trollope also has degraded herself in the *Widow Barnaby*. How good was her *Vicar of Wrexhill, Jefferson Laidlaw* [*Whitlaw*], *Trenore* [*Tremordyn*] *Cliff*, all admirable ; but not the *Widow*, nor her last written against the Poor Law System. There are rumours afloat,

---

[1] Lady Holland wrote earlier in the month : " I do not know whether you read *Custine* on Russia. If you have, you will not be surprised that the Emperor Nicholas should send for Balzac to Petersburgh to answer the book. All who know Russia affirm that is a correct account of that country, to which much might be added in aggravation, but with truth. What a dreadful disclosure it makes of the existence there."

[2] Sarah Austin (1793–1867), translator, *née* Taylor.

[3] Frances Trollope (1780–1863), novelist, and mother of Thomas Adolphus and Anthony Trollope. It is clearly the first-named to whom Lady Holland refers, as he was in Italy at this time.

[4] As Ambassador. (*See ante*, p. 177.)

of the Govt intending to drop the prosecution against O'Connell, on account of the blunder committed in the outset by the main witness, but this requires confirmation. They have got a nut which they do not know how to crack. The Duc de Guiche is going to Alton Towers to meet the Duc de Bordeaux, an unwise move on his part, as every one says *he* is not to be received by the Queen at Windsor.[1] Why did he come to England?

November 3d, [1843].

. . . Baron Dedel [2] gave an amusing account of an incident which occurred at Drayton when the Gd Duke was going away.[3] Both Sir R. Peel & Lady accompanied him to his carriage, a calèche in which he & Capt. Meynell travelled. A spacious hired omnibus was behind to hold the suite. Just as they were driving off, six little dwarfish dirty Cossacks rushed by, clambered up the carriage, sticking on as they could on the top & sides. The astonishment of the Peels was great; they had never seen or heard of the existence of these inmates, who upon enquiry it appeared had been closely confined to the Gd Duke's apartment; held no intercourse whatever with the servants of the family. They slept at his door, & about his room. How strangely barbarous! It was the same at Chatsworth. The Queen, to whom Dedel told the story, was diverted, & said she should set about making enquiries if they had also been in the Castle.

Many of the Carlists are come from Paris to pay their respects to the D. of Bordeaux. There is a great gathering to meet him at Lord Shrewsbury's today. . . . The young man is not reckoned in the least clever, but pleasing from good nature, fat, awkward, and rather ugly.

---

[1] The Duc de Bordeaux (Comte de Chambord) (1820–83), posthumous son of the Duc de Berri. His visit made a great stir in French political circles, as he on several occasions gave hints as his claim to the throne. Lady Holland wrote later in the month: " . . . The Carlists at Paris are quite wild at this visit of the D. de Bordeaux, holding forcible language against this Country & our dear little Queen. She, they say, is a *vile Reine*, a *cochon de Pays*, etc. Sorry was I to hear these terms were used by a lady whom we know well: and sorry that the Duc de Guiche is here on a visit to the D. of B . . ."

[2] (1776–1846). Dutch Minister in London, 1833–46.

[3] Later Czar Alexander II.

CHAPTER XIII

1844–1845

January 23d, 1844.

. . . Poor Sir Francis Burdett died this morning, a victim to the cold water practice. He was warned by Pennington, his apothecary, not to venture upon it ; but too late. I am sorry for him, as with all his blemishes there were high, reclaiming qualities in his nature, great good nature and a generous feeling of indignation against oppression in every form.

March 29th, [1844].

. . . Politics are in a very strange state. It would require the pen of Ellice to disintangle them or make them comprehensible. All parties are mixed ; and the strictest on each side have changed about, & vote with their enemies. The holidays will shake them all right again ; only I hope some of our *best* men may not have offended too deeply their supporters. Ld Lyndhurst is much pleased at Sir J. Graham's use of " the companion of Jack Cade " : [1] says he thinks he shall hear no more of " aliens in blood," that Jack Cade will absorb all the shots against the Ministry. Our friend Brougham conducted himself strangely indeed at the Drawing Room, got *into conversation* with the Queen & Albert, offering to carry letters to Paris for her, & then turning most familiarly to her, " and *parcels* also." [2] He told the Dss of Kent she only looked 24, by the bye younger than her daughter. Yet with all this wildness he went to H. of Lords, & made the most rational speech he has made for years.

April 2d, [1844].

. . . I last evening dined with Baring Wall, who knowing I had not seen the dwarf, had him in the evening. He is a wonderful

---

[1] Lord Ashley's " Ten Hours Bill " was largely responsible for the confusion. The likening of it by Sir James Graham, then Home Secretary, to " Jack Cade Legislation " infuriated the Whigs. Lyndhurst, who had called the Irish, " aliens," in 1836, was correspondingly delighted.

[2] Lady Holland added in another letter : " You will see that this has reached *Punch,* who makes good fun of it. It is perfectly true that he made the offer ; at which her little Majesty was indignant and tossed her head."

little being, only 25 inches high, weighing 15 lbs. He is not in the least deformed, perfectly well made, with all his faculties, rather sharp, answers questions aptly, seems good tempered. It is really curious, & not in the least offensive. You will probably see him ; as he is *sold* for £3000 for a year, & will make the tour of Europe.

April 5th, 1844.

You will be glad to hear that the Duke of Sutherland, who had become stone deaf latterly, has entirely recovered his hearing. They are going to finish their holidays at Trentham. He jokingly ascribes his recovery to the sight of an immense cargo of *trumpets* sent to him to Brighton : like a dentist driving off a tooth ache by the sight of the instrument.

Friday, [April ?].

. . . Your friend, H. Greville, the world chose to marry to Ly Essex.[1] Her giving up her house for a theatrical exhibition in which he plays the hero, rather confirmed the report ; but I disbelieve it much from the manner in which she speaks of him, quite at her ease, without any reserve. The persons most admired yesterday were Lady Ormonde, Ly C. Villiers, and an American girl, a niece of Lady Wellesley's, Miss Macvigor. Rachel [2] is much improved, was praised for her figure & graceful maintien. She will, I hope, have great success, for she is extremely clever, modest & agreable. Ld Melbourne does not come from Brocket till 3d May. He is wise to enjoy the beauties of his charming place as long as possible. I suspect he delayed coming in order not to be in town on the Birthday, which he knew he ought in prudence not to attend, & yet felt annoyed at the necessity.

Notwithstanding Lady Holland's doubts, Sir Hugh Gough won great praise for his conduct of the war in China, and as Commander-in-Chief against the Sikhs in 1845, Hardinge serving under him as second-in-command. The latter had succeeded Lord Ellenborough, who had been recalled, as his record as to Afghanistan and India had not been outstanding.

[1] The Dowager-Countess of Essex (Catherine Stephens, the singer). The marriage did not come off.
[2] The 6th Duke of Bedford's youngest daughter. She married Lord James Butler.

May 7th, 1844.

. . . The Indian business is so far settled that Sir H. Hardinge is appointed.[1] His nomination is considered as a *sop* to the D. of W., whose man he is. The choice is of a doubtful good (?) ; as H. is impetuous, not likely to be a good administrator for the civil Govt. He will be Commander in Chief, by which appointment the Ministers will be extricated from employing Sir H. Gough, in whom little confidence is placed, & whose achievements in China are ascribed solely to Sir Wm Parker [2] & Pottinger. S. Herbert is to move from the Admiralty to the War Office without the Cabinet ; & a rising man connected with the manufacturing interest is to succeed S. H. at the Admiralty, Mr Cardwell, who distinguished himself by making the best answer to Ld Ashley's Factory question, & seconded the Address on the meeting of Parliament.

May 24th.

I dined yesterday with Spencer Cowper in his pretty house, the late Duke of Argyll's. He lives very handsomely without profusion, not with vulgar profusion like a parvenu. All is in good taste, the plate beautiful ; poor Motteux's crest, a bird, has a very pretty effect on the tops of the dishes. The cellars are abundantly stored with the best of wines, very choice & excellent. He now only wants a suitable wife to make him perfectly happy ; for his eye I believe to be very safe. People are diverted at the defeat of a job of Brougham's upon a Railway Bill. He was very wrath with Ld Clanricarde upon the subject, & has said more, they say, about Ld Grey's opinion than he was justified in doing. The accounts from Howick are, I fear, *very bad.*

June 4th.

. . . I cannot press on Lord Aberdeen your wishes & my own, till the commotion of the Emperor's arrival is over.[3] Said Emperor came suddenly. It will hardly amount to a nine days wonder ; he having announced his intention of quitting England next Sunday.

[1] Sir Henry Hardinge, created Viscount in 1846 (1785–1856), Governor-General of India, 1844–8.

[2] Vice-Admiral Sir William Parker, 1st Bart. (1781–1868). Sir Henry Pottinger (1789–1859), soldier and diplomatist, was also created a Baronet.

[3] Lady Granville wrote to her brother, the Duke of Devonshire, on June 1 : " What a surprise on the world is the Emperor Nicholas—expected today to play with Saxony, to bet at Ascot, & puzzle the ladies who head the Polish ball " (ii. 384).

He travels under the name of Cte Orloff, being accompanied by the real Cte. The police are put upon a close watch of the Poles ; *one* Pole is watched day & nights. He is to go to Windsor today till Friday. It is lucky he came in Ascot week, as it is among the few sights quite *unique*. No other country could shew him such a sport & pastime. It is silly to give reviews to great Continental powers ; we have such a handful only of troops, compared to other powers. The Prussians laughed in their sleeve at those we exhibited to the King. The poor King of Saxony [1] is quite dimmed by the Imperial effulgence. It is said he has not pleased the House of Coburg, by his ordonnance as to the rank & title they pretend to ask for, that of Royal Highness.

Your Aunt has sent you *Coningsby*, D'Israeli's novel. When you read it, you may like to know what is said to be the glossary. Rigby, Mr Croker : Lord Eskdale, Ld Lonsdale : Oswald Millbank, young Mr Walter, Editor of the *Times* : Gay, Theodore Hook : Taper & another of the same stamp, Messrs Ross & Bonham : Coningsby, Mr Smythe : Ld Monmouth, Ld Hertford, not exactly his biography but many traits & incidents similar to what occurred in his career : Sidonia, Israeli himself. It is a work full of talent ; the most impudent, brilliant & tedious I ever read. Macaulay calls it, " Young England, written by old Jewry " : well said.

Poor Naworth[2] is to be patched up. The £10,000 insurance upon the building is to be expended in roofing & restoring, so as to make a few rooms habitable. The whole family are passionately fond of the place.

June 7th. S. St.

The Emperor's visit has hitherto been successful : he gives & spends largely, both virtues in the eyes of John Bull. He is also chevaleresque about women : shocked at our Court etiquette of *brisking* (?) to the Royalties, a fashion unknown in other Courts : shocked on his visit to the Dss of Gloucester, that the *Lady* in waiting opened the battens (?) for him. A man interposed, caught the door, exclaiming, " Ah ! Madame, c'est impossible," rather a lesson to our great folks. The papers give an account of his donation to Ascot. The Review was a failure, because the orders were disobeyed. The Queen had determined upon quitting the ground before the Artillery fired, & orders had been given to that effect ; when lo ! a volley was discharged close

---

[1] Frederick Augustus II.
[2] A disastrous fire had taken place at Lord Carlisle's, in Cumberland.

to the Queen. The D. of W. was in a towering passion, using strong expletives, D. D. D., D.s without end, ordered the Artillery off. When asked, said to H—., " If they liked." So this, the only good part of the show, was dismissed. It does not appear they have managed at Court very well for his amusement. Tonight there is to be a small party at the Palace, music, which he dislikes : & *mourning* still for old Papa Coburg. The invitations are confined to all persons more or less connected with Russia. They ought to have had a ball for the young beauties to be shewn to him. His conduct about Lady Conyngham was very pretty. He enquired about her, heard she was under a cloud, expressed his intention to see her before he left England, having been well received by her 27 years ago during her splendor : adding that he well knew where there was misfortune & calamity, there was also calumny. He saw her & was shocked. The good little, quizzical King of Saxony is delighted at being so eclipsed by the great autocrat; he is shy & modest. Your friend Lord Northampton, has written a mighty silly letter about the Poles, amounting to just nothing at all. Enough of Royalties.

Ld Albemarle has won the Cup at Ascot, at which I rejoice. His horse was one of his own breeding & occupied him much. The Cup is beautiful, both in taste & execution, one of Storr & Mortimer's design. Poor little Lady Barbara is no more ; & Wm Ponsonby [1] is greatly overcome by her loss. Whilst *herself*, she was a generous, sober minded soul ; witness her making him give up his own fortune, saying they had enough, to poor Fred. Ponsonby, who was deeply in debt. Then sheltering for upwards of 20 years Ld Bessborough, really reversing the position of parent & child. *Now* it is certainly a release from a life of long suffering.

The D. of Wellington swore that if he knew who had presumed to give the order for firing, they should be punished, dismissed. Nobody would tell ; but it's said to have been his own aide-de-camp, Capt. de Ros—probably, for they are a meddling race.

23d October 1844.

. . . I am going to quit my foyer for a visit to Bowood *per rail* : but I am not *yet* gone & my railroad friends advise postponing, should there be as heavy a fog as that of today. Luttrell will be my protector on the way. His conversation will distract my thoughts from the *imminent* perils of the trip. You will have heard all the anecdotes

---

[1] *See ante*, p. 44. He was created Lord de Mauley in 1838. Lady Barbara was daughter of 5th Earl of Shaftesbury.

of Louis Philippe & his visit.   The upshot has been that he has won
golden opinions everywhere ;   & probably each country will be
softened by such familiar intercourse.   You will soon have Neumann
& his illustrious bride.[1]   They set off after the ceremony for
Ostend ;   proceed straight to Florence.   She is a sensible young
woman :   she will be an addition to your society.   There is no harm
in him, a bon enfant disposed to be friendly.

Tuesday, [*October* or *November* ?   Bowood ?   1844].

Thank you, my dear Henry, for the sketch of the appearance of
the Chiaja [2] during the inundation.   What a wonderful escape for
the pretty bridge.   It would have been a sad privation to Florence,
had it been destroyed.   I hope measures will be taken in time, & with
scientific skill, to ward off another overflow.   Tell me what are the
means projected for that purpose.   Have you any expert civil
engineers ?

The Dsse Stephanie de Baden is arrived.[3]   She exacts much,
attempting to form a sort of Court, giving audiences, & having a
circle.   Lady Canning unintentionally displeased by enquiring how
the Marquise de Douglas was.   " Qui ?   Qui ?   qui ? "   Lady C.
saw her error, & then said, " La Princesse Marie," to which a most
gracious answer was given.   The Duke of Hamilton calls his daughter
in law, the Marchioness Princess.   Our little Queen is less gracious,
not having spared Prince Albert to take her in to dinner.   These silly
stories make topics for the gossips.   Ld Bessborough is returned in
excellent health,[4] but very *lame* ;   he limps much, & obliged to use a
stick.   He gives a reluctant consent to the marriage, which will take
place immediately after Lent.   I hope it may answer.   Did I tell you
that Talleyrand, struck with the beauty of Ly Kerry, said, " Elle est
belle comme Ève avant le Péché " ?

I can give you but a hearsay account of Ly Lansdowne, who has
been very ill, as she is still in her rooms upstairs ;   & the house is

[1] Baron Philipp von Neumann had married Lady Charlotte Augusta Somerset,
daughter of 7th Duke of Beaufort.   He was Austrian Minister in Tuscany.

[2] The Arno broke its banks in Florence on November 3.

[3] *See ante*, p. 103.   Her youngest daughter, Princess Marie, married 11th
Duke of Hamilton (Marquis of Douglas) in 1843.

[4] Previously known to us as Viscount Duncannon (1781–1847).   He had
succeeded his father as 4th Earl in February.   His daughter, Augusta Lavinia,
had married Lord Kerry, who died in 1836.   She was now engaged to Hon.
Charles Gore, whom she married in April 1845.

crowded with models for the monument in W. Abbey.[1] I am afraid
of my nerves, which may be affected as to be painful before servants.
In a few days you shall have a sketch of what I am going to put up
at Millbrook. The observation on Ly Kerry was made by Pozzo
at Bowood to your Aunt, not by Talleyrand, who I believe never
saw her.

25th November, 1844.

I have but a slender budget of gossips. My best story you had,
of Lady Pollington & the County of Norfolk. She is very wild &
gay ; but most people believe it is merely from excess of animal
spirits, & that her " Boys," as she calls her troop of suitors, are merely
her playfellows. But as her husband is perfectly satisfied, the dragons
of Virtue must be silent.[2]

December 3d, [1844].

Neumann came to take leave of me yesterday. He is to be married
on Thursday, & proceed to Paris, to Nice, & by the Corniche to
Florence, where he has the offer of two houses. . . . There is a
sharp man who writes to all Ld Byron's friends, representing himself
as his son, the issue of an amour Ld B. is said to have had with a
Spanish lady of rank at Cadiz. The existence of such a being was
never notified to Lord Byron till shortly before his death ; the letter
did not reach its destination till after his death. The man begins by
asking a loan of £900, & to Ld C— (?) : upon his refusal begs for £9.
It is altogether an imposture ; & Sir J. Hobhouse, who has received
a similar application, is satisfied of the falsehood of the man's story.[3]

[1] Lord Lansdowne was responsible for a subscription raised to erect a monument to the late Lord Holland in Westminster Abbey. £5,000 was collected ;
and the design selected was by Edward Hodges Bailey. It stands at the north-
west end of the nave, but has no inscription or name on it. Lord Holland was
buried at Millbrook Church, near Ampthill.

[2] Lady Holland wrote elsewhere : " They say in Norfolk that Lady Pollington's introduction of the Polka at the Norwich balls has produced almost
as much sensation in the country, as when Ld Townshend first introduced
Turnips." Viscountess Pollington was a daughter of the 3rd Earl of Orford, and
therefore a sister-in-law of Lady Holland's own grand-daughter, Harriet
Walpole. Viscount Pollington succeeded his father as Earl of Mexborough.

[3] Hobhouse wrote to Lady Holland that Byron had never had an intrigue
with any Spanish lady in Cadiz, and that the man was clearly an impostor.
George Gordon Byron, self-styled, was also a clever forger of his reputed father's
letters, and commenced a publication in America, *The Unedited works of Lord
Byron*, which ceased when its unreliability came to be recognized.

Poor Rogers ! He bears up with great calmness.[1] I cannot give any authentic particulars beyond what you read in the papers. However, the general opinion is the loss will be far less than originally stated . . .

December 10th, [1844].

. . . Miss Martineau [2] has gone wild upon mesmerism. She is a highly vain person, restless when not before the public. One is sorry the *Athenaeum* should disgrace its character by such a publication. The medical men for these last two years pronounced her complaint as one likely to be subdued, & never of a dangerous nature. She quarrelled outright with her brother-in-law last year, upon his telling her she could walk as well as he did, if she would only get up & try. This folly has done her reputation great harm. Her former admirers scoff and laugh at her now. The folly of magnetism or clairvoyance is still going on. Arthur Kinnaird went to Rogers about the robbery, telling him a cock & bull story of a French lady having (in her sleep) been present at the theft, describing the room & two Jews in slouched hats carrying off the spoil, then getting to the River, embarking, & then finally depositing it in a crowded part of the town in the hands of another Jew in a garret in G[th] Street, but the *name* of the street deficient. Could you believe any person silly enough upon such a serious occasion to make a communication of the sort ? Rogers assured me they had no clue whatever, but Mr Hohler (?) is satisfied some opening will be made ere long. The suspense is most painful ; and already one can perceive anxiety has worn upon poor Rogers. Forrester, the expert policeman, when he examined the premises said to the people *there*, that *they* knew more about [it] than he did, very conclusive of his opinion.

I have heard great praises of Ld Napier's talents & acquirements ; that he is sure of making his way in his career, as he is very clever, & learning all the languages, Russian, Turkish, & others that our diplomats do not dream of having.[3] He must fight his way up, as he is very poor, & his pretty wife not richer.

---

[1] £40,000 apparently had been stolen from Rogers's Bank. Lord Lansdowne, writing to Lady Holland, was sanguine that £35,000 would be ultimately recovered.

[2] Harriet Martineau (1802–76), writer of many works. Her *Letters on Mesmerism* were first published in the *Athenaeum*.

[3] Francis, 10th Lord Napier (1819–98), a successful diplomatist. He married the only daughter of Thomas Manners Lockwood.

December 17th, 1844.   S. St.

. . . Dickens's Xmas book [1] I fully intended sending to you today ; but it is such a failure, that I cannot finish it myself.   So how would you, who do not relish Dickens, endure it ?

There is a report of Wm Cowper's marriage with a beautiful Miss Tollemache, a grand-daughter of our old friend Lady Aldborough. [2] Her sisters are numerous, Lady Cardigan, Mrs Lock, & half a dozen more ; & Mrs De Burgh, the only steady one who is married.   The mother, Lady Elizabeth, took fright at the misdeeds of her daughters, fell into great devotion, & has brought up the young lady in question *very* strictly.   She does not go into society, or ever saw the inside of a theatre.   These tastes are very consonant with those of Wm Cowper.

Our dear little Queen must have imbibed some German sentiment from her two connexions, by sparing the life of the ox, because it licked the hand of Prince Albert ! at the Cattle Show.

[end of 1844.]

. . . Mrs Norton is out of danger.   She was on the verge of a brain fever, brought on by nervousness about her *Poem,*[3] which she wished should appear before the close of the year, & sat up all night for corrections of the press.   Her brother Brinsley, who was sent for to her, very judiciously stopped the publication, so that by calm & complete repose for a fortnight she may return to London.   Her condition really made me quite uneasy about her.   I was much pleased with her brother Brinsley, whom I had known but little before. What beauty there is in that family.   *He,* who is the least well looking, is certainly very handsome.

Ld Lansdowne himself *officially* announced to me the marriage of Louisa with Kenneth Howard.[4]   It has long been known, like the Secret de la Comédie, but was not to be mentioned till his sanction was given.   It is a very happy affair to all parties, & will conduce, I think, much to Ld L.'s own comfort.   However, he may be at first annoyed by losing her.

[1] *The Chimes.*

[2] William Cowper's first wife, Miss Gurney, died two months after their marriage in 1843.   He did not marry Miss Georgina Tollemache, daughter of Vice-Admiral John Tollemache, until the end of 1848.

[3] On the sufferings of the poor.   Her brother, Richard Brinsley Sheridan, who died in 1888, married Miss Marcia Grant, the heiress of Frampton Court, Dorchester.

[4] Hon. James Kenneth Howard (1814–82), son of 16th Earl of Suffolk married Lady Louisa Fitzmaurice in February.

January 3d, [1845].

. . . Ld & Ly Londonderry had a narrow escape. Just before, scarcely two minutes, entering a tunnel near Hexham, the top fell in & entirely covered the rail road. With some difficulty they got back to the station, & were obliged to scour the country for horses to take them on. It will be an affair of some months before the line can be opened. Lady Le Despencer is about making a foolish marriage, not only so from want of money but that she has chosen a weak man, Mr Boscawen, a cousin of Lord Falmouth's.[1] I am going to venture out today to dine in this street with the Ponsonbys. I shall go in a sedan chair ! a mode of conveyance quite obsolete ; & chairmen are with difficulty procured. Our excellent friend Brodie [2] is much worried by the Medical Bill, and feels it more. It has really affected his health & appearance. Alas ! I cannot say anything about dear Sydney the least consolatory. Hopes of recovery are very slender. He suffers greatly from breathlessness, which of all sufferings is said to be the most distressing. What a loss !

January 14, 1845.

. . . The two numbers of *Punch* [sent] are clever, the parody on the " Miller & his men," also the Boys' lessons in little words of few syllables [" Little lessons for little politicians "]. Brougham is always the victim. They say that when O'Connell was condemned to a year's imprisonment, Sheil overheard Brougham say he would much dislike 12 months in Kilmainham Gaol. " Better," said Sheil, " than 6 in *Punch*."

The Dss of Sutherland came here last night in great beauty. The physicians say she need not remain ; so they go off to Castle Howard, where all is doing well, & he still holds his wish & intention of coming to London in April. The Palmerstons have been at Windsor, where they saw the picture of Winterhalter, a beautiful work of L. Phillippe's visit here. Nothing, she says, can be better than the likeness of the Queen & the grouping of the four children about her, so graceful & well done. It altogether promises to be very successful ; the likenesses good, St Aulaire striking, Lady Gainsborough beautiful, Sir Robt Peel's *left leg*, as in nature, very remarkable ! ! ! [3] The Queen talked very eagerly of another speedy Continental trip.

[1] Mary Frances Elizabeth Stapleton, Baroness Le Despencer in her own right (1822-91). She married Evelyn Boscawen in July 1845, who succeeded, in 1852, as 6th Viscount Falmouth.

[2] Sir Benjamin Brodie (1783-1862), the celebrated surgeon, and President of Royal College of Surgeons.   [3] The picture is still at Windsor.

Alexander Lieven [1] is come to England. The on dit is a marriage with Ly Powerscourt, [2] with whom he has been passionately in love sometime. She has smarted from a bad match with a half crazed man. She ought to consider ; as Russians, according to Mirabeau, have always the *peau d'un ours* about them however disguised by an embroidered gilet. Mde de Lieven has been shut up 5 weeks from an inflammation in her eyes. The position of Guizot would make the full use of both necessary. I am told she thinks Neumann quite wretched, & full of repentance at his marriage. The French are sure of saying so ; for he is not popular at Paris. Everett, [3] the American Minister, has wisely determined to wait his recall, not to take the initiative : but evidently is apprehensive. They talk of sending Mr Stevenson again ; he would hardly be welcome here.

Gladstone had resigned his post on Peel's proposal largely to increase the grant to Maynooth College for training Roman Catholic clergy, as incompatible with the view expressed in his book, *The State and its relations with the Church*, published in 1838. He spoke for an hour in explaining his reasons for leaving the Government. Francis Charteris (1818–1914), best known to the last generation as Lord Wemyss, moved the Address. The two Lords here mentioned moved and seconded in the Upper House.

February 7th, 1845.

The meeting of Parlt always makes a little stir & bustle ; but nothing very material has arisen. Mr Gladstone's explanation threw but little light upon his motives for resignation, beyond what was supposed. He was as obscure & unintelligible as his own book. He may be a very clever, well informed man of business, but certainly can be no loss in *Council*, as he is far from *sensible*, & very vain. F. Charteris did extremely well on seconding the Address. In Lords, it was a race which did worse, Lds Camden or Glenlyon. Ld Jocelyn is to have a place ; it is a secret which, so I cannot tell you ; but it pleases all his friends that he should be employed, as he has very good abilities & the salary will be convenient, for they are wretchedly poor.

Both Sydney and Bobus Smith died within a fortnight of one

---

[1] Alexander Lieven was a son of the Princess.

[2] Richard, 4th Viscount Powerscourt had died in 1844 ; and his widow (Lady Elizabeth Jocelyn, daughter of 3rd Earl of Roden) married, in 1846, Frederick, later 4th Marquis of Londonderry.

[3] Edward Everett was American Minister in London 1841–5. He succeeded Andrew Stevenson (*see ante*, p. 164).

another. A further blow was imminent, though fully expected, the death of Caroline Fox, so beloved in the family, early in March. She had had a seizure at the end of the preceding year, but lingered on for some months. Lady Holland wrote on March 14 : " I was stunned and much bewildered at the rapid succession of calamities. Mr Smith [Bobus] has been a cruel blow to me. He was so staunch a friend, and such a delightful companion."

28th February, 1845.

I am not very well & quite overcome The enclosed corroborates too well my apprehensions. It is dreadful to outlive all ones old friends. My heart is quite oppressed.

John Wortley dined here, & was very agreable. I was rather in a *fuss*, as Ld Fitzwilliam had offered himself shortly before dinner to dine, & I fancied there was a feud between the great Yorkshire potentates. On the contrary they were very amiable. Macaulay made a splendid speech the other night on the Sugar Duties. The House was tumultuous in applause.

March 7th.

. . . You will have been diverted at some of the debates in House of Commons, particularly Israeli's retort upon Sir Robt Peel.[1] The stealing the clothes of the Whigs when they were bathing is as witty as possible, so short, & true an image of the facts. Most of the stolen property was used last night by Peel, who means to do away with the disabilities of the Jews for holding civil & corporate offices. They will thus be eligible to everything but Parliament ; which doubtless will come in due time. Tonight there was to have been a motion for enquiry of Papers upon the Indian affairs under Ld Ellenboro', but somehow it has dropped till after Easter, & then no wise fixed. It would almost seem as if Hume had been cajoled by some influence to give it up, either Directors or Govt.

Good Friday, [March 21st, 1845].

. . . The Duc de Broglie [2] is in no respect changed. Among his first visits was one to me. He was much affected. Each had undergone equal sorrows in the 14 years we had not met. When we were at Paris, he sent up from his château in Normandy a friend to express

---

[1] In debate on February 28, on the opening of letters by the Post Office.

[2] See ante, p. 11. He had married Madame de Staël's daughter, Albertine, who died in 1838. When the Hollands were in Paris for the last time. He was a great friend of Bobus Smith.

regret at not being in Paris to receive us, but that he should follow in two days. Alas ! poor man, Albertine died, whom he was so fondly attending ; & my grief subsequently he did not hear with dry eyes. He was shocked on landing to hear of Mr Smith's death ; he had looked forward to many delightful hours with him. He had known him long : & had passed a winter at Pisa with him & Mde de Staël. The negotiation in which he is engaged is important, & may tend to very useful measures for the good fellowship & peace of both countries. His character for probity, truth & frankness is a guarantee for sincerity. His fellow negotiator is a very zealous, honest man. Neither would undertake the business unless convinced of the fair intentions of their employers. The only inconvenience is their not being well able to communicate easily. Dr Lushington cannot *speak* French, nor Broglie very readily English ; but each understand both languages perfectly.

I have not sent *Punch*, as you take it in. The last number is very clever. " The Honor of the Bar " is levelled against Fitzroy Kelly,[1] a very eminent lawyer. If you have read his speech in defence of the Quaker Mcadam at Ailesbury, you will understand many of the biting criticisms. It is said he is the son of my poor old friend Monk Lewis. His brother, by the same mother, is acknowledged as such in Lewis's will, who left him a provision. He is one of the leading men at the Bar, but does not enjoy a very good reputation on account of some supposed irregularity on an Election Committee.

" *25th March.* A melancholy day." 1845.[2]

You must have been diverted at all that Ld Malmesbury narrates of the Court of Brunswick & the wretched woman he brought over.[3] Sir Arthur Paget was always supposed to be the person who infused such disgust against her into the mind of the Prince. You may be

---

[1] Sir Fitzroy Kelly (1796–1880), Lord Chief Baron, 1866. Knighted in 1845. He was unseated on petition for Ipswich in 1835. " Monk " Lewis was Matthew Gregory Lewis, the author.

[2] Her own birthday.

[3] The *Diaries* of James Harris, 1st Earl of Malmesbury, were published in 1844. He had brought Queen Caroline to England. Sir Arthur Paget (1771–1848), diplomatist, was brother to the 1st Marquis of Anglesey. Lady Holland (then Lady Webster) had met Harris at Lord Elgin's house in Brussels in 1793, where the latter was British envoy 1792–5. She was then on her way back to England, and dined with the Duke of York, who was besieging Dunkirk (see *Journal of Elizabeth, Lady Holland*, pp. 86–95). The passage in question in the *Diaries* was : " Got a late dinner at Lord Elgin's, Lady Webster there—strange woman, sensible, learned, flighty and coquettish—they say not gallant."

surprised at Ld Malmesbury's grand-son retaining that passage concerning me ; & the more so, when you hear that he had sent me a message of enquiry to know whether I should dislike my name being mentioned in a very complimentary manner. My answer was that for *many* years Ld M. was so intimate & friendly, that I felt confident all he would say would be kind. My intimacy with him was *after* that first unlucky interview. I certainly was a singular person when he first knew me, thoroughly ignorant of life & manners, but very innocent and unwary. The *only* word that annoyed me in the paragraph was calling me *coquettish*, which was wholly false & totally repugnant to my nature & habits. My weakness was a desire to be reckoned what I never was, clever. But enough of self. . . .

11th April, [1845].

Did you hear of Ly Seymour's practical joke on 1st of April. She wrote to Lady Ailesbury,[1] they were both in Paris at the time, that she had just received an authentic account that Sir R. Peel was out ; that she was sorry on account of Sir James Graham, but very glad for B— (?) sake. Ly Ailesbury, très empressée, went to Molé to tell him ; & in the course of a short time the news got to the *Bourse*, & the fonds affected. Ly A. gambles in railway shares. She cleared £17,000, which she has not quite lost back.

May 2d, [1845].

. . . Ld Melbourne has been *very ill* in consequence of the fall, which has shattered him much & produced great debility. Add to this the gout & a painful gumboil. In short, there has been great uneasiness about him ; nor can one feel much satisfaction just at present. The Queen Dowager is to give a mid-day ball to the Royal children next week. They are very young for such an exploit. The Dss of Kent, who is now out of debt, has begun a course of parties somewhat grim & dull. O'Connell seems to have changed his note, which was one of triumph & welcome at the prospect of the Queen's visit, but is now in a very different key. So if her Majesty & her Ministers are timid, the project of going there will be frustrated.

May 10th.

I made a blunder from ignorant report. The Queen's Fancy Ball, which is for 6th of June, embraces only the period of 10 years, from

---

[1] The second wife of 1st Marquis of Ailesbury, Maria Elizabeth, daughter of Hon. Charles Tollemache. She was celebrated in the annals of Victorian society, and lived till 1893.

1740 to 1750. It includes the Rebellion of '45. The costumes of that period are not graceful ; tho' Hogarth makes his pretty faces carry off the dress. If by any sketches you could help your lady friends in England, it would be a great benefit to them.

June 6th.

. . . The Seafords have been in town on a visit to Ld Granville. They leave tomorrow with lessened hopes of his recovery. This extreme debility is what alarms most.[1] From the first my hopes were never strong, having it deeply impressed on my mind what Chambers & others said after dear Allen's case, that after 70 a man did not recover from jaundice. His case & Mr Motteux's strongly confirmed that opinion of the medical men but too fatally. This is the day of the Ball. When it is over, it will be well for the peace of the town, & make people more rational. You see from the enclosures how wild all are.

The marriage of Ly E. de Burgh will be declared immediately with Ld Lascelles, the son of Ld Harewood.[2] I never saw him. He is very young & said to be pleasing ; she is handsome and sensible.

June 10th, 1845.

Never was anything more complete than the success of the Queen's Ball. Strange to say all were pleased, young & old ; & even those who did not go enjoyed the success. The streets were crowded ; large groups assembled at the doors of those invited, to catch a glimpse of their costume ; & many persons in their strange fashions stopped to shew themselves to the assembled crowd & got cheers for their obligingness. Among the *non* invited & much displeased, was B[rougham], who wanted the Lords to sit on that day, & abused Barry for the delay about the building of the Houses of Parlt, addressing in a bye *sotto voce* something injurious to Albert & his *ugly* wife !

Midsummer eve, 1845.

The fatigues of the rail road so completely overwhelmed me, that not one of my good intentions could I fulfil, especially that of writing a long cozy letter to you. I much enjoyed my visit to Althorp.

---

[1] Lord Granville died in January 1846. Lord Howard de Walden had just succeeded his father as Lord Seaford.

[2] Lady Elizabeth was daughter of the Clanricardes. Lord Lascelles succeeded as 4th Earl of Harewood in 1857. Lady Holland wrote in July : " In going to Church, St George's, the very frisky horses of Ld C. took fright at the wood pavement, & broke the carriage. However all went prosperously at the altar."

My host was so kind in his reception, so cheerful & pleasant all day long, that I really felt almost happy myself. The house is most comfortable & spacious, 8 or 9 good sized rooms contain the library, which you know is composed of the rarest & most beautiful specimens of the Art of Printing The pictures & collections of portraits are most valuable and curious. The latter are well seen, & placed in a noble gallery of great size, well proportioned. The trees are very fine ; & country just about the Park very pretty, which is not the character-istic of the county, usually very ugly. Shortly before setting off on my return per rail, the account came of the great overthrow on the Western Railway,[1] not encouraging to one especially so much alarmed as I always am when travelling by that mode. However, I achieved my labors perfectly well.

July 29th.

. . . Norfolk House [2] was opened last night for the first time since its renovation. Those who were there were much struck by the display of good taste & great magnificence ; but for residence it wants the light & space around, as in Devonshire or Chesterfield House. By the bye I dined at the latter lately, for the first time since many years. I was much pleased. The society was rather new to me ; but it is impossible not to like it, from the great good nature, courtesy & good breeding of the society. I was unfeignedly pleased with all of them. I had a similar party at George Anson's. Lord Hertford [3] is a most singularly agreable & distinguished man ; but he is rarely to be found in society, the more the pity. He has been very ill-used about Dorchester House. The executors of the Duke of Dorset sold it over his head, without the common usual civility of giving the refusal to the tenant in occupation. He would in all probability live more in England, if he possessed such a house permanently.

August 2d.

. . . The first opening of Norfolk House since it has been under a new régime, took place last week, splendid & showy. Sneyd, who has good taste, says it is more gaudy than gorgeous, objects to some

[1] Near Slough. 40 people were injured, but no one was killed, though part of the train fell down an embankment 12 or 15 feet deep.

[2] In St James Square. Henry Charles, 13th Duke of Norfolk succeeded his father in the titles in 1842.

[3] Richard, 4th Marquis (1800–70). He bought Hertford House, which he left to his reputed half-brother, Sir Richard Wallace, with his collections.

paper hangings instead of silk ; but upon the whole it is admired. Goodwood has a most successful party, one day fine, that for the principal race. The King of Holland [1] was there. The D. of Richmond introduced to him Ld Stanley, as a member of a *very bad Government*.

Psse Lieven is over on account of her eyes, which I am glad to say are not seriously injured, merely her eye lids ; the vision is present. She came only for a week, returning immediately. She lives at the Clarendon. The reception of the K. of Holland has not been very gracious on the part of the higher Powers, but most cordial & warm in society & in the public. It is curious how spiteful Leopold is said to be to him, enough so to influence our Court towards him in their behaviour. The great Miss Lawrence is dead. [2] Her will as usual displeases. She has divided her Yorkshire estates into two portions equal, giving Studley & Fountains Abbey to Ld de Grey for his life only ; the other half to Ld Ripon, with Studley, etc. to himself & son after the death of Ld de Grey. She had £250,000 in ready money, which she has distributed among many obscure people, some relations. To her man of business, the Vice Chancellor Shadwell £30,000 : two god-sons £20,000 each. To a man of the name of Warner an estate of £5000 per am in Nottinghamshire. From what is said, it should seem the De Greys are not very well pleased. They go to the funeral nevertheless. I am going next Saturday to the Grove, Ld Clarendon's, & probably from there to Panshanger. I have floating visions of further journeys, but tremble about rail road conveyance, which really seems most perilous. My writing is so bad that you will hardly decipher it.

Yesterday the Beauforts gave a dinner to the King of Holland, quite one of form & etiquette. The D. of Wellington was to take out according to precedence, Ly G. Coddington as a Duke's daughter. Lady Jersey bustled up, shoved her off, & said to the Duke, " Which will you take ? " He very gravely & properly kept to his destined lady, without answering Lady Jersey. They say she is really too impudent & pushing.

---

[1] William II, the rejected suitor of Princess Charlotte.

[2] Elizabeth Sophia Lawrence, daughter of Capt. William Lawrence and granddaughter of John Aislabie, Chancellor of the Exchequer at the time of the South Sea Bubble. Thomas Philip, 2nd Earl de Grey's great-grandfather, Sir W. Robinson, married Aislabie's sister. He was son of 2nd Lord Grantham, and succeeded to the Earldom in 1833 from his mother. On his death in 1859, his nephew, 2nd Earl of Ripon, succeeded him, whose father, best known as the Prime Minister Lord Goderich, had died earlier in the same year.

28th August, 1845.   Norman Court.

I have, in addition to leading a *vie vagabonde*, been very suffering
& so languid that I had not the energy to hold my pen.   This must
plead my apology.   At Broadlands our party was most agreable,
richly composed ; if my health would have let me have relished it.
Ld Melbourne is at times as clever as ever ; but the great change is
that it is not an uniform state.   He often sinks for hours into gloomy
silence & reverie.   He is stronger, & means to go to his estates at
Melbourne & Nottinghamshire this autumn. . . .

September 15*th*, 1845.

. . . The baths will take you from Florence just at the moment
Charles Buller will be there.[1]   He is a most agreable, witty, clever
person.   His society would be most agreable to you & to Augusta.
He is gone to Italy to see his parents, who pass the winter for heath in
Lombardy.   C. B. distinguished himself on the New Zealand business
very much last session : greatly annoyed Ld Stanley whom he brought
to terms of capitulation on the subject.   He is much connected with
the Ashburtons & Bingham Barings.

Dickens is going to act at an amateur theatre with some artists and
most all of the *Punch* people.   He says Macready is in a perfect agony
of expectation to see him act.   The play is " Every man in his
Humour." [2]   Dickens will do Bobadil ; Mr Foster [J. Forster], a
writer in the *Examiner*, Kitely.   Stanfield is to paint a scene.

Lady Holland had serious thoughts apparently this autumn, the last
of her life, of going to Florence to see her son and daughter-in-law.
But her health was unequal to the effort ; and she suggested that
Henry should get leave and come home.   When at Bowood in
October she caught a chill : but she continued to entertain at dinner
in London until November 9.   From that day she grew worse rapidly,
and died peacefully on November 17.   The last letter of the long
series is dated October 28.

October 6*th*, 1845.   Bowood.

. . . I left town on Thursday, spent two delightful days at
Beckett (Lord Barrington's) & his charming family, in an excellent,
very handsome house.   They are captivating people.   The daughter

---

[1] Charles Buller (1806–48), Liberal politician.
[2] By Ben Jonson.   They acted in the Fanny Kelly Theatre.

Charlotte,[1] who met with the disastrous accident of burning herself, is quite lovely. Luckily no mischief to her beauty has taken place, only still some irritation about the arms & shoulders. She is really perfectly handsome, totally without any tricks too common with acknowledged beauties. I never spent two days *honestly* & truly more enjoyable. Their reception of me was friendly, frank & cordial— quite *cousinly*, rather spoiling me too much. Augustus B., aware of my terror of rail roads, most gallantly came up entirely on my account & met me at the station, a great feat for an old bachelor loving his comforts & college independance. From thence by turnpike road I came here, & had the real pleasure of finding Lady Lansdowne in very *good* health, which from the state she has been in all the spring & summer appeared unlikely ; but thank God she is safe. Ld L. is well. We have the Robt Grosvenors ; & the B. Barings are expected today.

[1] Hon. Charlotte Barrington, daughter of 6th Viscount, married 12th Earl of Strathmore in 1850, and died four years later. Elizabeth, daughter of Lady Holland's grandfather, Florentius Vassall, married Major-General John Barrington, son of the 1st Viscount, about the middle of the XVIII century : hence the relationship.

INDEX

(Customary abbreviations have been made use of, to save space. Ladies' names follow those of their husbands, their maiden names being given in brackets. Reference numbers in italics denote descriptive mention in footnotes.)